The Revolution Has

COME

ROBYN C. SPENCER

The Revolution Has

COME

Black Power, Gender, and
the Black Panther Party in Oakland

Duke University Press · Durham and London · 2016

Interior design by Courtney Leigh Baker
Cover design by Amy Ruth Buchanan
Typeset in Trade Gothic and Whitman
by Westchester Publishing Services

Library of Congress Cataloging-in-Publication Data
Names: Spencer, Robyn C., [date] author.
Title: The revolution has come : Black Power, gender,
and the Black Panther Party in Oakland / Robyn C. Spencer.
Description: Durham : Duke University Press, 2016. | Includes
bibliographical references and index.
Identifiers:
LCCN 2016023568 (print)
LCCN 2016024533 (ebook)
ISBN 9780822362753 (hardcover)
ISBN 9780822362869 (pbk.)
ISBN 9780822373537 (e-book)
Subjects: LCSH: Black Panther Party. | Black power—California—Oakland—History—
20th century. | Black power—United States—History—20th century. | African
American political activists—Interviews. | African American social reformers—
Interviews. | Civil rights movements—United States—History—20th century.
Classification: LCC E185.615.S697 2016 (print) | LCC E185.615 (ebook) |
DDC 322.4/20973—dc23
LC record available at https://lccn.loc.gov/2016023568

Cover art: Kathleen Cleaver (*left*) and Tarika Lewis (*far right*), De Fremery Park,
Oakland, 1968 © 2016, Stephen Shames / Polaris Images.

For my mother, Pansy Spencer,
and my daughter, Sira Imani Basse

———————

In loving memory of my father,
John A. Spencer

Contents

Acknowledgments

I took my first research trip to the Bay Area in the summer of 1996. Melvin Dickson, a Panther rank-and-file member and lifelong community organizer, invited me to come along with him as he did some community work. Eager to meet people and immerse myself in unfamiliar Oakland neighborhoods, I said yes without hesitation. It was just me, him, and a folding table, intrepidly set up on a street corner in the hood, with the Panthers' well-known powder blue banner hanging on the front. We set out literature, a newspaper dedicated to commemorating the Panther cofounder Huey P. Newton, a few pamphlets about political initiatives, and a donation can. Melvin engaged everyone who walked by with humor and sincerity, and soon enough so did I. One woman literally stumbled by, barefoot, her face marred by addiction. She ignored my hesitant "Excuse me, sis" as she went by. She went into a liquor store and emerged minutes later with a brown paper bag. As she went by this time, I caught her eye again and she stopped. "Ya'll the Panthers?" she asked. "Yeah" seemed to be the simplest answer. There was a long pause as she took us in from head to toe. "Well, right on," she said. "We need you out here." Then she dropped a fistful of precious coins into the can. Later Melvin and I went to the nearby housing project and knocked on doors to offer people services at a free health clinic. Explaining to people that the clinic, with limited hours and a modest array of services, was 100 percent free, remains one of the most politicizing moments of my life. That summer I met almost a dozen Panthers and logged seven hours a day going through the newly deposited Huey P. Newton Foundation records and visiting other local archives. I earnestly wrote in my journal, "I feel like I am writing a book for the first time." I could never have imagined that half my life would unfold between that first unforgettable summer and the year of this book's publication.

I owe immense debts of gratitude to the many people and institutions who sustained me along this path. Eric Foner, Farah Jasmine Griffin, Winston James, Manning Marable, and Lynette Jackson served as my dissertation committee at Columbia University, providing encouragement and inspiration, and also as examples of the type of engaged scholar that I wanted to be. Manning Marable's arrival at Columbia as the founding director of the Institute for Research in African-American Studies transformed my graduate experience. I appreciate Manning's careful commentary on my dissertation, his commitment to lobbying for financial support for his graduate students, and his willingness to share from his ever ready Rolodex of scholars and activists. Daryl Scott's open-door policy and ready ear were invaluable to me as I struggled to organize my ideas. His blunt phone calls urging me to finish helped me to do just that. Beth Bates, Tami Friedman, and Premilla Nadasen, then graduate students at Columbia, surrounded me in a web of love and support. Talking to them about feminism, socialism, imperialism, and the world we wanted to create with our scholarship and activism was central to helping me navigate the demands of graduate school and grow as a scholar. While Columbia provided the context for my growing politicization around issues of race, class, gender, and sexuality, it was the Center for Women's Development at Medgar Evers College that showed me the path from the academy to the streets. I volunteered at the Center for many years under the tutelage of its founding director, Safiya Bandele, and together we launched or participated in dozens of community initiatives. Safiya demonstrated grassroots black feminism in action and reinforced my commitment (urged by the women scholars on my dissertation committee and the countless phone conversations with my friends) that no matter what else it did, this book would also tell the stories of Panther women. I met the Caribbean Marxist Lloyd D'Aguilar when I wrote a letter to the newspaper he edited, *Third World Viewpoint*. I eventually joined the publication team, and the global perspectives we featured in the magazine helped to flesh out the international frame for events in this book. I met the Pan-Africanist Thomas Deve on a trip to southern Africa encouraged by Marcia Wright, and we became lifelong friends. He connected me to African feminists and Pan-Africanists when I relocated to South Africa for a year and continually reminded me to imagine a global audience for the Panther story. This early coterie of mentors inside and outside of the academy helped me to believe in myself and find my voice.

There are many scholars whose work on the black freedom movement has enriched this study: Paul Alkebulan, Curtis Austin, Martha Biondi, Joshua Bloom, Scot Brown, Emilye Crosby, Daniel Edward Crowe, Angela Le-Blanc Earnest, Johanna Fernandez, Nishani Fraser, Dayo Gore, Wesley Hogan, Gerald Horne, Judson Jeffries, Charles Jones, Peniel Joseph, Waldo Martin, Tracye Matthews, Erik McDuffie, Todd Moye, Donna Murch, Premilla Nadasen, Jeffrey Ogbar, Mary Phillips, Jane Rhodes, Robert Self, Paula Marie Seniors, Nico Slate, Christopher Strain, Ula Taylor, Ekwueme Michael Thelwell, Rose Thevenin, Akinyele Umoja, Fanon Che Wilkins, Jakobi Williams, Rhonda Y. Williams, and Yohuru Williams. John Dittmer, Robin D. G. Kelley, Charles Payne, and Barbara Ransby deserve special mention for their brilliant scholarship. I turned to their books most often when I hit road blocks or simply needed inspiration. Komozi Woodard and Jeanne Theoharis invited me to disseminate my work on the Panthers to community-based audiences. They have helped build a community of scholars of the black freedom movement that has been a crucial source of camaraderie. I have appreciated Komozi's willingness to enrich his scholarly analysis with his participant-observer perspectives and Jeanne's model of engaged scholarship and activism. Nishani Fraser, Emilye Crosby, Wesley Hogan, and Hasan Jeffries have served as virtual touchstones, editors, and sometimes coauthors as we resolutely mined the common ground of civil rights and Black Power. Emilye in particular has become a cherished friend and collaborator. My work has been enriched by academic and activist collaborations with the Young Lords scholar Johanna Fernandez. Premilla Nadasen has traveled much of this road with me, from graduate student, to organizer, parent, CUNY professor, and author. Her example of political commitment, progressive parenting, and disciplined writing has been exemplary. Ula Taylor provided constant support and sisterhood through the completion of this manuscript as I returned to the Bay Area almost a dozen times. She picked me up at airports, dropped off groceries, pointed to holes in my research, shared the location of sources, and connected me to activists. When I became a parent, she sent me cards to encourage me to focus on self-care, took me to dinner, babysat my daughter, and opened up her guest room whenever we came to the Bay Area.

Participation in reading groups (Center for Place, Culture and Politics and US Gender and History Writing Group), summer institutes (Cornell University's Critical Theory, Black Womyn's Scholarship and Africana

Studies and Ohio State University's Thinking Transnational Feminisms), writing collectives (Ys women, Sisterscholars), and political education groups (Ella's Daughters) helped counter the isolation of academia at key moments and widen the circle of support around me. I particularly benefited from sharing writing with Aimee Meredith Cox, Dana-Ain Davis, Keesha Middlemass, Cheryl Mwaria, and Carla Shedd under the supportive eye of Leith Mullings in Sisterscholars. I first learned about the Panthers in Elsa Barkley Brown's course Women and Social Movements when I was an undergraduate at SUNY Binghamton. Her rigorous scholarship and honoring multiple ways of knowing indelibly shaped the historian I have become. I am eternally grateful to the many authors, colleagues, and teachers who have influenced me tremendously and the scholars who have become like family.

This book would not be possible without the archival collections held at the Bancroft Library at the University of California at Berkeley, the San Francisco African American Historical and Cultural Society, Stanford University's Huey P. Newton Foundation Records at Green Library, the Schomburg Center for Research in African American Studies, Oakland Public Library, and Berkeley Public Library. Clayborne Carson helped me get authorization to do research in the Huey P. Newton Foundation Records at an early stage of processing. I couldn't have started my research without his faith and trust. Heartfelt thanks to Billy X Jennings and Gail Shaw at the It's About Time archives. Billy X's passion and commitment to preserving and sharing the history of the Black Panther Party through exhibits and public programs is unparalleled. Thank you for your careful stewardship of Panther history and your ongoing love for the people.

Grants from the Professional Staff Congress–City University of New York Research Foundation, the Minority Faculty Development Support Grant from Penn State University, and Columbia University's Dissertation Writing Fellowship provided crucial travel and writing support to complete this book. A yearlong postdoctoral fellowship at the Center for African American Urban Studies and the Economy at Carnegie Mellon University came at a pivotal time in my thinking, and I am grateful for Tera Hunter's and Joe Trotter's mentorship. I presented this work at different stages at conferences and would like to thank the audiences at the Labor and Working Class History Association, the Women's History Conference at Sarah Lawrence College, the American Sociological Association, the Organization of American Historians, the Association for the Study of African American

Life and History, and the National Council for Black Studies for their insightful comments.

My colleagues at Penn State University's Department of African and African American Studies and Lehman College's Department of History, Department of Africana Studies, and Department of Women's Studies supported me as I moved through the publication process. Cindy Lobel and Timothy Alborn in Lehman's History Department deserve special mention for their role as excellent sounding boards and generous mentors. At Duke University Press, Gisela Fosado's enthusiasm for this project, gentle encouragement, and accessibility have helped move the project over the finish line. This book was made stronger by readers who painstakingly provided suggestions, feedback, and constructive criticism that helped me shape this work. Early editorial work with Grey Osterud jump-started the book and put it back on the right track. I am grateful for her editorial suggestions.

In the process of writing and revising this book I made contact with dozens of members of the Black Panther Party. In New York in the 1990s I joined Euriah Bennet, George "SEN One" Morillo, and others in the Black Panther Collective, an attempt by Panthers to provide political education for younger generations. Many members of the Panther 21 and the Black Liberation Army volunteered their time on Saturdays to connect the lessons of the past to the present. Bob Collier and Thomas McCreary were central to these efforts, and being part of this collective gave me a small sense of the comradeship that bonded Panthers to each other and undergirded their political commitments. I am grateful to Melvin Dickson, the Huey P. Newton Commemoration Committee, the Black Panther Collective, and all the grassroots activists who taught me the spirit of the 1960s outside of traditional classrooms. I worked alongside Sam Anderson, Safiya Bandele, Safiya Bukhari, Lloyd D'Aguilar, Johanna Fernandez, Mae Jackson, Sadiki "Bro.Shep" Ojore Olugbala, and Dequi Kioni-Sadiki in several political formations and am grateful for their example of commitment and integrity. I appreciate the time that Janet Cyril, Ali Bey Hassan, Curtis Powell, Michael Tabor, and other New York Panthers who have now passed took in sharing their experiences. Thank you, Paul Coates, Pamela Hannah, Rosemari Mealy, Cappy Pinderhughes, and other East Coast Panthers who spoke with me. From these interactions I was able to gain a different perspective on Oakland. Most of the core interviewees in this book are based around the Panthers in Oakland. I am grateful to James Abron, Clark

"Santa Rita" Bailey, Elendar Barnes, Ruth Beckford, Bobby Bowen, Amar Casey, Kathleen Cleaver, Terry Cotton, Emory Douglas, Sherwin Forte, Janice Garret-Forte, Veronica "Roni" Hagopian, Ericka Huggins, Bill Jennings, Tarika Lewis, Bobby McCall, Thomas McCreary, Steve McCutchen, Darron Perkins, Brenda Presley, Bobby Seale, and Mary Williams for sharing their life stories with humor and honesty and for enveloping me in kindness. Some of my best memories are when interviewees extended themselves to me. Thank you, Ericka Huggins, for the shawl you offered me, a clueless New Yorker who wasn't prepared for the fog and evening chill of Bay Area summers. Thank you, Bobby Seale, for letting me spend one of the most unforgettable days of my life accompanying you on a tour of Panther sites in Oakland as you were being filmed for a documentary. Thanks, Kiilu Nyasha, for giving me a place to stay when my roommate situation tanked. Thank you, Tarika Lewis, for allowing me to tag along and talk to you on the road because that was all the time you had. Thanks, Clark "Santa Rita" Bailey, for driving from Sacramento to pick me up when my train was delayed. Thank you, Billy X, for always being a phone call away with a fountain of information. Space prevents me from adding more acknowledgments, but it is no exaggeration to say that the shared commitment to Panther history often became the building blocks of lasting relationships of mutual respect.

I have to extend a special thanks to Phyllis Jackson for the countless hours of long-distance sisterfriend advice, historical insight, tough love, and encouragement as you walked me through mental missteps and rescued me from analytical dead ends in the beginning of this book project. Quick witted and intense, you were the first Black Panther I met, and you held me to a high standard that has strengthened this book.

The path to completing this book was filled with moments of soul-shattering grief as I lost my dear father, John Spencer; my husband, Karim Basse; and my grandmother, Miriam Kingston, along the way. Family and friends' support helped me to keep moving forward. My dear sisterfriends Kimberly Ellis, Tami Friedman, Charmaine Gentles, Cheryl Hicks, and Laura Lomas carried me more times than I can count. They kept me company, made me laugh, and helped me find the path to survival. They knew when to not ask about the book and when to provide gentle encouragement to keep chipping away. My family has been my strongest foundation. I want to thank my mother, Pansy Spencer; aunts Joan Hamlin and Giftay Kingston; cousins Alesa Andrew, Tramain Andrew, Winrock Andrew, and Shayla Hamlin; and brother, Treyvon Spencer, for their support as I worked toward a goal that likely seemed amorphous in a career that seemed opaque. Thanks to my brother-in-law, Yssa Basse, who has remained a consistent and loving presence in our lives.

My parents were my first teachers. It pains me not to be able to put this book into my father's hand. His passion for politics and abiding love for black history and culture planted seeds that grew into this book. My mother has championed my educational goals from kindergarten and made innumerable sacrifices to ensure that my upbringing provided more opportunities than she was afforded. She has supported me in immeasurable ways. It is only because of her help with child care that I have been able to do the traveling, reading, and writing that I needed to complete this book. I thank her for shouldering some of the workload of solo parenting and for her unflagging patience and love.

My daughter, Sira Imani, has lived with this book for a decade and has tolerated the space it has occupied in our home life. I have coped with balancing the joys and demands of parenting with the realities of research and writing by incorporating her into as much of my work world as feasible. Her sticky fingers and muddy footprints are all over this book. I want to thank Sira for sharing me with this book. Through the travel we do and the political meetings we attend, I have tried to show her that this book is not just an individual quest. It is a contribution to the collective history of black resistance. Decades ago it was conceived in the context of the outrage and activism spurred by the Rodney King beating, the Gulf War, Clarence Thomas's nomination to the Supreme Court, torture in Guantanamo Bay, the campaign to free the political prisoner Mumia Abu-Jamal, the afterlife of apartheid in South Africa, the World Trade Organization protests in Seattle, and the execution of Shaka Sankofa (Larry Graham). It is being published in the context of a movement proclaiming "Black Lives Matter" and "#SayHerName." This is the world that Sira has inherited. As the onslaught of state-sanctioned killing of black women, men, and children has increasingly dawned on her young consciousness, the need for Mommy's book has become less and less abstract. She is my greatest inspiration. I wrote this book to make it possible for ten-year-old black girls like her to imagine themselves seizing the time.

Introduction

In the summer of 2014 I visited Broad Street Historical Park in Greenwood, Mississippi, the site where Stokely Carmichael threw the phrase *Black Power* into a crowd of movement activists and the echo that roared back was heard around the world. Despite the fact that the site had been immortalized in popular memory, documentary films, and oral history accounts, a Freedom Trail marker had been placed there only in 2013. It was that marker that drew my attention and had likely resulted in a trickle of visitors through the black side of town. While scholarly research and oral history had long decentered the place and time of Carmichael's call in favor of alternative chronologies and genealogies, there was still something momentous about being there. Then and now the scene was framed by a poverty line that was almost tangible. Shotgun houses, abandoned storefronts, and unpaved roads told a story clearer than any statistics. It was easy to imagine that there hadn't been much change between the call for Black Power in 1966 and 2014. In the waning years of the first black presidential administration, which some had argued represented one of the greatest symbols of black progress, Greenwood, known as the "Mississippi of Mississippi," stood as a stark testament to the changing same. It was a place that raises questions about Black Power then and now. The movement for Black Power was a response to the crises and opportunities in working-class black America in the 1960s and 1970s. It was irreverent, bold, and brash. It was also organized, rooted in black political culture, and deeply analytical. It was as much substance as style, as much intellectual rigor as revolutionary freedom dream. And it faced an almost unprecedented attack from the state. Activists developed this movement to transform places like Greenwood. A full accounting of the fate of the political organizations that grew in the wake of the cry for Black Power provides one means of rectifying the present we live in with the past that Black Power activists struggled to transform and the future they imagined.

This book analyzes the political evolution of one of the leading Black Power organizations, the Black Panther Party (BPP), in the city where it was founded: Oakland, California. Although the BPP found expression largely in urban America, the young men and women who joined the Panthers in Oakland were the children of those who had migrated from the South to the West during World War II. When wartime opportunities closed down and state violence and economic forces conspired to push this aspirant population to the bottom rungs of the social and economic ladder, their resistance transformed politics in Oakland.

Today Huey Newton and Bobby Seale, the founders of the Black Panther Party, might be written off as stereotypes or statistics. Newton was an ex-convict and a seasoned hustler who straddled the formal and informal economy with ease. Like many youth seeking skills and an income, Seale had spent time in the military. Both men were community college students who grappled with international political theory, activists who debated strategies for revolution, and employees at a local War on Poverty program office. Neither was a stranger to guns, alcohol, or marijuana. In the richness of their lived experiences, none of these social, economic, or political positions was mutually exclusive or contradictory. Newton and Seale lived the complexity of everyday life in working-class black America.

They were part of the nationwide decision by grassroots activists to address pervasive police brutality against men and women in their communities. Los Angeles activists had been early pioneers of this approach in the wake of the Watts riots. Inspired by activists in other cities, the Panthers launched armed patrols of the Oakland police. One incident at a time they refashioned the fear, intimidation, and anger caused by daily indignities from the police into empowerment, education, and street theater. In the process they turned strangers into comrades and built community. When the state retaliated by removing the legal foundations of their public arms, the BPP adopted many other tactics. Self-defense was not their only solution to police violence. The gun turned out to be a weapon turned on them more than they ever turned it on others, and the BPP existed as an organization under siege for much of its history. However, they also launched ideological warfare and sought community-based and public policy solutions to the brutality that faced black communities. They issued political statements against police violence and on many different occasions sought to connect the daily brutality of life in black America to the heightened surveillance and repression its membership faced, much as contemporary activists in the movement to free political prisoners have continually connected with the larger movement against mass incarceration in the early twenty-first century. The solutions the Panthers sought, such as community control of the police, freedom for political prisoners, and an end to poverty and war, remain central in many struggles for justice today.

Although this book centers on Oakland, I argue that the BPP's commitment to making linkages with revolutionaries in Europe, Africa, the Middle East, and the Caribbean made it one of the most effective ambassadors for Black Power. African and Asian decolonization and the Vietnam War framed the Panthers' attempt to provide an organizational vehicle and an ideological framework to allow working-class black people to explore linkages between antiracism and anti-imperialism. At the same time, the Panthers understood Black Power as home-grown resistance inspired by the Declaration of Independence and the U.S. Constitution. They tried to hold America accountable to its most democratic promises and dared to suggest that justice for black people would be the beginning of a revolutionary overhaul that would free everyone at the bottom of society. In 1970 the Panthers brought between ten thousand and fifteen thousand people from the movements for gay and lesbian liberation and women's liberation and those representing Third World politics, anticapitalists, Native Americans, Chicanos, Puerto Ricans, radical whites, and other people of African descent to Philadelphia to rewrite the Constitution. Their ability to highlight areas of cross-pollination between social movements, embrace a diversity of allies, and connect to global struggles and worldwide challenges negates any simplistic condemnation of Black Power as racial chauvinism or the politics of exclusion. It suggests that the legacy of Black Power is rooted in black America but remains relevant to marginalized people in all communities.

The BPP's activities were framed by state political repression nimble enough to go from the sledgehammer of arrests, shootouts, and raids to the delicacy of planting infidelity accusations between husband and wife. The FBI's Counter-Intelligence Program (COINTELPRO) had an indelible impact on the lives of leadership and the rank and file and eroded the political community the Panthers sought to build and that was its greatest strength. Hundreds of young people came to political awareness and journeyed to adulthood under the aegis of the Black Panther Party, and their raw and youthful energy brought the organization to life. Rank-and-file members interpreted, implemented, and influenced party ideology and programs and helped shape the growth and development of the organization. The Panthers believed that revolution was both internal and external and strove to create an organization that would be a microcosm of the world they were trying to create. Party members grappled with sexism, classism, individualism, and materialism and attempted to create alternative structures, institutions, and lifestyles. Their goal was not only to challenge and change the conditions in America but to politicize their membership and their mass following. In short, Black Panther Party members not only tried to transform the world; they tried to transform themselves. This struggle within the struggle unfolded in the day-to-day realities of the rank and file—those who occupied the most democratic layer of the organization. For many of these members the attempts to shed individualism, confront ingrained ideas about gender and sexuality, build genuine bonds of mutual trust and respect with comrades, and provide social services to both comrades and communities in need were some of the most politicizing experiences of Black Power. Panthers grappled with social reproduction, collective living, housework, individual autonomy, and leisure. While the resolution of these struggles was not always egalitarian, the debates speak to how women and men sought to define their freedom-within-a-freedom movement.

Facing the organized power of the state, the Panthers pursued electoral political and community survival programs in the 1970s, with some striking successes. They faced organizational revitalization under the leadership of women and experimented with truly collective organizational structures for health, child care, and education. This era has been the least studied aspect of their history, but their engagement with urban renewal, alternative education, and community control reflects a continuation of their quest for Black Power. The impact of mass incarceration, the growing drug epidemic, and the adaptability of political repression would continually shape the possibilities for social change that the Panthers pursued. The party came to an end in Oakland in 1982 with the closure of its last community program, the Oakland Community School. Fifty years have passed since the founding of the Black Panther Party. The economic downturn for black and brown Oakland has continued unabated, and the cry for Black Power and the need for "land, bread, housing, education, clothing, justice and peace" is echoed in contemporary activists' insistence that "Black Lives Matter."[1]

Today's activists are seeking lessons from the past with the urgency of now. What does Black Power have to offer in the context of drone warfare, deepening poverty, unemployment, immigrant detention, and a criminal justice infrastructure that is an engine of destruction in black and brown communities? The study of Black Power doesn't just fill holes in the scholarly literature; it fills holes in the tapestry of the American past. It fills bullet holes. The young black men and women who joined the Black Panther Party attempted to create a revolutionary political vehicle in the context of a burgeoning movement for Black Power that unfolded within the context of deindustrialization, state violence, and global revolution. It is time to examine the roadblocks they faced, the tune-ups needed, the drivers (including those who steered even when they were not in the driver's seat), the devastating breakdowns, and those moments of joy and optimism when the road, and the possibilities, seemed endless.

SEIZE THE TIME

The Roots of the Black Panther Party
in Oakland, California

———

In 1944 the *Observer*, a local white newspaper in Oakland, bemoaned the "new race problem" caused by "the influx of what might be called socially-liberated or uninhibited Negroes who are not bound by the old peaceful understanding between the Negro and the white" and who insisted on "barging into the white man and becoming an integral part of the white man's society."[1] This comment came on the heels of a railroad station brawl between black and white servicemen and civilians that had turned into a full-scale race riot involving two thousand people. World War II had unleashed the winds of change in Oakland, but the problems of race were hardly new. During the war thousands of African Americans migrated to Oakland from Louisiana, Texas, Oklahoma, Arkansas, and other southern states. Drawn by the promise of work in war industries, these migrants swelled the city's black population from 8,462 in 1940 to over 20,000 four years later.[2] They transformed West Oakland, a magnet for 85 percent of Oakland's black population, into a bustling, vibrant community complete with its own retail corridor that became known as the "black downtown."[3] These migrants had a profound impact on racial politics in Oakland. Spurred to action by a growing collective consciousness and sense of empowerment as well as visceral experiences of racial discrimination, they challenged the fragile racial balance between the historic black community and the white majority. Their struggles against racism, housing discrimination, poverty, educational inequities, and police brutality in the postwar period would radicalize a new generation of activists who were, literally and figuratively, their children. This new generation would come of age politically as part of the nationwide upsurge of civil rights, social justice, and antipoverty activism in the 1960s.

The Black Panther Party was part of this groundswell. Founded in 1966 by Huey Newton and Bobby Seale, children of migrants from Louisiana and Texas, the BPP would grow to over forty chapters and branches and become one of the leading organizations of the Black Power movement. The roots of the Panthers lay in the responses of African Americans to the economic inequities and racial indignities of postwar Oakland. Postwar demobilization displaced working-class blacks from the toehold they had been able to gain in shipbuilding and other defense industries.[4] Manufacturing jobs disappeared as trucks replaced ships and trains as the major commercial freight carriers. Some African Americans were able to find work on railroads and docks, in local canneries, government installations, and, to a lesser extent, in domestic service. However, overall economic depression, high unemployment, underemployment, and low wages were the economic fate of many blacks in this period.[5] These structural economic conditions and visceral experiences of racism combined with the limitations of government initiatives such as urban renewal and the War on Poverty in the 1960s to galvanize Oakland's black working class.

The emergence of the BPP is the story of this uprising. It reflects the attempt of the poor to organize for social justice, economic and political transformation, and cultural self-determination. It is the story of individuals: Newton and Seale and the comradeship that developed between them as they journeyed down intersecting paths of political exploration; local activists like Mark Comfort, who laid the groundwork for grassroots black activism before the BPP; regional activists in Los Angeles and Berkeley whose struggles reverberated locally; and the many rank-and-file members who would swell the Panthers' ranks. While some members would come from Oakland's grittiest streets and were politically inexperienced, others were veterans of Oakland's civil rights struggles, student activists from local community colleges, high school students who had participated in boycotts, and former members of Oakland's many local black nationalist formations. They were united by their sense of purpose, collective identity, and commitment to seize the time.

THE FLATLANDS

The Black Panther Party was born of the problems and potential of Oakland's flatlands, a region within the city that was defined by both topography and politics. Historically, flatlands neighborhoods included West Oakland and downtown Oakland as well as East Oakland—a middle-class area that was racially diverse and contained majority-white neighborhoods in the foothills—and Fruitvale, the core of the Mexican community.[6] However, in the postwar period segregation and exclusion made the term *flatlands* synonymous with the poorest and most dispossessed areas of the city that were hardest hit by Oakland's economic downturn. In March 1966 the inaugural issue of the *Flatlands* newspaper editorialized that race, class, and place determined whether you experienced Oakland as "the all-America city" embodied by the upscale lifestyle of Oakland's hills or as the "city of pain," experienced by the largely black and brown residents of the flatlands. The editorial's message of crisis-level socioeconomic conditions and gaping disparities of wealth was delivered alongside a message of hope: the flatlands were both the spatial expression of oppression and a crucible for resistance. They were a place that "spill[ed] over with people" and "stank with decay" and where "things were getting worst," but that also had the potential for transformation if residents would unite to fight back and declare, "We're not taking it anymore." Founded by a group of local black activists, the *Flatlands* reflected, nurtured, and reported about this spirit of mobilization. The editorial urged action: "We've got to decide what to do. If we're going to change things around this city, we're going to have to change ourselves too. . . . This is a challenge for you [the poor] as much as for the people who sit up high and let things go on as they are."[7]

The economic underdevelopment of the flatlands was not accidental. The downturn there was tied to structural economic transformations, institutionalized racism, and government policies in the postwar period. By 1946 more than half of the black families in Oakland lived in the flat-lands in overcrowded government housing constructed in 1942 as temporary shelters for incoming workers drawn to the war industries.[8] White prop-erty owners would often refuse to rent or sell to "minorities," and racial dis-crimination in the private market hindered the ability of blacks to spread out into other locales.[9] Zoning restrictions and restrictive covenants barred black people from model suburbs created by federally sponsored wartime construction programs, and the banking industry practiced discrimina-tory policies in allocating real estate loans.[10] A 1965 survey of real estate brokers starkly revealed the constellation of discriminatory practices that reinforced the residential color line: "refusing to open listings to Negro brokers, block-busting, outright refusal to sell or rent to minorities, fast-talking or shaming a client out of the desire to buy or rent, raising the fear of being unwelcome, soliciting neighborhood opinions on race, charging higher interest rates, higher prices, and more discount points, and giving shorter loan terms."[11]

By 1966 Oakland had become a segregated city: whites had left neigh-borhoods in East and North Oakland and run for the hills and the foothills. With few other choices, middle-class African Americans spread into East Oakland locales that were increasingly abandoned by whites. An estimated 100,000 white middle-class homeowners left Oakland between 1950 and 1960 and were replaced by black and Chicano renters.[12] Between 1960 and 1966, while the white population in Oakland decreased by 36,000, the black population increased by 33,500 and there was a dramatic increase in the number of Japanese, Korean, and Filipino residents.[13]

Residential segregation was not just a result of discrimination in the real estate and home finance industry; it was reinforced by local and federal government.[14] Suburbanization was aided by the availability of inexpensive housing and the relocation of jobs outside of the city, while transportation projects had a devastating impact on the West Oakland economy.[15] Ferry service for train passengers arriving in Oakland and crossing over to San Francisco declined in the 1950s, and train service to Oakland was discon-tinued altogether in 1958, resulting in the loss of a traditional source of em-ployment for blacks.[16] The Nimitz Freeway, completed that same year, cut through the heart of West Oakland, dividing it in half and destroying many homes and businesses in the process. The black downtown, the economic center of the West Oakland community, never recovered from these losses.

While federal and local initiatives would prove detrimental to all flat-lands neighborhoods, West Oakland was hardest hit. City Council's designation of West Oakland as a "blighted area" in 1954 meant that it was targeted for "revitalization" projects, which had a devastating impact on the community.[17] Local government agencies destroyed many units of low-rent housing without providing affordable replacements. Between 1946 and 1966 fewer than four hundred units of public housing were built in Oakland. During the same period over seven thousand units—the vast majority of which were in high-poverty areas—were eliminated. Of the 2,334 new single-family dwellings constructed between 1960 and 1965, 1,716 of them, or over 73 percent, were built in six of the lowest-density and highest-income census tracts in the city. In contrast only ten new single-family houses were constructed in the four most densely populated tracts in West Oakland during the same period. Forty-three percent of the new multiple-unit dwellings, 4,099 units in all, built between 1960 and 1965 were around the expensive Lake Merritt area. During the same period in West Oakland only 210 new apartment buildings were built.[18] Poor people's only choice was public housing—less than 1 percent of the city's 146,000 housing units.[19] It was a recipe for displacement, overcrowding, and home-lessness.[20] According to the *Flatlands*, West Oakland had become known as "Niggersville" by the mid-1960s.[21]

Although "slum removal" and transportation projects were billed as mechanisms to improve Oakland's economy, they did little to stem capital flight. Oakland was not able to attract new profit-oriented corporations and growth industries. As early as 1935 the Oakland Chamber of Commerce had established the Metropolitan Oakland Area Program to encourage the development of industry outside of the city. As a result, from 1952 to 1962 Oakland, formerly the only major industrial center in the county, accounted for a mere 28 percent of the county's industrial investments. Established businesses and industries left the city in search of more attractive locales. The loss of companies like Cal Pak, which employed between one thousand and five thousand people seasonally, and Marchant Calculators and Nordstrom Value, which each had a workforce of approximately one thousand, had a devastating impact on the local economy.[22] Eighty businesses left town or simply went bankrupt between 1958 and 1963. By 1975 one third of Oakland's manufacturing jobs were gone.[23]

Government initiatives and an infusion of federal money were no panacea for flatlands residents. The War on Poverty, launched in 1964 by the federal Equal Opportunity Act, did little to change the material conditions of Oakland's poor. Eighty percent of all black people lived in War on Poverty target areas—East Oakland, West Oakland, North Oakland, and Fruitvale—"where the average age of the residents was lower, household income was lower and household size was larger than elsewhere in Oakland."[24] The War on Poverty was administered by four poverty centers in the target areas, four Adult Minority Employment Project offices, and a large skills center—housed, ironically, in a building whose former occupant was a manufacturer that had moved to the suburbs.[25] Sixty-three percent of $5,935,234, the total approved budget from 1964 to 1967, was slated for service, education, and administration. The majority of the job creation allocation, $1,886,354, went to the creation of temporary summer jobs through Neighborhood Youth Corps rather than address the long-term employment needs of the "hard-core poor."[26]

Business interests dominated the Oakland Economic Development Council, the major governing body for poverty programs. Twenty-eight of the Council's forty members were appointed by the mayor. Oakland's poor communities had only twelve representatives, three members from each of Oakland's four Target Area Advisory Committee (TAAC) areas: East Oakland, West Oakland, North Oakland, and Fruitvale.[27] African Americans complained that too many "fat cats" had administrative power over the program as compared to ordinary flatlanders.[28] The *Flatlands* editorialized, "All this government money's has been pouring in—so's the poor can pull themselves up by their bootstraps. But FLATLANDS can tell you how the poor see it; the poor say there isn't nothing that's been done."[29]

Police brutality was a persistent problem in Oakland history, especially in the flatlands. Brutality was not simply a matter of isolated instances of individual police misconduct; it was a reflection of how racial inequalities permeated the maintenance of law and order.[30] Oakland's police force was overwhelmingly white, and many were recruited from the Deep South. Despite the fact that the number of blacks rose from 5 to 35 percent of the city's population from the mid-1940s through the 1970s, black police officers were never more than 3 to 4 percent of the total police force.[31] The police enforced the racial status quo, forcing blacks to either remain subordinate or face the consequences.[32] In 1931 the National Commission on Law Observance and Enforcement, which produced the very first federal review of the police, described Oakland as a place of "unjustifiable brutality by police towards citizens."[33] One observer commented that the police would beat "a

Black man within an inch of your life back in the late '30s and all through the '40s." During this period black residents often described the police as "cold blooded" and gave them nicknames such as "'Ass Kicking' Slim."[34] In 1947 the Alameda County chapter of the National Negro Congress called for an end to the police's "campaign of terror and intimidation" in testimony in front of the City Council after a black woman's arm was twisted and her clothes torn during the issuance of a traffic citation.[35] In June 1948 the Oakland Committee for Civic Unity recommended prohibitions on police use of "violence, abusive language, and other indications of improper respect, regardless of race, color, creed, and social or economic status."[36] Despite the many charges of police misconduct and brutality in the 1940s, by 1950 not one officer had been suspended for using illegal force. By this time Oakland school authorities had begun to coordinate with social service agencies, including recreation agencies, police departments, and prisons, to monitor the behavior of youth defined as delinquent. This led to increased police scrutiny of black Oakland youth.[37]

In January 1950 Oakland held the first hearings in the country that "brought a state investigating body into a certain community to specifically investigate the single charge of police brutality particularly directed towards racial groups."[38] These hearings provided a voice for victims of police brutality and misconduct. Several local residents complained of brutality toward black men and harassment and disrespect aimed at black women, such as when women riding in cars with white male friends were accused of being prostitutes.[39] The Bay Area Civil Rights Council testified that black Oakland residents "live in daily and nightly terror of the Oakland police department."[40] Although Police Chief Lester J. Devine acknowledged that there was a problem of civility and issued orders that "police should no longer refer to Negroes as 'knotheads' and 'Jigs,'" he denied the existence of "systematic racial discrimination." The irony of Devine's comments was not lost on the majority-black audience. When he opined that the police force "compares favorably with that of any Police Department in the country," the crowd erupted in derisive laughter.[41]

By the mid-1950s the prevalence of brutality charges against Oakland police led one newspaper to editorialize, "This treatment of Negroes in Oakland has become almost a tradition. It has happened to so many Negroes, over and over, without any action on the part of the department heads[,] the feeling has grown that Negroes can look for nothing better at the hands of the police."[42] There were over twenty demonstrations protesting police violence in Oakland between 1965 and 1966, and the California Advisory Commission of the U.S. Civil Rights Commission heard testimony at local hearings.[43]

By 1966 the flatlands were facing residential segregation, poverty, unemployment, and police brutality. It had become a cauldron of discontent. Observers noted that the condition of African Americans in Oakland were so dire that "Black Dynamite," wide-scale protest, might erupt, making "the city of Oakland . . . tremble from top to bottom."[44] In August 1965, less than ten days after the passage of the Voting Rights Act, the neighborhood of Watts in Los Angeles exploded in urban rebellion. At least thirty-four people died, a thousand were injured, and four thousand were arrested, and property damage tallied $200 million.[45] The catalyst was an incident of police brutality. The very next month the U.S. Community Relations Service identified Oakland and Los Angeles as two of eleven cities outside of the South likely to explode in racial violence.[46] The idea of Oakland being "another Watts" and containing "one of the most dismal and explosive ghettoes in the nation" became part of public discourse.[47] The *Flatlands* described the local reverberations of Watts: "Seems like Watts made the federal government jumpy. People from Washington, they come all the way down here. They ask us what's going on in the flatlands. They want to know how long we can wait. Some of these national magazines and newspapers write about us too. They say the flatlands is an area in which we have a so called 'potential explosion.' "[48] Oakland's explosion would come, but not in the form of spontaneous urban rebellion. It would take the form of organized resistance.

FROM BLACK DYNAMITE TO BLACK POWER

In the 1960s a vibrant grassroots movement spilled out from local high schools and colleges, neighborhood centers, and street corners, spearheaded by Oakland's most dispossessed residents and rooted in the flatlands. These activists drew upon Oakland's long history of political activism to create organizations tackling everything from poverty and housing to police brutality and entrenched racial hierarchies. They included black nationalists influenced by national spokespeople such as Malcolm X; traditional civil rights organizations like the National Association for the Advancement of Colored People (NAACP) and the Congress of Racial Equality (CORE); local coalitions representing churches, civic groups, and fraternal organ-

Civil Rights Coordinating Committee; and trade union
Negro American Labor Council. This local movement
'd by the civil rights movement, which had emerged
with the goal of ending racial segregation and secur-
ights through legislation using the tactic of nonviolent
as well as grassroots black nationalist activism represented
on of Islam and other community-based organizations advocating black cultural self-determination, economic justice, and dignity.

As the nationwide movement for social change evolved, debates about defining and achieving black liberation increasingly took center stage. These debates were also present in Oakland, where grassroots activists worked in tension and in tandem with "respectable Negro leaders," New Leftists, and white liberals who often bemoaned the apathy of the black poor and saw the flatlands as part of the problem rather than part of the solution. Divisions became more evident as the local movement achieved incremental victories, embraced a diversity of strategies and tactics, and experienced hardening resistance. However, national events influenced rather than prefigured the evolution of local protest. The Oakland movement was also influenced tactically and ideologically by events in nearby Berkeley, San Francisco, and Los Angeles—cities that were national centers of anti–Vietnam War activism, college student protests, and anti–police brutality mobilizations.

Mark Comfort stood at the epicenter of grassroots Oakland's political explosion. Although he would never formally join the Black Panther Party, he played a crucial role in its early evolution and laid the groundwork for the emergence of the organization. Born in Oklahoma City in 1934, Comfort moved to Oakland in 1941 and grew up in West Oakland. He dropped out of school and got involved with local gangs and amassed a police record and jail time for fighting, sometimes in turf battles with white peers brought on by shifting spatial boundaries due to changing demographics. Comfort was politicized by his experiences with low-paying jobs, inequities in the judicial system, and interactions with Mexicans and other people of color. He became a visible leader in the local political scene and joined the staff of the *Flatlands*. Comfort was deeply influenced by the Student Nonviolent Coordinating Committee (SNCC), which fostered grassroots leadership, and by activists who immersed themselves in the community. Since 1960 SNCC members had been on the front lines of southern white violence and had engaged in grassroots organizing among some of the most politically

disenfranchised black people in the South. Comfort was also influe[...]
leftist ideas and black nationalist thinkers. His marriage to Gloria B[...]
a white activist whose father was a communist and active in union orga[...]
izing, doubtless furthered his exposure to the Old Left. By the mid-1960s
he had traveled to many of the social protest hot spots around the country,
forging links between Oakland and the wider world of activism.[49]

Although protest politics in Oakland were too diverse and complex to be
reduced to one individual, Comfort's political path wound through many
of the major protest activities and organizations in the 1960s. His activism
provides a window into the evolution of community organization among
blacks at the grassroots level as they sought to work with (and pose alterna-
tives to) movements aimed at achieving economic justice and integration
through nonviolent direct action. His commitment to interracial activism,
his embrace of black self-determination, his focus on nourishing grassroots
activism in the black community, and his nationwide connections laid the
groundwork for the Black Panther Party.[50]

The year 1963 was pivotal for grassroots protest in the Bay Area. The
Southern Christian Leadership Conference's spring civil rights campaigns
in Birmingham, Alabama, had galvanized national attention and invigo-
rated protests nationwide. The Ad Hoc Committee to End Discrimination
was formed by activists committed to challenging racial discrimination in
employment. It began as a multiracial coalition of organizations that included a representative from the W. E. B. Du Bois club, a Communist Party
affiliate; members of the Congress of Racial Equality from Oakland, Berkeley, and San Francisco; and local college students. The Committee was
involved in several direct action demonstrations addressing long-standing
issues of racial inequality and became one of the most visible organizations
on Oakland's civil rights landscape. One of their initiatives was protesting against discriminatory hiring practices by Mel's Drive-in Restaurant, a
popular local eatery. The Ad Hoc Committee embraced tactical flexibility.
Rather than adopting an explicit commitment to nonviolence, they promised,
"We'll defend our line. There was singing, shouting, clapping, smoking, talking, walking two abreast, dancing, and all types of dress on the line." One
observer noted that this self-conscious abandonment of respectability politics "consolidated the image of militancy and new notions of protocol."[51]
Protesters picketed the restaurant and marched to the home of Harold
Dobbs, the co-owner of Mel's who was running for mayor. Dobbs caved to

the pressure after losing the election and agreed to hire African Americans in more visible positions.[52]

Comfort took part in this activist wave. He was particularly concerned with youth activism and unemployment and was a vocal critic of the War on Poverty. In 1963 in Oakland he joined Youth for Jobs, an organization that sought unemployment insurance for high school–age youth and held protests at the local unemployment office.[53] Youth for Jobs played an important role in organizing demonstrations in Oakland and San Francisco to protest the Birmingham church bombings on 15 September 1963 that resulted in the death of four young girls and occurred in the wake of the March on Washington. According to Comfort, who was cochair of the Youth for Jobs Oakland protest march, hundreds of black students, many of them from West Oakland's McClymonds High School, attended the demonstration and marched to a local police station chanting "Now is the hour" and "We want our rights now."[54] Comfort commented on the vibrant spirit of the march: "We blew these people's minds; we caught the police off guard. They went ape."[55] Along with members of the NAACP he addressed the marchers, demanding that the Birmingham killers be brought to justice and a federal investigation be launched. One local newspaper speculated that the "current racial violence" in Alabama "has made the feelings of local Negroes run high" and helped fuel racial tensions between black and white students at local high schools over everything from open enrollment to attacks on students by nonstudents.[56]

By 1964 Comfort had left Youth for Jobs, citing its increasing bureaucracy, and joined the Ad Hoc Committee, playing a pivotal role along with its leaders Mike Myerson, a white student activist from Berkeley, Tracy Simms, and Roy Ballard. In 1963–64 the Committee attacked Jim Crow employment practices in nearby San Francisco at the Sheraton-Palace Hotel and Cadillac Row car dealerships. These massive campaigns mobilized hundreds of college students and resulted in mass arrests and the intervention of both the mayor and the California Fair Employment Practices Commission. The Ad Hoc Committee won important concessions from these industries, securing nondiscrimination policies and commitments to achieve specific percentages of black employees. However, despite the visible and vocal leadership of African Americans in the protest and the endorsement of the head of the NAACP, the black masses were not galvanized. The complexion of protesters prompted one newspaper to point out,

"To the credit of our fellow Negro citizens, let it be noted that their part in these unfortunate events has been minimal."[57]

Ironically the local movement that was deeply inspired by black activism nationwide struggled around the issue of black involvement.[58] CORE exemplified these realities; it had gained strength on and off campus in Berkeley in 1963, and its membership base was among liberal whites as well as college students from Berkeley, many of whom would go on to be active in the Free Speech Movement.[59] CORE attacked discriminatory hiring practices and segregated public accommodations using nonviolent direct action campaigns. One of their most visible campaigns was a series of protests in 1964 and 1965 at Jack London Square, an area near the Port of Oakland filled with restaurants and shops.[60] CORE activists picketed restaurants and held "sip-ins" and "nibble-ins" (where activists would linger interminably over light meals) to protest many restaurants' unstated "white–up front policy," which limited black employees to back room labor. Assemblyman Don Mulford called for an investigation of the protests by the legislature, claiming, "[The] masses are taking over the public streets." Those masses were predominantly white. This was partly due to the isolated location of Jack London Square, but it was also a reflection of local priorities. CORE activists acknowledged, "Discriminatory hiring in the fancier restaurants is a symptom of Oakland's general sickness but does not immediately affront most of Oakland's Negroes." As a result the campaign failed to "gain any significant involvement from Oakland's black community." CORE's acknowledgment of the limitations of their strategy didn't prevent them from castigating the black community and speculating about whether "repeated civil rights arrests [in the restaurant campaign] might break the traditional apathy of the Negro community." Eventually they moved from Jack London Square to large department stores downtown to gain more visibility and diversify support.[61]

Like many civil rights coalitions the Ad Hoc Committee's liberal premises, which had provided points of unity and attracted a committed core of black and white activists, unraveled over time around defining goals, embracing tactical diversity, and race. Comfort's ability to tap into the political priorities of grassroots blacks while working in coalition with liberal whites gave him increasing visibility on the Ad Hoc Committee and in local protests. He gained local prominence during the Committee's campaign against the *Oakland Tribune*, the city's only daily paper. The *Tribune* was run by William Knowland, a conservative Republican and former senator who had campaigned for Barry Goldwater in the early 1960s. Knowland had been a staunch critic of New Left Bay Area social movements, and to many activists the newspaper represented the white conservative establishment. The Ad Hoc Committee launched protests in 1964 focused on the *Tribune's* hiring practices. Knowland initially responded with a series of meetings with activists and unions, but after negotiations broke down the Committee organized persistent demonstrations, a letter-writing campaign, and a call for subscription cancellation and even advocated a boycott of the paper.[62] In December they launched a massive direct action protest that included rallies, marches, letters of protest, a request that supporters cancel subscriptions, and demonstrators blocking the trucks at the *Tribune's* distribution gates.[63] The police swept in and arrested eighteen people.

Comfort had been a vocal critic of the *Tribune* and was arrested several times over the course of the Ad Hoc Committee campaign, including in the 14 December mobilization. Even though he was not directly participating in the sit-in he was accused of being a public nuisance and of failure to disperse and received a six-month sentence.[64] Comfort's visibility increased as supporters raised money for his bail. He believed that greater black involvement was the key to successful protest: "If the Knowland grip is ever to be broken, only the people in the Oakland ghetto can do it." The Ad Hoc Committee called the *Tribune* protests the beginning of a citywide thrust, envisioning "a full-scale project for Oakland like the SNCC Mississippi project" and a follow-up conference at UC Berkeley.

The Bay Area was propelled into the national spotlight as the streams of activism between white and black activists converged. In 1964 the Free Speech Movement was begun by veterans of the civil rights movement's southern campaigns and local activists at the University of California at Berkeley in response to the university's ban on political canvassing outside of its gates. Black students in high schools and community colleges and university campuses formed black history study groups and militant black student unions and demanded black studies courses. San Francisco State University was a center of black student activism and would eventually give rise to one of the first black studies programs in the United States.

Several organizations in 1965 demanded "real solutions" for "real problems" from the City Council. One of these groups, called ACTION, was formed in the fall of 1965 as "an association of ministers, civil rights groups, and local leaders" whose goal was to use direct action to agitate for a civilian review board, more black officers, residency requirements, and a police academy.[65] These multiple political cross-currents overlapped in re-inforcing and collaborative as well as antagonistic ways. In the mid-1960s the *Oakland Tribune* reported on the divisions between, on one side, the NAACP, the Urban League, the Oakland Economic Development Council, city councilmen, ministers, and attorneys who had been active in social improvements and civil rights for the black community for a long time, and, on the other side, the "so-called indigenous leaders" such as Curtis Lee Baker and Comfort, who had been getting press and had the ear of the white civil rights establishment.[66] Comfort was clearly part of a larger activist tradition but represented a different and increasingly more visible alternative to mainstream organizations.

Comfort left the Ad Hoc Committee and went on to found the Oak-land Direct Action Committee (ODAC) in 1965.[67] An organization that em-bodied his activist vision of doing community work to address racism and poverty, ODAC was multiracial but firmly based in the black community. In addition to Comfort three white activists took the lead to demonstrate that "there can be a black and white unity in working on human problems without 'white control.'" Rather than begin with a platform and try to gain community support, ODAC put the impetus in the hands of the community and sought to bring black "people together so that *they* can decide how *they* want to live" and define "*real* freedom and *true* democracy." Although there was some initial support from white college students, the type of sustained face-to-face organizing that Comfort called "block work" and that was cen-tral to ODAC's mission proved challenging. Comfort recalled, "No one has been back because it's hard, going from door to door talking to people, and a lot of people don't like to do it because it's a long, drawn out process. But it's very important, because how are you going to know exactly what is hap-pening in the black community unless you talk to the people themselves to find out exactly what they would like to see done, what seem to be the biggest problems in the community, and what type of activity they would be willing to participate in?"[68]

Comfort saw no contradiction between embracing the politics of black pride and unity being advocated by spokespeople like Malcolm X and Rob-ert Williams while working in interracial alliances. Nationalism in Oakland was a pivotal political force, and Malcolm X's visits to local mosques dove-tailed with growing student activism around a black history course at Oak-land City College, which became Merritt College. Comfort worked closely with local nationalist allies such as Curtis Lee Baker, a flamboyant activist who promoted self-defense and black pride to local youth.[69] Comfort believed, "The whole thing is black liberation, and what the white people have to realize is that the black people in this country are no longer waiting, that they are going on, beginning to call their own leaders, beginning to take some steps forward for themselves." He engaged with the organized left, such as the Communist Party and the Progressive Labor Party, but articulated a nonsectarian leftism rooted in grassroots organizing. "It's going to take the *people* to make the revolution. Just poor, working people striving for a better way of living will bring about the revolution and set up a government. And it doesn't matter what kind of government it is, just so long as it isn't a capitalist, fascist government. That's what counts."[70]

ODAC started as a small but dedicated group that focused on the major concerns of the black community: jobs, schools, and police brutality. The organization tackled police brutality by getting local residents involved in fighting back and raising awareness about local cases. They saw their activism as in line with SNCC, reflecting "the same esprit, the same urgency, direct confrontation."[71] ODAC quickly gained community support; their office was dubbed "Freedom Now Headquarters." Melvin Soriano, a fifteen-year-old ODAC field secretary and a member of the Alm Boy Dukes, a local gang and social club, spearheaded ODAC's work with teenagers. His goal was to unify warring gangs and politicize their activities.[72] Comfort hoped to send some of these youths to the South to work in SNCC projects to learn organizing skills they could bring back to Oakland. He wanted to create a cadre of youth who would "come back to organize people into opposition to end local white rule in Oakland, and to join with their brothers and sisters in the South, and all over this country, to bring about real democracy in America."[73]

This was just one way that protest politics in Oakland were connected to civil rights activism nationwide. Some groups traveled to demonstrations and saw their local activities as an extension of the national movement. In 1965 local CORE chapters sent representatives to Selma, Alabama, to join the demonstrations for equality. They argued, "We think that the most important thing to do is to let the people of Selma know that we are really with them, that we are willing to fight for our own freedom, here in Oakland, now."[74] Other groups were more explicitly focused on marshaling local resources and support for the southern movement. Organizations like Bay Area Friends of SNCC supported southern civil rights activities through fund-raising and community development work. They took the official position that while they were "not indifferent to racial problems close to home," their priority was "significant change in the political and economic status of the Southern Negro" as a "prerequisite to permanent change in race relations throughout the nation."[75] This official stance belied the local impact of Friends of SNCC. The organization served as a conduit through which southern civil rights leaders like John Lewis traveled through the Bay Area for fund-raising and speaking engagements.

By 1966 Comfort had made connections with activists in fourteen states. His links to the larger black liberation movement provided one conduit through which the imagery and symbolism of the Black Panther came to the Bay Area. The panther was the symbol of the Lowndes County Freedom Organization (LCFO), an independent black third party in Alabama founded in 1965 by SNCC activists. It would eventually become known as the Black Panther Party.[76] Comfort had gone to Lowndes to work on voter registration activities. In September 1965 he was interviewed in the SNCC newspaper the *Movement* talking about ODAC, the local impact of the Watts riots, and his work with young people following the SNCC model. He argued, "You have to stay with them like the SNCC workers in the South. You live in the houses: people respect this. You don't run in and run out, and then say you got arrested for the Negro people." Comfort would return to Lowndes in 1967 to donate twenty-two tons of food.[77] The cover of the *Flatlands* for 1–20 January 1966 had a picture of Comfort wearing a beret featuring a button of a snarling black panther.[78] Several issues over the course of the year show him wearing the beret and button.[79]

Panther imagery was a reflection of the connective tissue linking protests nationwide. In Berkeley the campus-based Friends of SNCC organized meetings to support the LCFO, and in 1966 John Hullett, an LCFO leader, spoke in the Bay Area at a public meeting against the war in Vietnam and asked for support for their organizing efforts.[80] An organization called the Committee for Lowndes County sprang up in Berkeley for the purpose of organizing locally. Their literature pointed out, "Negroes in northern ghettos have the vote, but they suffer under the same conditions that Southern Negroes do namely, poor schools, poor housing, and either poor jobs or no jobs at all."[81] Oakland's connections to multiple and shifting currents of activism around the country could not be more evident.

Black-led organizations arose to address bread-and-butter issues, and the War on Poverty's limited delivery on lofty promises made it a prime target. The first statewide convention of the poor was held in Oakland in February 1966 and brought together 175 to 200 delegates from fifty statewide antipoverty organizations to discuss welfare rights, housing issues, fair employment, and the federal antipoverty program. Criticism of government policies and initiatives was a unifying theme, and the groups present demanded "a full voice in policy levels and in policy decisions."[82] The California Federation of the Poor grew out of this meeting and was established in March 1966.[83] In the spring of 1966 antipoverty activists demanded major changes in the local War on Poverty administration to shift power from the "fat cats" to community members in the TAACs. They demanded policymaking power and 51 percent membership in the Oakland Economic Development Council for the TAACs, which had only "advisory authority and the power to initiate proposals, but not final authority over any program or over the community organizers paid to report on neighborhood conditions."[84]

This antipoverty activity buoyed ODAC's efforts, which continued to expand the scope of their activism to reflect the concerns of Oakland's young people. Education remained a key issue; a state commission on equal opportunities in education had issued a report that connected the tension in the schools to tensions in the community and suggested that the Board of Education act decisively in response to protests about historic inequities. Educational segregation had closely followed residential segregation in Oakland's history. In 1956 four elementary schools in the hills were created with a $40 million budget, while the population-dense flatlands received only four portable schools. In 1958 hot lunches were terminated in flatlands schools, and parents increasingly protested how school attendance boundaries were determined.[85]

The creation of Skyline High School in 1959 was a turning point in segregation debates in Oakland. Skyline's district boundaries were created to include only the hill areas, which would lead to an all-white school district.[86] Black teachers who spoke up about educational inequities were fired.[87] In 1966 a coalition of activists from civil rights groups, teachers, parents, and education groups founded the Ad Hoc Committee for Quality Education to advocate for flatlands children. The Committee demanded a review board investigate suspensions of teachers in flatland schools and ask for restrictions in the police's ability to question children in schools, free hot lunches, and equal equipment in hill schools and flatland schools. They threatened direct action if their demands were not met.[88] ODAC worked with the Committee to organize a three-day boycott of schools. One-third of flatlands high school students participated in this boycott, attending alternative "freedom schools," where they discussed everything from local politics to U.S. involvement in Vietnam.[89] A few weeks later students at Castlemont High School took out their frustration at police brutality outside of school and poor conditions inside in spontaneous acts of vandalism and confrontations with authorities.[90]

Comfort turned to electoral politics; he ran for the 15th Assembly District in Oakland and began to speak out against the war in Vietnam.[91] But his campaign was derailed when he was sentenced for the *Tribune* demonstrations and had to serve a six-month sentence beginning in May 1966.[92] Although he was subsequently released from jail due to a state supreme court stay, the *Flatlands* editorialized that Comfort's incarceration signaled a turning point in the consciousness of local activists because it meant that protesters who used "channels available within the system under which they live (votes, rallies, strikes, pickets, etc.)" that represented "faith in the basic rules of the system" were increasingly ineffective.[93] Driven by local and national events, many activists had come to this same conclusion.

Under the leadership of Stokely Carmichael, SNCC moved away from integration and tactical nonviolence. Carmichael and Willie Ricks popularized the phrase *Black Power* during one of the last southern civil rights marches in Mississippi, in June 1966. In its urgency and pride the phrase captured the mood of blacks nationwide. In Oakland Black Power provided a language for the evolution and radicalization of social protest and a broad umbrella under which various political and grassroots groups could coalesce. Activists seized on the term and rooted it in black self-determination, unity, political power, and knowledge of self and history. The chair of the NAACP defined Black Power as black politicians "doing what the people want and not what the power structure wants." A local SNCC representative pointed out that "Black power is opposed to assimilation. It means no longer being absorbed into a white liberal consensus with no real power." The local activist Curtis Baker explained that Black Power "isn't necessarily for violence, but it does include the power to defend oneself when attacked. White people had that power a long time ago." Comfort defined Black Power expansively, as a movement with the potential to remind blacks that "they will never be anything until we win full human rights for anyone."[94]

Black Power continued, rather than began, Oakland's connections to nationwide activist trends. It was a concept that progressive whites who had played a visible role in local struggles tried to adapt and fit into. But it belonged to the black community, where it was bandied from campus to street corner, from dinner table to community meeting in organizations fighting against poverty, police brutality, housing shortages, unequal education, and racial discrimination. It was cross-generational, engaging seasoned activists like Comfort, a veteran of many organizations and campaigns, as well as blacks who were just cutting their political teeth. It was deeply intellectual, visceral, explosive, and uncontainable. The black dynamite activists had been warned about for so long had arrived.

GRASSROOTS BLACK NATIONALISM

The Black Panther Party was one of the organizations founded during the explosion of Black Power in Oakland. While activists in San Francisco, New York, and other cities around the country had been inspired by the LCFO's panther symbolism and strong stance of black self-determination to create organizations bearing the panther name, it would be the Oakland organization that would lay ultimate claim to the name that Carmichael believed belonged "to the people."[95] The BPP was conceived in a War on Poverty community center by Huey Newton and Bobby Seale, two black men with prison time, military service, nationalist organizations, and college activism under their belt. Newton and Seale were among the wave of children of migrant parents that swelled Oakland's grassroots formations. Seale, born on 22 October 1936 in Dallas, migrated to Oakland with his family in 1942. Newton, born in Monroe, Louisiana, on 17 February 1942, did the same in 1945.[96] Both men had come of age amid harsh socioeconomic realities in Oakland's flatlands. Housing shortages forced Newton's family to move several times around West and North Oakland searching for decent accommodations. Newton had many disciplinary problems growing up and was expelled from school after school. Filled with a sense of alienation from the teachers and the learning process, he soon became involved in petty crime.[97] Seale's family lived in an overcrowded government housing project in Berkeley before moving to Oakland. Like Newton's, his family struggled economically and he grew up poor. He joined the military, but a conflict with white authority led to a bad conduct discharge after almost four years. Afterward he worked on and off around the state as a sheet-metal mechanic, draftsman, and comedian.[98]

Newton's and Seale's paths crossed at Oakland City College, a junior college in North Oakland. Seale had been attending the college part time since late 1958; Newton enrolled in 1959. As Merritt College it had become a center of political activism for first-generation college students, and the demand for black studies was fueled by strong student organizations and the presence of seasoned community activists. The atmosphere on campus had become very charged. Debates about the civil rights movement and discussions of black history and politics spilled out from classrooms to lunchrooms, sidewalks, and street corners. After school and during lunch black students mounted their sidewalk soapboxes at informal street rallies where political debate and jive talk were common. Newton and Seale were often in the thick of these debates; according to Seale, the two men solidified their friendship during a sidewalk discussion of the U.S. blockade against Cuba.[99] They gravitated to the same political circles and college courses and would move in and out of many of the same organizations. Seale recalled a memorable meeting with Newton when they shared their backgrounds and copious amounts of fast food: "This when we first get to know each other. This is 1963. So I want to find out about Huey. I asked him why he went to college, he said really, ah, more than anything to entertain my mind. I liked that. It was a good answer. . . . And I thought Huey had a lot of good theory and a lot of good heart. And I liked him."[100] Seale's down-to-earth wit and life experience were apt complements to Newton's mix of street smarts and intellect, and their friendship flourished. Together they embarked on a journey through Oakland's local political formations on and off campus that brought them into contact with national and international political trends growing in their own backyard. Their politicization process reveals the confluence of forces that would give rise to the Black Panther Party. While Comfort's brand of grassroots activism laid the groundwork, the Black Panther Party's origins would also be derived from the increasingly seamless nexus between the campus and the community.

Like many urban youths, Newton and Seale gravitated toward the message of pride, unity, and self-determination articulated by black nationalists. In their political universe black nationalism was both a local and a national phenomenon. Malcolm X, the fiery spokesperson of the Nation of Islam's largest mosque, had emerged as a vocal critic of nonviolent resistance and one of the most forceful advocates for black nationalism and self-determination. He urged black people to protect themselves against white violence, arguing, "We should be peaceful, law abiding—but the time has come for the American Negro to fight back in self-defense whenever and wherever he is being unjustly and unlawfully attacked."[101] Although both men encountered Malcolm's ideology in radio addresses and the Nation of Islam's newspaper, he also delivered his message to Oakland in a series of speeches in Bay Area mosques and community institutions in the early 1960s.[102] After attending one of these speeches Newton began to go to political discussions at Nation of Islam mosques in Oakland and San Francisco.[103] Seale saw Malcolm X speak at McClymonds High School in Oakland.

Malcolm X's critique of nonviolent civil rights strategies and advocacy of armed self-defense resonated with both men, who had grown up with the stark reality of police brutality. Seale recalled, "We dug quite specifically how he talked about the right of the people by the Constitution of the U.S. to defend themselves with guns, because the U.S. government wasn't doing its job to protect the poor, oppressed people."[104] Seale took Newton to his house one day and showed him an impressive collection of weapons, including pistols and shotguns. His long history with weapons demonstrated the impact of transplanted rural traditions in Oakland: "I was raised a hunter and a fisherman. . . . I was using guns from age ten. When I was ten and eleven, my brother and I would be hunting and fishing in northern California. . . . We would shoot the squirrels with the .22. Then at twelve my father bought me my first high-powered rifle. He bought me a .30-30 Winchester and bought me deer tags because at age twelve with the approval of your parents you could have a high-powered rifle in the state of California."[105]

Newton and Seale joined organizations that were influenced by Malcolm X's vision. Seale joined the Revolutionary Action Movement (RAM) in the early 1960s.[106] Formed in 1962 in Philadelphia, RAM openly called for international black revolution and preached revolutionary nationalism: "RAM is dedicated to the *national liberation and self*-determination of our captive non–self governing African nation–Black America and all oppressed dark nations of the world." They would achieve this "by using any means necessary."[107] RAM operated covertly and focused on political education and study. Seale remained active in the West Coast branch for two years but would eventually leave the organization, criticizing its focus on cultural activities.[108]

Both men played pivotal roles in the Afro-American Association led by Donald Warden, a popular black talk show host and nationalist voice.

Founded on the Berkeley campus of the University of California, the Afro-American Association grew outward into the Bay Area's black communities and would provide a space for the area's black college and high school students to discuss nationalist theory and practice. Newton and Seale became active participants in book discussion groups on black history and attended street rallies, forging many crucial political ties. It wasn't long, however, before both became critical of Warden's leadership and disillusioned by the focus on capitalism as the solution to the economic problems blacks faced. They eventually left the organization.[109]

Newton's academic activities and growing political consciousness blended seamlessly with his street life. While he was a student he continued to participate in petty thefts, credit card scams, and short-change scams, and he remained a familiar face in Oakland hangout spots. He had cultivated a street-tough, fearless reputation, and people had grown to respect his intelligence and his debating skills. At the time, he justified his petty theft activities in his own mind as stealing from the oppressor. Newton had begun to take classes at San Francisco Law School and studied the California penal code intensely. He was arrested several times, but because of the legal knowledge he had acquired he was able to defeat some charges, get out on bail, or be paroled. After being arrested for assault with a deadly weapon after an altercation at a party, Newton was sentenced on 8 October 1964 to serve six months in jail and a three-year probation period.[110] After his release in 1965, he continued his political involvement, and the friendship with Seale began to deepen.

Malcolm X's political trajectory was a frequent topic of their conversation. Malcolm had moved toward a more secular activist political stance when he broke with the Nation of Islam in early 1964. Although attracted to his political philosophy, both men had rejected the theological foundations of the Nation of Islam, which Seale had dubbed "unscientific stuff about Yacoub." Seale recalled raising a cheer when Malcolm traveled to the Middle East and Africa to meet with activists and heads of state and began talking about human rights: "I said yea! A whole lot of us did. I'm talking about all across this country. . . . Then he [Malcolm] defined it as a civil rights struggle in terms of human rights. Yes. It's much more three-dimensional when you start talking about human rights."[111] When Malcolm returned from abroad he articulated an anti-imperialist, internationalist philosophy rooted in black self-determination. He founded the Organization of African American Unity, reflecting his anti-imperialist stance and growing conception of the black liberation movement in the United States in terms of a worldwide struggle for human rights. He began to advocate that black Americans seek justice through the United Nations for the violation of their human rights.

Malcolm X's assassination in February 1965 was one of the catalysts that led Seale, Newton, and other students in a study group called Black History Fact Group to initiate the first black studies course at Merritt College. Newton and Seale joined the Soul Students Advisory Council, whose goal was to "develop Black student leadership, advocate for a more inclusive curriculum and to connect the university to the community." However, differences of opinion about the allocation of funds, acceptance of donations from whites, and the issue of armed self-defense divided the fledgling organization, and Newton and Seale eventually resigned.[112]

By this time Seale and Newton felt empowered to see themselves as agents of change. Seale's house, located right around the corner from Merritt College, became the site of heated discussions and debates over the black struggle on local, national, and international levels. Rather than joining yet another organization, creating one that they could customize became an imperative. They envisioned a blueprint for the type of organization they felt was needed to transform black people's conditions. Newton and Seale fused nationalist paradigms with understandings derived from their study of Malcolm X. They believed that black America was an internal colony of the United States and that the relationship between the black colony and the "mother country" was one of pure exploitation of labor and resources. As such, their goal was to create a political vehicle that would raise political consciousness in the black colony and forward the struggle for self-determination there. However, they did not see black self-determination as an end unto itself. They posited that black control of the black nation-state, or national liberation of the black colony, was a part of the larger goal to transform America and eventually the rest of the world.[113]

The civil rights movement had been framed by the international context of African independence movements, the reality of the cold war, and the escalating protest movement against the Vietnam War. Civil rights leaders had made explicit in their speeches the connection between the struggle of blacks in America and the struggle of African nations for their freedom. This connection was more than a rhetorical flourish; it had concrete expression in the consciousness of movement participants. In the fall of 1964 a SNCC delegation traveled to newly independent Guinea and met with

President Sékou Touré, a vocal proponent of socialism. One SNCC leader observed that year, "Something is happening to people in the southern Negro community. They're identifying with people because of color. . . . They're conscious of things that happen in Cuba, in Latin America, and in Africa."[114] The ideological soil in black America had become more receptive to international revolutionary theorists like Amílcar Cabral, Kwame Nkrumah, Fidel Castro, Frantz Fanon, and Mao Zedong.

Newton and Seale turned to Marxist theoreticians at home and abroad to explain the poverty they saw all around them. They identified capitalism as the root cause of oppression worldwide and linked the cause of African Americans with the cause of Third World liberation movements. They studied anticolonial movements worldwide and tried to apply the tactics of liberation struggle to the African American situation. They were particularly influenced by theories that posited that a small, armed group of dedicated people could lead the revolutionary struggle and that guerrilla warfare could be an effective strategy for progressive social change. They avidly read Mao's writings on the crucial role of the guerrilla in the struggle for national liberation. Mao argued that the guerrilla acted as both a political theoretician and a military commander, gaining support among the masses through his participation in the struggle and leading the masses to a higher state of consciousness by his words and example. Cuba's Castro further sanctioned the role of the guerrilla as a conduit through which revolutionary consciousness was transported to the masses. He declared, "It was enough for the ideas to take root in a sufficient number of men for revolutionary action to be initiated. . . . The masses started to acquire these ideals . . . and consciousness."[115] Mao's and Castro's theoretical depictions of the guerrilla fighter's role in the struggle for national liberation were especially relevant in the context of Vietnam, where guerrillas were stubbornly and effectively holding their ground, despite the superior technology of the United States.

Fanon, who analyzed the Algerian political situation and argued that national identity, culture, and pride could be achieved only through violent struggle, particularly influenced Newton and Seale. To Fanon violence was not only an effective tactic but also a psychological imperative to liberation. In the preface to *The Wretched of the Earth*, Jean-Paul Sartre explained that Fanon "shows clearly that this irrepressible violence is neither sound, nor fury, nor the resurrection of savage instincts, nor even the effect of resentment: it is man re-creating himself." Fanon asserted, "The armed struggle mobilizes the people; that is to say it throws them in one way and in one direction." Furthermore "the mobilization of the masses, when it rises out of the war of liberation, introduces into each man's consciousness the ideas of a common cause, of a national destiny and of a collective history."[116] Newton and Seale had also read Lenin and believed that a small group of people could act as a vanguard to lead the way to liberation. They saw themselves as that vanguard and resolved to put their ideas into action.

Newton and Seale were filled with optimism and determination and cognizant of the upsurge of activism and consciousness locally. They believed the revolutionary moment had arrived. Newton wrote in his autobiography:

> We had seen Watts rise up the previous year. We had seen how the police attacked the Watts community after causing trouble in the first place. We had seen Martin Luther King come to Watts in an effort to calm the people, and we had seen his philosophy of non-violence rejected. . . . We had seen the Oakland police and the California Highway Patrol begin to carry their shotguns in full view as another way of striking fear into the community. We had seen all this, and we recognized that the rising consciousness of Black people was at the point of explosion. One must relate to the history of one's community and to its future. Everything we had seen convinced us that our time had come.[117]

On 15 October 1966 Newton and Seale drafted a program for their organization in the back room of the North Oakland Neighborhood Anti-Poverty Center, where Seale worked. After all those months of discussion it took only a short time to create the founding principles and a statement of goals of their ten-point platform and program. It was separated into two sections: "What We Want" and "What We Believe." The first point called for self-determination: "We want freedom. We want power to determine the destiny of our black community. We believe that black people will not be free until we are able to determine our destiny." The ten-point platform and program went on to demand full employment, reparations from the federal government, decent housing, education representative of the black experience, and exemption of all black men from military service. Point 7 called for an end to police brutality and affirmed black people's right to organize self-defense groups. It took its justification from the Second Amendment's guarantee of the right to bear arms. Point 8 called for freedom for black prisoners, and point 9 called for a jury of peers for black defendants, as guaranteed in the Fourteenth Amendment. Point 10 demanded "land, bread, housing, education, clothing, justice and peace."[118]

This ten-point platform and program was not a revolutionary manifesto, a blueprint for radical social change, or a carefully thought-out plan of action. Instead it was a program of radical reform rooted in the nexus between visceral lived experiences of discrimination in Oakland's flatlands and the strong sense of connection with forces of radical social change around the country and the world. Newton and Seale starkly enumerated the failures of American democracy to its black citizens and sought justification for their points from the U.S. Constitution. Their platform and program fell squarely within the radical democratic tradition of American protest. It did not put forward a systematic analysis or critique of capitalism or imperialism. Instead it named "white landlords," "white American businessmen," "the American racist," "racist police," "racist government," and "racist military" as the oppressors of the black community. It did not call for the overthrow of government but instead sought to make the government antiracist and responsive to black citizens, whether that meant providing reparations or creating housing. They ended with an excerpt from the strongest statement for political independence and nascent nationhood in the history of the United States: the Declaration of Independence. Point 10 concluded with the statement that all men are created equal and are endowed with inalienable rights, and "whenever any form of government becomes destructive of these ends, it is the right of the people to alter or abolish it, and to institute a new government."[119]

Tactically the ten-point platform and program had the potential for broad mass appeal. Newton emphasized that the program had to be accessible to "the brothers on the block"—the brothers whom he had engaged in rap sessions on street corners and at parties.[120] One such block was 84th to 85th Avenue on East 14 in Oakland. This area was known as "the Block" and was typical of poor areas in Oakland.

For two young men who had experienced everything from prison to college, this commitment to the streets cast a net wider than their gendered articulation of the streets allowed. The goal was "a program for the people. A program that relates to the people. A program that the people can read and see, and which expresses their desires and needs at the same time."[121] These people were potentially from the streets, the campuses, local political organizations, and nationwide social protest groups. They were men and, potentially, women. To all who answered the call the ten-point platform and program would provide a foundation on which a more specific framework of implementation and action could be built. Armed with a thousand mimeographed copies of their program, the two founding Black Panthers hit the streets of Oakland in October 1966, determined to seize the time.

The type of political study and activism that led to the formation of the Black Panthers was central to the movement of Black Power. It was not just action, but discourse—both practice and theory. In Oakland this translated into two conferences that reflected local engagement with notions of Black Power. On 21 October 1966 the Committee for Lowndes County sponsored a symposium on Black Power at Merritt College.[122] All proceeds would go to the Black Panther Party in Alabama. A constellation of black grassroots activists from the *Flatlands*, CORE in Oakland, Soul Students Advisory Council, San Francisco State's black student union, and the editor of the Friends of SNCC newsletter, *The Movement*, met to share information and chart future directions.[123]

Students for a Democratic Society, one of the leading New Left organizations, held a second Black Power conference in Berkeley in October. The visible role of white students in planning the conference became a source of controversy, and student leaders at three Bay Area campuses threatened to boycott. The organizers argued that their goal was to educate whites about the need to organize in the white community, while critics pointed out that white commitment to the cause of Black Power might be fleeting: "If this fine strategy should backfire, some of those people in [Students for a Democratic Society] are merely going to shave and go back to New York."[124] Despite this tension, many Oakland activists did not use Black Power as a vehicle to express racial animus or political skepticism toward whites. Instead they offered a sharp critique of white racism, urged black activists to avoid white control, and suggested that sympathetic whites focus their efforts in their own communities. One activist summed up this spirit: "Black power has some enemies who are Negroes and some friends who are white."[125] The Berkeley conference went forward with a program that included panels on "Black Power in local communities," "Black Power and violence," "black culture and integration," and "organizing whites."[126] Local leaders such as Mark Comfort and regional activists like the Los Angeles nationalist Ron Karenga spoke alongside Stokely Carmichael, who offered intellectual analysis, historical insights, and searing polemics, urging white allies to answer the question "Can the white activist not try to be a Pepsi generation who comes alive in the black community but can he be a man who moves into the white community and starts organizing where the organizing is needed." The *Flatlands* reported an audience of ten thousand.[127] It was a scene that played out all over the country as people gathered to give voice to multiple understandings of Black Power. But it would soon become clear that the Black Panthers would define Black Power, even as it defined them.

2

IN DEFENSE OF SELF-DEFENSE

BRUTALIZERS AND EXPLOITERS

The Black Panther Party for Self-Defense began with two members, no funds, and no office. Newton and Seale's main resources were their sheer determination to build the organization and their commitment to each other. Their initial strategy to gain membership was to focus on the basic needs enumerated in the ten-point platform and program. They diligently circulated the document among their social and political networks and reached out to a cross-section of Oakland's black working-class and poor communities, including "all the Black brothers and sisters off the block," "mothers who had been scrubbing Miss Ann's kitchen," "brothers and sisters in college, in high schools, who were on parole, on probation, who'd been in jails, who'd just gotten out of jail, and brothers and sisters who looked like they were on their way to jail."[1] As byproducts themselves of a politicized college campus, Newton and Seale understood students were a key potential constituency. A witness to their organizing technique at San Francisco State recalled that they were a formidable tag team who "worked both sides of the fence" in "the lunchroom where people used to hang out and play cards." Seale would engage people socially, with a style that was more "'street' and down," while Newton was more "quiet, kinda introverted," but with a "finesse" that made him the center of attention when he did speak.[2]

However, in Oakland's flourishing political landscape the Panthers were just one of several groups attempting to organize young people. Their initial actions, such as agitating for the installation of a traffic light at a busy intersection, brought visibility but not bodies. Then they began to center their efforts on one of the most pressing community concerns among Oakland blacks: police brutality. The Panthers advocated armed self-defense as a means to address police violence, and their initial actions contributed to ongoing debates over what the strategy would involve.[3] The Panthers' stance was part of a nationwide conversation about armed self-defense among black nationalists and elements of the New Left. There was no single definition of self-defense; the debate that engaged Black Power advocates was not whether armed self-defense was more effective than nonviolent resistance but what self-defense would and would not entail.[4] Some activists defined self-defense in uncompromising terms, advocating a prescriptive course of action. The exiled former head of the NAACP Robert Williams, one of the most vocal advocates for meeting "machine gun with machine gun, hand grenade with hand grenade," had urged American blacks to "use whatever method in our possession" including "gas bombs, the lye can, the ice pick, the switchblade, the axe, the hatchet, the razor, the brick and the bullet."[5] Influenced by Williams and the Revolutionary Action Movement, some African Americans had organized gun clubs in urban areas. The founding charter of the Organization of African American Unity defined self-defense as self-preservation—a necessary step to take in the face of government's inability and unwillingness to "protect the lives and property of our people": "It is the duty of every Afro-American and every Afro-American community throughout this country to protect its people against mass murderers, bombers, lynchers, floggers, brutalizers and exploiters."[6] While influenced by both Williams and Malcolm X, the Panthers would chart their own path.

Newton and Seale realized that the "brutalizers and exploiters" that loomed the largest in the lives of Oakland blacks were those very agents of government who were not just "unable and unwilling" to protect blacks but were complicit in the maintenance of the racial status quo: the police. The defense that the Panthers would call for and the protection they hoped to provide would be against the violence that black people faced at the hands of the police. Point 7 of the ten-point program called for the end of police brutality and proclaimed that the key was "organizing Black self-defense groups that are dedicated to defending our Black community from racist police oppression and brutality." The justification for this was drawn from the Second Amendment's right to bear arms.[7] The self-defense that the Panthers embraced staked its claims from within as well as from outside of the system. Its radical edge was in conceiving African Americans within the American political contract, challenging the historic correlation of a constitutionally protected right to bear arms with white privilege. Newton and Seale understood police brutality as an issue of dignity and disempowerment experienced by individuals. For blacks, hostile and violent interactions with the police were part of the fabric of daily life, and negative experiences with the police linked people across age, gender, and class. However, they also hoped to clearly connect the heightened police presence in Oakland's black communities to structural discrimination and raise awareness of the role the police played in reinforcing the racial status quo. Self-defense was not a means to an end but an organizing tool. They implemented it by pairing bold and confrontational rhetoric with the assiduous avoidance of any offensive action and an awareness of the parameters of the law.

Emphasizing self-defense in the BPP's early actions would heighten the party's visibility, attract their first members, and garner national attention. However, it also created publicity that Newton and Seale were unable to define or control as they gained notoriety not for their political analyses but for their armed stance. They uncritically embraced the gendered assumptions of masculinist self-defense rhetoric, and their initial members were men. Despite the fact that women too were supporters and practitioners of armed self-defense, the prevailing dialogue had at its core the assumption that men would be on the front lines of white violence serving as protectors of the black community. Yet black women in Oakland boldly cast themselves in the image of a Black Panther. They trickled into the organization, drawn by a sense of self-empowerment and out of a growing consciousness about the role racism, poverty, and violence played in their lives. These women would push the Panthers to broaden their conceptions of self-defense in ways they had never conceived. The Panthers forged their understandings of self-defense and their strategies to combat police brutality in the fire of these debates. It was part and parcel of organization building, but it also held the seeds of organizational destruction. Armed self-defense exposed the raw nerve of state repression as Oakland's local police forces responded to the Panthers' armed initiatives with surveillance and harassment and conservative politicians sought to sew shut the loophole that made the Panthers' weapons legal.

PATROLLING THE POLICE

The Panthers' advocacy of self-defense was an outgrowth of their engagement with international theorists, a reflection of their ability to address local concerns, and a continuation of earlier grassroots attempts to organize against police brutality. Oakland blacks had sought solutions to police brutality as far back the 1940s through civil rights organizations and other groups, and by 1966 grassroots activists had taken up the call. Conditions in Oakland were ripe for the Panthers' focus on police violence as public conversations and activism around this issues increased in 1966. The Oakland Direct Action Committee was a leading voice against police violence. They solicited the Ford Foundation for funds to establish the Police Affairs Committee, despite strong resistance from City Council. The new committee, made up of a cross-section of activists, religious leaders, and local politicians, investigated cases of police brutality and held public hearings.[8] In March 1966 they called for a demonstration and a walkout by local high school students to protest a case in which three sisters were beaten up by the police.[9] This mirrored a successful protest at the end of 1965, when hundreds of students walked out of McClymonds High School to rally against police brutality.[10]

Local activists spoke out at hearings on police-community relations before the California Advisory Commission of the U.S. Civil Rights Commission. Curtis Baker pointed out that in addition to brutality, disrespect was also an issue to be addressed as the police commonly addressed black men as "boy" and women as "gal," racially laden terms that dated back to slavery. John George, an activist lawyer and politician, argued that Oakland was "an American brothel" as "the fundamental principles of American democracy" were prostituted daily in the city.[11] Mainstream politicians and police spokespersons responded to these allegations during National Police Week. District Attorney J. Frank Coakley stated, "There is nothing wrong with the Oakland police department. The Communist conspiracy has created disrespect for law and constituted authority." Police Captain Palmer Stinson echoed this view, claiming that "nearly all critics of the police are from the radical left."[12] Relations between the police and the community had reached a crisis not just in Oakland but nationwide. The Report of the National Advisory Commission on Civil Disorders, set up to examine the causes of urban unrest in 1966, concluded that most of the forty-three rebellions reported that year were rooted in animosity between the black community and the police.[13] Mark Comfort spearheaded citizen patrols of the Oakland police with a group from East Oakland called the Police Affairs Committee in an attempt to address increased police scrutiny and rumors and fears about riots and violence in Oakland in the wake of Watts.[14] Although Oakland did not experience social unrest, Mark Mullins, president of the Oakland Police Department Welfare Association, acknowledged that the renewed demands by various groups for a police complaint review board "indicate[d] a deep suspicion of our entire system of government since the advocates, by asking for a review board, are saying that they are unable to obtain justice through normal established democratic processes."[15]

Comfort's actions echoed the types of mobilizations going on regionally. Influenced by similar initiatives in Seattle, a broad coalition of black organizations in Watts, ranging from civil rights groups to the Slausons, an increasingly politicized street gang, came together after an incident of police brutality to create the Temporary Alliance of Local Organizations under the direction of local leaders such as Clifford Vaughs, a SNCC field secretary.[16] The Alliance created Citizens' Area Patrols (CAP; later changed to Citizens' Alert Patrol) to monitor police, sometimes with cameras and tape recorders, to deter brutality. To these activists CAP represented community empowerment and self-determination; the goal was not just to decrease incidents of brutality but to confront the feeling of helplessness.[17] Reporters who shadowed the patrols argued that CAP had "the same esprit, the same urgency, [and] direct confrontation" as SNCC. One reporter described a scene in which police had stopped a carload of young people and two CAP members observed from ten feet away and recorded details of the interaction. Another described being witness to the often hostile police reaction to CAP cars, often clearly marked with Black Panther bumper stickers, including issuing spurious tickets.[18] The program received praise too; for example, the president of the local NAACP chapter called CAP "one of, if not the most, effective programs that we have seen actually reach the people in this community for some time."[19]

Activists also discussed having Watts secede from the city of Los Angeles and becoming "Freedom City," with its own police force. This secession movement had adopted as its emblem the Lowndes County black panther as a "symbol of independent Negro power."[20]

Newton and Seale launched their own patrols in the fall of 1966. Newton familiarized himself with all of the particularities of the Oakland gun law, learning that civilians could legally carry unconcealed weapons in public in Oakland, when it was legal for the weapons to be loaded, and what restrictions applied to persons on probation and those under the age of eighteen. In November he and Seale secured a donation of a shotgun and a pistol from Richard Aoki, a Japanese radical in the Bay Area. A few weeks later they began to monitor the actions of the Oakland Police Department, poised to intervene with tape recorders, cameras, law books, and legally carried firearms. Typically Newton and Seale would observe police as they arrested people to make sure the officers were not breaking laws or using excessive force. Their goal was to educate people about their legal rights, to legitimize self-defense, and to gain the attention of Oakland blacks. Their efforts soon paid off. The sight of two young black men, carrying guns, loudly asserting their right to bear arms and warning the police not to be the aggressors repeatedly drew crowds. The Oakland police reacted with surprise at the sight of the armed youths, and tense verbal confrontations often ensued. Newton's fast talk and Seale's sharp wit would turn these moments into dramatic street theater. The fact that the police were often the ones to back away from these potentially volatile situations and were powerless to strip the Panthers of their weapons was empowering in almost palatable ways. Afterward Newton and Seale would distribute copies of the ten-point platform and program to onlookers and talk about the need for black people to organize politically. These patrols earned the Panthers a reputation in the community, and within a few months the Panthers welcomed their first recruits.

Newton and Seale embraced a militant masculism; appeals to manhood infused their organizing strategy, shaped how they were received in the community, and attracted an initial membership base of young men.[21] Although Artie Seale, Bobby Seale's wife, Laverne Williams, Newton's girlfriend, and other women had helped in the Party's operations from its inception, they had not made a political commitment to the organization and were not considered members.

The first new member of the Black Panther Party for Self-Defense was sixteen-year-old Bobby Hutton, affectionately dubbed "Lil Bobby," who met Seale while attending the North Oakland Anti-Poverty Center. Seale had arranged a job for him at the Center, and Hutton took part in political discussions with Newton and Seale. Eventually he joined the Panthers and was given the title of treasurer.[22] Seale, Newton, and Hutton pooled their paychecks and rented a space for meetings, and on 1 January 1967 the first Black Panther Party for Self-Defense office opened at 5624 Grove Street. The office was a sparsely furnished storefront in the heart of North Oakland, with a boldly lettered sign on the window, announcing the BPP's presence.[23] Just a few blocks away were Seale's home and Merritt College; the seamless border between the campus and the community meant that the politically charged atmosphere of the college often spilled into the office.

They created an advisory board of older community members, some of whom had been involved in the North Oakland Poverty Program, to broaden their growing base of support. One of these advisory board members, Ruth Beckford, donated office supplies and made curtains for the Panthers' first office.[24] To further increase visibility in the community they devised chic and stylish uniforms: black slacks, a powder blue shirt or turtleneck, a black leather jacket, and a black beret, rakishly tilted to one side. The aesthetic flair was not lost on community members, who saw the uniforms as "sharp and clean and organized." According to Seale, the uniform represented organization and was a symbol of powerful masculinity to be emulated: "To the brother on the block, the lumpen, 'Man, them dudes sho' is sharp. Baby I sho' wish I had me some knobs and some pimp socks like that,' you know what I mean. But at the same time, it gave us a chance to talk with people about the ten point platform and program, really what we were about."[25]

The police patrols embodied power, protection, and defense, characteristics that were often gendered male. Newton and Seale spoke of the "brothers" on the block standing up and acting as the protectors of the black community. One early member recalled, "The whole thing of packing guns to protect yourself was real for a lot of Black males."[26]

The young men who began to trickle into the Black Panther Party for Self-Defense came from many different paths and from all levels of income, education, and political consciousness. Most had grown up in the Bay Area and often came to the BPP through their association with someone else. Membership spread throughout social and political circles, in what one member described as "waves of curiosity, interest, acknowledgment, concern."[27] Willingness to join and work was initially the only criterion of membership.[28] Some recruits were unemployed, had prison records, or had been involved in gangs. These were the "brothers off the block" whom Newton and Seale wanted to make sure their organization spoke to. Others were student activists at Bay Area high schools or colleges. These early recruits were attracted to the BPP for different reasons. Some wanted the sense of "doing something" to change the conditions around them and were drawn to the concept of black people standing up for themselves. Others were attracted by the party's ten-point platform and program, while still others were drawn in by the party's armed stance. Some recruits fit into one of these categories; others fit into all of them.

What united these early members was their optimism and pride. The Panthers were a mirror that reflected an entirely new self-conception: the rejection of what some had seen as the weakness of a nonviolent strategy and the embrace of Black Power. One BPP member described it as both a "coming of age" and a "coming of consciousness": "The party was started from people realizing that turning the other cheek, singing, letting no fucking dogs bite you, just ain't the way—and the fact that we are black and we are proud of it and we gonna do something for our own. You can't market that, you can't never go back and get that again because when you forever had a slave mentality, not knowing your history, not knowing your place in society and coming to know that. You can never go back."[29]

Sherwin Forte was one of these early recruits. Forte became involved in the BPP in early 1967, when he was in his late teens. His family had migrated from Birmingham, Alabama, to Berkeley, and then to North Oakland. He grew up being conscious of police brutality and frequently witnessed the police harassing black teenagers. He had become an avid admirer of Malcolm X, and the Vietnam War had a major impact on his consciousness:

I had a choice whether I would go and fight the country's battles in Vietnam or whether I wanted to take my life and use it to redress some wrongs in this country. I didn't see the Vietnamese as the enemy. I saw the enemy as racist America. . . . And you know when you are young, you have a lot of fervor, a lot of strength. I think I felt like the way a majority of young people felt at that time given the riotous atmosphere, the killings, the national guard, the helicopters, the protest in Berkeley, the antidraft movement. It was a period of action and tension, and a lot of blacks focused on the political system.[30]

In the context of Vietnam the Panthers were the literal embodiment of the Black Power soldier who was committed to the war at home. Forte wanted to do something about the social, economic, and political status of black people in the United States, and the Panthers' emphasis on the issue of police brutality resonated deeply with him. Self-defense was also a draw. Forte saw membership was a way to "have the same tools that the oppressor had: guns." At the time he joined he was a student at Merritt College and had taken part in many "bull sessions," where students would sit on the steps of buildings and debate and discuss "the black man in America, the draft, what Stokely Carmichael was saying, what H. Rap Brown was saying." Forte met Seale at one of these sessions and learned about the Panthers. He was intrigued. His younger brother, Reginald, was attending Oakland Technical High School at the time and had heard about the organization from Hutton. The Forte brothers decided to attend a meeting; they experienced an "instantaneous connection" and vowed to come back. Sherwin recalled, "By the second meeting they were presenting me with this nine-millimeter semi-automatic pistol. . . . And you pick it up and . . . you feel a little bit of power. You feel like you have some righteous equipment to begin to address these wrongs."[31] Both of them joined.

As more people became involved in the BPP, the number of patrols increased and the geographic area covered grew as well.[32] The party began to offer other services, such as explaining the law, coordinating bail, and notifying family members of arrests.[33]Although patrolling often consisted of reading the penal code or simple observation, there were several major confrontations and standoffs with the police in which the Panthers refused to back down. These adrenalin-filled experiences had an indelible impact on Panther participants. When Sherwin Forte went on patrols and saw Newton explain the law to the police and saw the officers react with frustration and shock, he felt empowered: "[It] confirmed that we could gain respect, command respect. I think that bolstered our egos, made us feel very powerful, like we were a force to be reckoned with, and it was something that we became less and less afraid of doing."[34]

David Hilliard, one of Newton's closest friends, soon joined the BPP. Hilliard was born in Alabama, and his family migrated to Oakland when he was nine. He lived around the corner from Newton, and the two had become fast friends. Growing up, Hilliard had been somewhat of a rebel who often chose hanging out and drinking over attending school. Then Malcolm X shaped his consciousness, and when he heard about the Panthers' ten-point platform and program and about the armed police patrols he challenged himself to "take the intellectual and moral leap from the street corner into this world of action, ideas and revolution."[35]

Eldridge Cleaver and Emory Douglas joined the Panthers in February 1967. While in prison serving a nine-year sentence for rape, Cleaver had become politicized by reading Malcolm X's work. After being paroled in December 1966, Cleaver and several others rented a house in San Francisco's Fillmore district that served as a political and cultural center for various black organizations. Cleaver's writing and oratorical skills landed him a position as a journalist for *Ramparts*, a popular magazine in the Bay Area.[36] His prison essays, which were later published as *Soul on Ice*, received much acclaim in both black and white radical circles. The eloquent writing, critique of white supremacy, and raw account of his political evolution overshadowed the fact that the book was also a paean to machismo and heterosexual manhood that excused the violent rape of women. Cleaver's uncritical embrace by such a wide swath of movement activists speaks to the consensus around patriarchy and the promotion of manhood that was so central to movement culture at this time.

Newton and Seale encountered Cleaver at a planning meeting for the Malcolm X Grassroots Memorial, a conference on Malcolm's legacy to be held on the anniversary of his assassination, organized by the Black Panther Party of Northern California (BPPNC). A black nationalist organization based in San Francisco that promoted self-determination, cultural pride, and black independent politics, the BPPNC was one of many organizations that had been inspired to take up the symbol and name of the black panther.[37] Newton and Seale agreed to work with the BPPNC as part of an armed delegation to escort Betty Shabazz, Malcolm X's widow, from the airport to the *Ramparts* offices.

The Panthers made an indelible impression at that planning meeting. Cleaver described them as "the most beautiful sight I had ever seen: four black men wearing black berets, powder blue shirts, black leather jackets, black trousers, shiny black shoes—and each with a gun! . . . Where was my mind at? Blown!"[38] Emory Douglas, a twenty-two-year-old student activist at City College in San Francisco and a skilled artist, was also in attendance and marked this meeting as the moment that he knew he would join the organization: "I was very impressed with how they articulated themselves. They were armed and wearing uniforms. It was at that time that I knew that I wanted to be part of the Black Panther Party."[39]

The delegation of Panthers arrived at the San Francisco airport and escorted Shabazz without incident. But by the time they arrived at the *Ramparts* office, police, the local media, and onlookers had congregated outside. In a dramatic flourish Newton faced down a police officer who confronted him, and both the Panthers and the police drew their weapons. This tension-filled moment ended with the police officer backing down. This incident contributed to the Panthers' growing reputation.[40]

After this incident Douglas joined the organization and began patrolling the police.[41] Cleaver also joined, and Newton and Seale immediately elevated him to the third highest position in the organizational hierarchy: minister of information. In April 1967 Cleaver added the Panther voice and symbolism to an antiwar rally in San Francisco that was part of the Program for the Spring Mobilization against the War in Vietnam. He promoted the Panther ten-point platform and program and linked the struggle of blacks in America with the struggle of the National Liberation Front in Vietnam.[42] He represented the uncompromising militancy, strength, and powerful manhood that the Panthers would come to be associated with. However, gender politics in the Panthers, even in this early period, cannot be reduced to the politics of manhood.

COMRADE SISTER

The Panthers did not simply replicate the sexist assumptions, role patterns, and rhetoric that were promoted by some Black Power advocates who felt that male supremacy was part and parcel of fighting white supremacy. While much of their rhetoric revolved around the idea of brothers on the block standing up and acting as protectors of the black community, they also preached a nondogmatic message of activism that assumed a unified

FIGURE 2.1. Black Panthers from Sacramento at the "Free Huey Rally," Bobby Hutton Memorial Park, Oakland, California. No. 62 from the series Black Panthers 1968 by Pirkle Jones, Pirkle Jones Collection © 2014 Marin Community Foundation.

community where women were political actors.[43] They theorized about the need for strong manhood but didn't counter that with descriptions of submissive womanhood. Black women turned these theoretical loopholes into open doors.

The Black Panther Party appealed to black women in Oakland who faced issues of poverty and political powerlessness similar to those black men faced and felt the same desire to do something. These young women had come to political consciousness in the context of the growing women's movement and the public dialogue about women's equality, rights, and liberation. They understood the commitment to armed self-defense as a marker of strength and determination exemplified not just by men but by women, including the nationally known activists Mabel Williams and Gloria Richardson, as well as women in their families and communities. Many of these women had been involved in activism at their school or as part of the burgeoning black arts movement and were seeking to connect to an organization whose racial politics they agreed with and whose gender politics seemed malleable. For them, pragmatically, the Panthers posed a viable alternative to the strictly hierarchical gender roles advocated by some local nationalist organizations, such as the Nation of Islam.

Sixteen-year-old Tarika Lewis was the first young woman to join the BPP, in the spring of 1967. Like Bobby Hutton and Reginald Forte, she was a student at Oakland Technical High School and a member of the Black Student Union. She was one of the first students to agitate for a black history club and to proudly wear her hair in an afro. Lewis attended forums on black history and culture with her activist older cousins and often cut school to hang out and attend courses at Merritt College. One day she boldly walked into the Panther office and declared, "Ya'll have a nice program and everything. It sounds like me. Can I join? 'Cause ya'll don't have no sisters up in here." Seale said yes and Lewis was swiftly incorporated into the organization.[44]

Elendar Barnes also joined the BPP in the spring of 1967 in her late teens. Her family had migrated from Louisiana and she was raised in West Oakland. She was a student at Merritt College and involved in the Black Student Union as well as the local cultural resurgence around African dance. She learned about the Panthers through Laverne Williams, her best friend and Huey Newton's girlfriend at the time. According to Barnes, her involvement in the Panthers was a natural evolution of the self-defense politics that she had grown up with:

> I became very involved in that level of politics because it was an extension of what I knew, an extension of what they called the Deacons [for Defense] down South. And my grandfather wasn't necessarily a member of the Deacons, but our family's stance was, you know, you protect your family by any means necessary and, you know, you use guns. My grandfather was the first person to buy land on what was considered the white part of town. I'd go visit him in the summers and I remember that the Ku Klux Klan burnt a cross on his yard because they opposed him living on that side of town. And my uncles, the males of my family, came from different parts of the country and, you know, there was a conflict. It ended with cars being blown up, all that kind of stuff. So my involvement in the party came from me seeing

certain things that occurred in terms of my family organizing down South and that stuff being carried. I remember asking, "Papa, why you always got a gun?" He'd reply, "It's for the white folks, baby." "Papa, why you get up so early?" "To keep up with the white folks, baby." That is from very young. That's why I joined the Panthers. I came from that idea of standing up. And I think a lot of people in Oakland have these southern roots and that whole connection with the idea of protecting your own. People were used to using and keeping guns because that's what they did in the country. My grandfather always kept a gun; it was invisible but it always was in the back of the car or up in the window in the back of the truck, and they always said in the South that they were for hunting but he said it was for the white man. And it wasn't for the white man who wasn't bothering you. It was for the KKK and the others. And that's what moved me into the Panthers.[45]

Judy Hart joined the Panthers in the summer of 1967 when she was twenty-two. She grew up in a middle-class neighborhood in East Oakland and was involved in the Black Student Union movement at San Francisco State University. She was attracted to the Panthers because she saw them as a group that was serious about combating police brutality.[46] Janice Garrett-Forte was also a student at San Francisco State and active in the Black Student Union movement when she first became involved in the BPP. She had met Newton and Seale when they came to speak on campus. She and her roommates had provided temporary housing for a few BPP members in their apartment, and soon their apartment became a meeting place. At first she was hesitant about the Panthers' armed stance, but as she learned more she came to accept the principle of self-defense. Being a supporter heightened her political consciousness. Soon she felt she had no choice but to make a stand. She officially joined later that year.[47]

These pioneering women opened the door for others. The political experience they brought, the expectations they had, and the challenges they raised would have an important impact on the Panthers' evolution.

THE LOADED GUN

As the party's ranks began to swell, Newton and Seale discovered that formal political education, leadership structures, and a plan for financing their activities were key components of organization building. Self-defense played a prominent role in all of these strategies. Looking for sources of income, the Panthers decided to sell copies of *Quotations from Chairman Mao* (also known as the *Red Book*) at the University of California at Berkeley. Berkeley was an important hub of white student activism in the nation, and students in its politically charged environment were ready consumers of Mao's ideas. The Panthers purchased the books for thirty cents and sold them for one dollar. What began as a chance idea turned into a profitable money-making strategy that they exploited for several months. Newton, Seale, and Hutton would prominently position themselves on Berkeley's bustling streets near the campus and aggressively hawk the books. Soon they were selling the books at rallies and other occasions.

The Panthers saw the sale of the *Red Book* as part of their larger strategy to politically educate their membership. They used the money to fund activities and buy guns for their police patrols, a prime tool for recruiting members whom they could politicize using ideas culled from the *Red Book*. It was a risky bait and switch as the weapons focus came to define the Panthers' public image. According to Seale, "Some brothers would come into the Party, and see us with guns, and they related *only* to the gun."[48] Some "sisters" fell into this trap as well. Tarika Lewis's second question to Seale on the day she joined was whether she could have a gun. Seale's answer was yes. Lewis quickly discovered, however, that membership meant learning BPP ideology and participating in a wide range of political programs. "I had to earn it [her weapon]. . . . I learned safety, I learned to respect it, I respected other people. I never pointed a weapon at anybody, and I followed the rules."[49] Lewis parlayed her gun skills into respect. When some Panthers questioned her emerging role in the organization, she invited them to "come on out to the weapons range," confident that she "could outshoot 'em."[50]

The Panthers played a critical role in the dialogue among nationalist organizations such as SNCC, the Revolutionary Action Movement, and the Republic of New Africa, an organization that sought to create an independent black republic, about the role of political violence in the black liberation movement. In the summer of 1967 the cities of Tampa, Cincinnati, Atlanta, Newark, Cleveland, and Detroit were marked by uprisings led by students and youths. The root causes of these incidents ranged from black political powerlessness in local government to poverty, unemployment, and inadequate housing and education—but the spark was usually an incident of police brutality.[51] The Panthers watched urban areas becoming battlefields, complete with national guard troops, looting, mass arrests, sniping, and fire bombing, and saw the seeds of revolution in these sporadic acts of defiance. As one of the most visible organizations openly carrying arms, they were thrust in the forefront of these debates.

Newton would issue three policy statements in the summer of 1967 that delineated the Panthers' analysis of these uprisings. He condemned rioting as unproductive and disorganized and argued that the black community should arm itself with weapons and with the ideology of self-defense because "force and brutality can only be eliminated by counterforce through self-defense." In this equation the gun was the "basic tool of liberation" that needed to be embraced to be abolished.[52]

To the Panthers these rebellions signaled the changing mood among black people and solidified a concrete role for the BPP: offering "guidance to extend and strengthen their resistance struggle." Pointing to examples of vanguard parties from Cuba, China, and Algeria and to the Russian Revolution, Newton theorized that the Panthers could serve the same leadership role in the United States. He used the bold, confrontational rhetoric that would become the Panthers' trademark. In one speech he said, "We were forced to build America, and if forced to, we will tear it down. The immediate result of this destruction will be suffering and bloodshed. But the end result will be the perpetual peace for all mankind." In another speech he compared the Panthers to the Vietcong, stating that "weapons must be taken from the oppressor."[53]

In reality, however, the Panthers were far from ready to wage guerrilla warfare as a vanguard organization. Armed self-defense had proven to be a successful tactic for visibility, but the gun had the potential to overshadow other aspects of their political program. The Panthers attempted to transform the consciousness of their early recruits and disseminate their ideology through political education classes. New recruits were challenged to memorize and understand the ten-point platform and program and familiarize themselves with the ideas of Fanon, Malcolm X, Che Guevara, and Mao. Seale noted that although the Panthers had focused on self-defense, they "didn't have any intention of having [members] identify only with the gun." Instead the goal was to "teach them that the gun was only a tool and it must be used by a mind that thinks."[54] Barnes recalled that members went through a "mind change" once they began to study politics, read, and participate in disciplined patrols.[55]

This "mind change," the idea of personal transformation, was key to the success of the organization, for the goal was not only to challenge and change the conditions in America but also to politicize their membership and their mass following. Early political education efforts ranged from formal classes to informal discussions at Seale's house, where he and Newton exposed people who were interested in the BPP to some of the ideas and thinkers who had influenced them.[56]

The Panthers held classes in political education and weapons training twice a week. Supporters with military experience, like John Sloane, taught members how to break the weapons down, clean them, and handle them in a safe manner. Seale and another early member, Elbert "Big Man" Howard, provided weapons training to new recruits.[57] The Panthers also focused on "coordinating various activities, and understanding the political significance of various actions we took."[58]

Soon the Panthers had a dedicated group of members and supporters. For those Panthers who had jobs or were in school, involvement in the BPP meant spending some of their spare time attending rallies, leafleting, attending meetings and classes, patrolling, or recruiting. Rules were created to specify standards of conduct and enforce organizational discipline. Some of the new members were undisciplined and brought habits such as smoking marijuana, gambling, and drinking into the organization.[59] The first three rules warned against using or possessing narcotics, marijuana, or alcohol while doing BPP work. Rule 4 covered office work and meetings; rule 6 stipulated that no member could be part of any army force except the hypothetical "Black Liberation Army"; rules 5 and 7 warned against improper decorum while possessing a weapon. The remaining rules specified that BPP members should understand legal first aid and the proper procedure if they were arrested. All members had to know and understand the ten-point platform and program.[60]

The Panthers' reputation began to spread beyond Oakland. On 1 April 1967 Denzil Dowell was killed by police in nearby Richmond, California. When conflicting police reports and eyewitness testimony raised suspicions about possible misconduct, the Dowell family turned to the community for support. Mark Comfort brought the case to the Panthers' attention. Although Comfort had not sought membership in the BPP, he was a key local ally for the fledgling organization. The Panthers worked with the Dowell family to put pressure on the Contra Costa Sheriff's Department and investigated the crime scene. A local newspaper reported on one of the Panthers' rallies in Richmond: "Some 150 Negroes listened as leaders of the group stood atop autos to make speeches and armed guards kept away all whites. The speakers reportedly advised the crowd what to do regarding the alleged police brutality. While Contra Costa deputies kept an eye on the gathering from a helicopter, no action was taken on the ground, since a sheriff's spokesman said the Black Panthers broke no laws and displayed their weapons openly."[61]

As part of mobilizing the community about the case, the Panthers published the first issue of their newspaper, the *Black Panther*, on 25 April 1967. Many of their armed actions had received negative coverage in the mainstream media, and the newspaper was a bold attempt to shape their own public image and disseminate their own propaganda.[62] The first issue was printed on both sides of two legal-size sheets of paper. It was hand-lettered and mimeographed and was distributed free. Emory Douglas was familiar with commercial art and worked on the layout; for this he was given the title minister of culture.[63] The masthead stated, "The Black Panther Black Community News Service, Volume 1 Number 1 published by the Black Panther Party for Self-Defense." The front-page headline queried, "Why was Denzil Dowell Killed?" There was a picture of Dowell, an article giving the "family's side" of the killing, and a list of eleven questionable facts in the police account. The newspaper urged people to attend a meeting in North Richmond. In an article titled "Let Us Organize to Defend Ourselves," the Panthers chronicled several incidents of police brutality that had taken place in Richmond, San Francisco, and Oakland and called for self-defense. The paper also contained an article titled "Armed Black Brothers in Richmond Community," which discussed an armed rally that the police had been powerless to prevent and stressed that organizing around a political perspective was just as important as being armed: "The beautiful thing about the Brothers who held the rally is that they are organized, disciplined and politically aware of all the ins and outs of the problems facing Black People throughout the Bay Area in particular."[64] The newspaper was an act of self-definition and a way to assert that weapons were a means to an end, not an end in themselves. But it was perhaps too little, too late.

SACRAMENTO INCIDENT

The legal underpinnings of the Panthers' self-defense strategy soon came under attack. A newspaper article published in April 1967 noted that the Panthers had avoided arrest because they had been meticulous in obeying the gun law: "Under California law, they have not violated any gun laws. They do not conceal the weapons, they do not carry loaded guns in vehicles—just guns and ammunition. It's legal." This article concluded with an interview with the state attorney general Thomas C. Lynch, who warned, "The time has come when we have to legislate against carrying or exhibiting guns in public places."[65] One month later the Mulford Bill, prohibiting carrying unconcealed firearms in public, was introduced in the state legislature, which would change the gun laws to make the Panthers' weapons illegal.

On 2 May 1967 the Panthers led a delegation to Sacramento to highlight their opposition to this bill. Among the thirty men and women were party members, such as Seale, Douglas, and Warren Tucker; relatives and friends of Denzil Dowell; and Comfort and other community activists.[66] Eldridge Cleaver's parole restrictions required him to go under the guise of an official assignment for *Ramparts*. Newton, also on parole, stayed behind.

In addition to protesting the bill, the Panthers saw a sure opportunity for media coverage. Twenty members of the delegation were armed. Seale planned to read a statement (Executive Manifesto #1) written by Newton declaring the right of black people to arm themselves in self-defense. It linked police aggression in black communities throughout the nation to American aggression in Vietnam and argued that the U.S. government had a policy of "repression, genocide, terror, and the big stick" toward communities of color, evidenced by the genocide of Native Americans and the internment of Japanese Americans during World War II.[67]

The Panthers caused a stir the moment they emerged from their cars, weapons in the air. As reporters swarmed, Seale read the manifesto on the steps of the legislative office building; then, with no real plan of how to proceed, the delegation marched inside. With police and reporters in tow, the group tried to head for the balcony to observe the proceedings but took a wrong turn and ended up on the floor of the legislature. The police briefly confronted them but eventually released them because they had broken no laws. Seale read Newton's statement again and they departed. When they stopped at a gas station after leaving the capital, police officers swooped in and arrested them on charges of conspiracy, carrying concealed weapons, and more.[68] Sherwin Forte recalled the tenseness of that moment: "There was a big question there when the police were trying to round us up after we were leaving the assembly and leaving the capital, and they began to get a sense of how to deal with us. . . . Because it was such a surprise, such a shock to the assemblymen, to the governor. . . . It merged into a confrontation between us and the Sacramento police. I really credit Bobby [Seale] with saving everyone's life there. Because he was the first one to say, 'Take the arrest.' "[69]

Cleaver and several others were soon released. Despite the fact that he had permission from his parole officer and was on an official assignment for *Ramparts*, Cleaver had further restrictions placed on his parole. Seale briefly considered going underground but decided to stand trial. He and several other delegation members were imprisoned.

This action, known as the "Sacramento incident," was broadcast nationally and internationally as a defiant assertion of the right to bear arms. Supporters of the Panthers held a rally at San Francisco State to raise money for the arrested members of the delegation. Stokely Carmichael spoke at the gathering and pledged his support. The Panthers deftly manipulated this surge of interest and tried to add complexity to the powerfully symbolic yet simplistic image of themselves as gun-toting, leather-wearing militants. They created flyers, posters, pamphlets, and buttons.[70] Newton spoke on several local radio stations and to newspapers to elaborate on the ten-point platform and program and the BPP's politics. On 15 May 1967 the Panthers published the second issue of the *Black Panther*, which featured stories that would tell "The truth about Sacramento" since "the mass media has indulged itself in an orgy of distortion, lying, and misrepresentation seldom equaled in the history of the racist USA."[71] The articles were written in vibrant language designed to capture the readers' imagination. The police were described as pigs: "an ill-natured beast who has no respect for law and order, a foul traducer who's usually found masquerading as a victim of an unprovoked attack."[72] This language symbolically stripped the police of their authority, dignity, and humanity. Douglas, a skilled graphic artist, and Lewis created captivating visuals portraying black people as powerful fighters while representing the police as fat, slovenly pigs.[73]

The Sacramento incident resulted in an increase in membership, especially among college students and other young people frustrated with police brutality.[74] Mary Williams recalled, "It was terrible here [Oakland], really terrible. And anyone who came along who had ideas about moving ahead, people would have listened, because it was really bad. You couldn't even talk to a policeman."[75] Williams, her husband, and her brother-in-law joined the BPP after the Sacramento incident. Terry Cotton was galvanized by the media coverage of the incident; he remembered seeing "li'l Bobby and Bobby when they went into the capitol" and hearing about "all the politicians . . . getting down under their desks." To him it was "really impressive": "I thought that everybody should have the right to bear arms for self-defense against harassment, police brutality, and ya know, Mass Genocide."[76]

The media coverage fueled interest in the Panthers around the country. Steve McCutchen recalled watching news of the Sacramento incident from Baltimore: "What caught my attention at the time was, one, black men with guns; two, black men who were there in a state capitol; and three, it was at a time where the Vietnam War was raging and I was caught in the conflict because I was in twelfth grade then and I had no clue how I was going to finish the twelfth grade, finish school, and stay out of Vietnam. That caught my attention."[77] Requests poured in from people who wanted to organize new Panther chapters or bring preexisting political formations under the Panther banner. While these local activists faced socioeconomic conditions that paralleled Oakland's, they had their own organizing traditions, political ideologies, and social networks. These local tendencies would be knit into a national movement, a dynamic process that was rarely led or directed from Oakland. Panther chapters would spring up in Michigan, Georgia, New York, Tennessee, and southern California. The Panthers quickly realized that they were not equipped to handle organizational growth in any systematic way; there was no "administrative body that could handle these requests and supervise a large-scale organization."[78] In a largely symbolic gesture, the Panthers drafted Carmichael, a skilled organizer, into the organization with the rank of field marshal.[79] Yet, although he considered the Panthers an ally and a promising manifestation of Black Power, his focus remained the growth and development of SNCC. In mid-1967 he visited Algeria, Syria, Egypt, Guinea, and Tanzania, leaving little time to recruit or organize on the Panthers' behalf.[80] So the question of how to expand was set aside for the more pressing business of survival.

BLASTED OFF THE STREETS

At the end of the BPP's first year its collision course with the state would come to its inevitable end. Prophetically Newton had written in his autobiography, "[I] did not think I would live for more than one year after we began; I thought we would be blasted off the streets."[81] Police harassment of the Panthers had begun soon after they initiated their police patrols. Armed Panthers who were supposed to intervene between the community and the police became the targets of an escalating police campaign to neutralize the organization. The police knew which cars were driven by BPP members and would often stop them for traffic violations. Criminal laws were used as a pretext to arrest Panthers and incarcerate them for as long as possible. This tied up limited BPP resources for bail and created adverse publicity.[82]

In July 1967 the Mulford Bill, which outlawed the carrying of loaded firearms on one's person or in vehicles and prohibited citizens from having loaded firearms in or near any state or government building, became law. It ended with a clear warning about the "increasing incidence of organized groups and individuals publicly arming themselves for purposes inimical to the peace and safety of the people of California."[83] Rhetoric to the contrary, the Panthers had been able to practice armed self-defense not because of Second Amendment rights but because of Oakland's liberal gun laws. The loophole in the law had been sewn tightly shut, and armed Panther patrols were now illegal.[84] Newton issued a directive ordering Panthers to stop carrying weapons publicly; as a result the arms went underground.[85]

In August Seale was sentenced to six months in jail for disturbing the peace in the Sacramento incident. The irony of Sacramento was that it had thrust the Panthers into the national spotlight while decimating their ranks. On 28 October 1967 Newton was arrested in an early morning melee that left him wounded and a police officer dead. Newton and his companion were driving his girlfriend's tan-colored Volkswagen; they had just left a party celebrating the end of Newton's parole after his 1964 arrest. The police officer, John Frey, identified the car as a Panther-affiliated vehicle with outstanding parking tickets and pulled it over. While Frey was examining Newton's registration, a second police car pulled up with officer Herbert Heanes inside. Heanes had heard Frey's request for backup, and as the closest officer in the vicinity he arrived on the scene a few minutes later.

Subsequent events are in dispute.[86] In one version Newton was ordered out of the car. He initially refused but eventually complied, holding his law book in his hand. A fight ensued in which Frey was killed and Newton and Heanes were wounded. Newton and his friend left the scene and asked the driver of a parked car nearby, Dell Ross, to give them a lift. They later jumped out of the car and fled on foot. In his autobiography David Hilliard revealed that Newton showed up at his home, and at approximately 5:30 a.m. he and his brother, June, dropped Newton off at Oakland's Kaiser Hospital.[87]

Newton's law book, with his name written inside, was found at the crime scene. It didn't take the police long to check local hospitals, locate Newton, and place him under arrest as the prime suspect. News of the incident spread, and the next morning a photograph of Newton handcuffed to a hospital gurney was featured on the front page of local newspapers. The killing of one police officer and the wounding of another in an incident that involved one of the leaders of the Black Panther Party for Self-Defense guaranteed the case would be high profile. Newton was hospitalized for two weeks for stomach wounds, then was transferred to the medical ward of San Quentin Prison, and then to the Alameda County Jail in downtown Oakland. On 13 November 1967 he was indicted for three felonies: the murder of Frey, assault with a deadly weapon against Heanes, and the kidnapping of Dell Ross.[88] He faced the death penalty.

The Panthers linked Newton's fate to the fate of armed self-defense, asserting, "What is at stake is first of all, Huey's life, and secondly, the right of black people to self-defense against armed aggression on the part of the police as the military arm of the racist power structure."[89]

The Panthers were not the only ones to feel the blast from this incident. Berkeley was the epicenter of nationwide domestic unrest over the U.S. government's involvement in Vietnam, and increasingly white student activists were challenging the social order and coming into conflict with the police. Just one week before Newton's arrest the police had clashed with thousands of antiwar demonstrators at the Oakland Induction Center. Photographers and reporters chronicled the indiscriminate clubbing and use of mace that police practiced against demonstrators who were determined to stand their ground. The Bay Area radical community dubbed this day, 17 October 1967, "Bloody Tuesday."

In the wake of Seale's and Newton's arrests, Cleaver stepped to the forefront as the Panthers' principal spokesperson. Despite warnings from the parole board, he made public speeches on behalf of the Panthers and published literature in Newton's defense. Cleaver brought his distinctive brand of Marxist political polemics to the organization. The Panthers continued to speak in terms of the national liberation of black America but began to shift toward leftist economic analyses that critiqued capitalism. While

FIGURE 2.2. Kathleen Cleaver, communications secretary of the Black Panther Party and wife of Eldridge Cleaver, De Fremery Park, Oakland, California. No. 5 from the series Black Panthers 1968 by Pirkle Jones, Pirkle Jones Collection © 2014 Marin Community Foundation.

Cleaver's role as a charismatic Panther leader was important, it would be the organizing skills of Kathleen Cleaver and other women that would play a decisive role in the Panthers' survival.

Kathleen Neal was working with SNCC when she met Cleaver in 1967 at a black student conference at Fisk College in Nashville. Cleaver recruited her to help him organize around Newton's case, and the two were subsequently married. Kathleen's organizing experience made her a valuable addition to the BPP.[90]

The period immediately following Newton's arrest was a time of crisis for the Panthers. Their core membership had dwindled from approximately seventy-five to fewer than thirty committed members, many of whom were incarcerated following the Sacramento incident.[91] The remaining members faced the formidable task of rebuilding the organization with both of its founders imprisoned.

Kathleen Cleaver initiated fund-raising activities, planned demonstrations to raise awareness about Newton's case, and served as a contact person for the press to inform them about Panther events. Soon she came to see herself as a Panther and called herself "communications secretary." The organizational structure was "in a total state of collapse"; there was no money for the office rent, no regular newspaper, and only a handful of active members.[92]

Despite their low numbers, the remaining Panthers mobilized behind Newton's case. They operated on a collective basis, met at different people's houses, and made decisions as they socialized.[93] Women played a central role in this process, asserting leadership and shaping policy not just despite the lack of formal structure but because of it. Janice Garrett-Forte recalled, "After Huey had gotten shot, we had a central committee that consisted of Kathleen, Eldridge, Huey, Bobby. I was in it 'cause I was his [Newton's] secretary. JoAnne Mitchell was the captain of the women, and we were lieutenants. We would have meetings about different policies within the party."[94] Kathleen Cleaver explained, "The party reconfigured itself in the midst of the 'Free Huey' movement. [It] allowed the party to reinvigorate [itself]."[95]

The Panthers worked with Newton's family to create the Huey Newton Defense Fund to coordinate fund-raising efforts. They chose "Free Huey" as their rallying cry rather than the more modest demand of a fair trial. While the mainstream media defined the case as criminal, the Panthers persistently focused on the underlying politics of his arrest. According to their propaganda, the criminal justice system was persecuting Newton because he was the leader of a radical political organization that was raising awareness of police brutality. He was a *political* prisoner, wrongfully accused and imprisoned, the victim of an ongoing campaign of police harassment against the black community in general and the Black Panthers in particular. The role of incarceration in derailing movements, draining resources, persecuting dissent, and sparking solidarity campaigns would grow evident over the course of the movement for Black Power.

In their first year of activism the Panthers had boldly and legally picked up the gun—and been forced to lay it back down. They had seen the power of armed self-defense to motivate, inspire, and empower both men and women. They had faced the reality of its inability to politicize, educate, and organize and witnessed its potential to unleash unheralded repression. Organizational development too was shaped by armed self-defense; it motivated the Panthers to create rules, weapons training, membership requirements, and political education classes. Going forward, Seale and Newton would continue to strategically advocate for self-defense but also prioritized developing other elements of their political program. Understanding that self-defense could be both a catalyst and a corrosive, they dropped the "for Self-Defense" from the party's name—an act of self-definition that largely escaped notice. It was a balancing act that would become increasingly untenable.

3

MOVING ON MANY FRONTS

The Black Panther Party's Transformation from
Local Organization to Mass Movement

THE DEATH OF NONVIOLENCE

Martin Luther King's assassination on 4 April 1968 in Memphis plunged the
country into shock, outrage, and mourning for King, whom many people
had considered one of America's greatest moral leaders. For the Panthers
and their supporters, the murder of the leading proponent of nonviolent resistance undermined the entire rationale of nonviolence. Kathleen Cleaver
called King's murder "probably the single most significant event in terms
of how the Panthers were perceived by the black community. . . . So, it's
like the Panthers were all of a sudden thrust into the forefront of being the
alternative."[1] King's death forced a reevaluation of the Panthers by those
who had dismissed them as irresponsible radicals. It helped fuel their expansion nationwide and bolstered their campaign to free Huey Newton. It

shaped the context of the political alliances they began to forge and opened the door to support from across the political spectrum and from celebrities such as Marlon Brando.

In the wake of King's death the Panthers tried to quell and channel discontent rather than advocate for spontaneous action. The murder sparked uprisings in poor communities of color all across the country. In Oakland the Panthers circulated throughout the streets spreading the word that spontaneous action was futile, hoping to set an example of organization and discipline. Partly as a result of their efforts, no disturbances broke out in Oakland. On 7 April 1968 they organized a barbecue picnic at DeFremery Park to channel the community's anger and raise funds for the Panther electoral campaigns as well as for Newton's defense fund. The night before that rally was to occur, Panthers clashed with the police. What started as a typical police stop resulted in a melee when Cleaver did not comply with police orders. Cleaver and Hutton fled the scene and hid in a nearby house; the police fired into the house with bullets and eventually tear gas. The two Panthers threw out the weapon they had in their possession and left the house with their hands in the air, ready to surrender. Hutton, the Panthers' first official member, was killed by the police when he emerged.[2]

In Oakland Hutton's death was inextricably linked to the death of King, both of which seemed to confirm the futility of nonviolence. The next day there was a huge turnout at the Panther rally, and thousands went to Hutton's funeral on 11 April. The funeral program contained photos of Hutton, Malcolm X, Newton, King, and Cleaver. The text described them as "freedom fighters."[3]

Although Hutton's murder pointed to police brutality and repression of the Panthers, the circumstances also hinted at an undercurrent of militarism within the BPP. Most of their actions were nonviolent, but the BPP had raised the question of the role of revolutionary violence in the black liberation struggle in language that sanctioned urban guerrilla warfare. The rhetoric ranged from invectives against police brutality to calls for armed revolution and threats of violent action—all delivered with a liberal sprinkling of profanity. Pictures of guns featured prominently on the Black Panther newspaper's masthead and were scattered in the margins of the interior, often accompanied by the caption "Guns, baby, guns."[4] Wayne Davis, an FBI agent, argued that from the government's perspective the Panthers' language evinced deep disrespect for law enforcers and the law and perhaps held "the seeds of anarchy."[5]

This mélange of messages was not easy to negotiate and shaped the context of Hutton's death. Hilliard implied that some Panthers were abusing the weapons and committing criminal acts. He admitted that he was one of them; before he learned that "revolution is a science, not simply a matter of risking a lot or acting like a rebel," he had been rebuked for randomly shooting at a police car.[6] Sherwin Forte recalled, "After Huey got shot, a few party members contemplated vengeful actions against the Oakland Police Department. That eventually led to some shootouts."[7] On the night Hutton was killed, Hilliard suggested, Cleaver and companions were seeking to retaliate against the police and to raise the level of resistance by "set[ting] an example of organized violence."[8] One Panther arrested that night claimed that they had decided to go on a police patrol; Eldridge suggested that "if the police stopped us from observing, . . . we would retaliate," and "everyone agreed."[9]

This incident points to what would become a tactical disagreement within the BPP as members grappled with how to implement armed self-defense. Cleaver, who had called King's death the start of war and a sign that "the violent phase of the black liberation struggle is here, and it will spread," would be a flash point for those debates.[10]

Incidents like Hutton's murder suggested that the Panthers needed to critically assess the implications of spontaneous uncoordinated military action by their membership. However, in the emotionally charged atmosphere of a beloved comrade's death, rigorous self-criticism was not the order of the day. After Hutton's death Panther leaders closed ranks internally, adopted a defensive posture, and presented a united front to the world. They focused on the injustice of the police in shooting an unarmed youth who was clearly surrendering, arguing that Hutton's murder was part of a larger repressive pattern. The Panthers placed Hutton's murder in the context of persistent police harassment, arrests, and threats of violence toward their members and supporters.

Kathleen Cleaver noted that the attention the Panthers received in the wake of the death of King and Hutton came at a cost: "Maybe [they] weren't quite anticipating as much attention as they got—neither the media attention nor the police repression. 'Cause they went hand in hand. The more repression, the more media attention; the more media attention, the more repression."[11]

On the local level police harassment increased as the Panthers' mobilization around Newton's case gained momentum. Frequent arrests, harassment, and intimidation drained emotional as well as financial resources. Eldridge Cleaver recalled, "Whenever we staged a large fund raising event, the Oakland Police would move, first, to try to prevent it from happening, then, failing that, they would arrest a lot of Party members and drain off whatever money was raised because we would then have to bail those party members out of jail and there were legal fees." The Panthers took every opportunity to publicly protest this situation. On 1 March 1968 Newton issued a third "executive mandate" from prison, with harassment as its subject. This document began by recounting the St. Valentine's Day Massacre in 1929 in Chicago, in which gangsters disguised themselves as policemen to gain entry into their rivals' homes. Newton drew parallels between this tactic and police harassment of Panthers, most notably raiding the houses of key leaders. He noted that on 16 January at 3:30 a.m. members of the San Francisco Police Department had raided the home of Eldridge Cleaver. Almost a month later, on 25 February, there was a similar raid on Bobby Seale's home. Cleaver recalled, "Bobby Seale and his wife, Artie, were drug from their bed in the wee hours of the morning and charged with Conspiracy to Commit Murder. There was a lot of public outcry against the police for this blatant harrassment and frameup and that charge was quickly dropped. But what a lot of people don't understand is that it was also very expensive to us. Even though the ridiculous charge was dropped, the real purpose of the cops was achieved successfully: to drain away our funds through exorbitant bails and legal fees."[12] In both of these cases the police produced no warrant to search or arrest. Newton mandated that all BPP members must have the technical equipment to defend and protect their homes. He proclaimed, "Those who approach our doors in the manner of outlaws; who seek to enter our homes illegally, unlawfully and in a rowdy fashion; those who kick our doors down with no authority and seek to ransack our homes in violation of our HUMAN RIGHTS will henceforth be treated as outlaws, as gangsters, as evil doers."[13]

He announced that the Panthers would resist arrest and fight back. However, the repression that the Panthers faced was greater than the local police forces. The FBI, led by J. Edgar Hoover, had created a program in late 1967 to target black nationalist organizations. A memo dated 25 August from the FBI director instructed all local offices to "immediately establish a control file, captioned . . . [Counterintelligence Program Black Nationalist–Hate Groups Internal Security], and to assign responsibility for following and coordinating this new . . . program to an experienced and imaginative Special Agent." The purpose of the program was to "expose, disrupt, misdirect, discredit, or otherwise neutralize the activities of black nationalist, hate-type organizations and groupings, their leadership, spokesmen, membership, and supporters and to contain their propensity for violence and civil disorder." The memo recommended:

> Activities of all such groups should be . . . followed on a continuous basis so we will be in a position to promptly take advantage of all opportunities for counterintelligence and to inspire action in instances where circumstances warrant. . . . Efforts of the various groups to consolidate their forces or to recruit new or youthful adherents must be frustrated. No opportunity must be missed to exploit through counterintelligence techniques the organizational and personal conflicts of the leaderships of the groups and where possible an effort should be made to capitalize upon existing conflicts between competing black nationalist organizations. When an opportunity is apparent to disrupt or neutralize black nationalist, hate-type organizations through the cooperation of established local news media contacts or through such contact with sources available to the Seat of Government, in every instance careful attention must be given to the proposal to insure the targeted group is disrupted, ridiculed, or discredited through the publicity and not merely publicized.[14]

This new counterintelligence program, dubbed COINTELPRO, specifically identified SNCC, the Southern Christian Leadership Conference, the Revolutionary Action Movement, Deacons for Defense and Justice, CORE, the Nation of Islam, and individuals such as Stokely Carmichael, H. "Rap" Brown, Elijah Muhammad, and Maxwell Stanford as targets for the bureau's "intensified attention." The memo concluded by warning agents, "You are cautioned that the nature of this new endeavor is such that under no circumstances should the existence of the program be made known outside the Bureau and appropriate within-office security should be afforded to sensitive operations and techniques considered under the program."[15]

Many top government officials condoned the FBI's actions against those who were trying to change the existing political order. An FBI memo dated 29 February 1968 announced the expansion of COINTELPRO from twenty-three to forty-one cities "to cover the great majority of black nationalist activity in this country."[16] Although neither of these memoranda specifically mentions the Panthers as a target, FBI offices in San Francisco would become the launching pad for COINTELPRO efforts aimed at the Oakland Panthers. Indeed it would not be long before the Panthers' activities would make them targets for "intensified attention."

Panther membership had become tantamount to being a target. This fact, plus the contradictions highlighted by Hutton's murder, pushed some members out of the BPP. Elendar Barnes grew up less than two blocks from where Hutton was killed. She had become concerned with breaches of security and undisciplined behavior and was suspicious when she observed in the Panther office people unknown in the Oakland community. She too would leave the organization in the wake of Hutton's death.[17]

However, the tiny outflow of people was dwarfed by the tremendous influx of new members and the Panthers' expansion internationally. Judy Hart saw Hutton's death as a clear example of everything that the BPP had been saying about police violence, and it reconfirmed her commitment to the organization.[18] Hutton's funeral changed the "entire life and mind" of Ericka Huggins, a future Panther leader: "I had direct confrontation with the brutality, the cruelty, and the doggishness of the police. His face had been entirely shot out. The entire portion of his face was gone and had been puttied into place and made up. He was no longer the seventeen year old person he had been, not physically or anything else. He wasn't."[19] Seale recalled that prior to the death of King and Hutton the Panthers never had more than four hundred members, but afterward membership increased. These new members came from colleges, especially the women: "Following Martin Luther King's death, it was those college students or those heading to college, or postponing their college that joined the party in masses and in droves." They brought a wide array of practical and technical skills and gave the organization increased organizational "efficiency."[20] The Panthers expanded internationally after Hutton's death. Cleaver fled the country in the wake of the shootout and emerged several months later in Algeria. He was able to utilize the Panthers' solidarity networks to establish an international presence for the Panthers in Algeria. This International Section would become a magnet for Panthers escaping repression and arrest.[21]

NATIONWIDE GROWTH

According to one Panther member, Bobby Bowen, "Free Huey" had become an engine of organizational growth: "Most of the work was highlighting Huey, but at the same time our newspaper was developing a national character, chapters and branches were opening up across the country, so other information and ideas began to have presence in our work and our organizing—not just local, even internationally. We were acknowledging other revolutionary struggles around the world in our newspaper and creating solidarity and collaborations with other communities. . . . We had a multiplicity of things going on all at the same time, and above all of that was 'Free Huey.' "[22]

Thousands of Chicano, white, Asian, and black demonstrators protested in front of the Alameda County Courthouse in the first days of Newton's trial in July 1968.[23] Bobby Seale recalled, "We used to have five thousand people jammed on these steps for those 'Free Huey' rallies. . . . Blacks, whites, young radicals, Mexican Americans. All chanting 'Power to the People.' "[24]

Concerned citizens formed the Community Mobilization for Huey Newton in Oakland. Their literature argued that Newton and the Panthers had been targets of the government because of their ideas, not because of their actions: "Some people begin by asking: 'Is Huey Newton guilty or not guilty of killing an Oakland policeman?' They are starting with the wrong question. The first question which must be asked is, 'Why was Huey Newton stopped by the police on October 28, 1967?' The answer to this question explains the reason Huey Newton has been called a political prisoner, and the demand has been made that he be set free." Although there were many organizations in support of Newton, the formation of this one showed that the Panthers were broadening their base of support. The Community Mobilization for Huey Newton promised to "bring the issues of this case into those sections of the community which will not otherwise be reached. We will hold community forums, speak at meetings of organizations, distribute literature, place advertisements in the papers, attempt to use the media, and picket the courthouse regularly . . . for the duration of the trial." The group's listed sponsors included three reverends and six professors.[25]

The Panthers had captured the imagination of African American youth nationwide. An FBI intelligence survey in May 1968 recorded substantial growth in the Panthers' bank account and noted that they were printing thirty thousand copies of the *Black Panther*. It also mentioned that Newton was having "considerable success" in bringing the Panthers' message to other black prisoners.[26] Another BPP branch office was opened in West Oakland, and Panthers based in San Francisco started a chapter there. New recruits were sectioned into work groups or cadres for greater efficiency.

Cadres served as an extended family for many members who had rebelled against their own family to join the organization. According to FBI surveillance material, the Panthers even held meetings for members' parents.[27]

Terry Cotton, then a new recruit, recalled that Seale, George Murray, who occupied the newly created post of minister of education, and many others taught weekly political education (PE) classes on Wednesdays.[28] According to Bowen, the Panthers read a rich selection of materials:

> Initially PE classes were specific to chapters and branches, and we would pick materials to read. It would usually be the paper, statements by leadership, or anything that had come out of prison from Huey. But there was also literature. We read the *Red Book* from Chairman Mao. It was a crucial book in terms of developing principles about organizations and operational relationships and ideas about liberalism, democracy, and democratic centralism. Party members became more politically articulate. Political education classes become weekly things at Central Headquarters [in Oakland]. They dealt with philosophical materials as well. It was always a very serious process. The party was always interested in developing a philosophical awareness and a theoretical awareness.[29]

Janice Garrett-Forte recalled that PE classes remained informal as well: "Father [Earl] Neil opened up his church and would let us have our PE classes and our organizational meetings there. His church was very supportive. Plus we had PE at people's houses. We did a lot of reading of the *Red Book*; that was the bible for a while."[30]

Bill Jennings learned about the BPP from Austin Allen, the *Black Panther* circulation manager, and joined in Oakland in July 1968. Reading was central to his interest and involvement. Jennings recalled being given a *Red Book* and told, "When it starts talking about the Communist Party, don't trip out about that. Just say 'the Black Panther Party.' So I just did that. It made sense to me." Jennings became a Panther in Training, joining a six-week program to orient new members. No longer could you show up at the office and gain instant entry:

> Within the six-week training period you must know the eight points of attention, the three main rules of discipline. . . . You must know criticism and self-criticism, . . . eleven points of liberalism, which is on page 254 in your *Red Book*. . . . You have to know them verbatim.

You have to read the paper, and you gotta read two hours a day, and if you don't that was twenty-five push-ups on the spot. You had to read constantly. You had to show up and do party work. . . . You had to sell the party newspaper. You had to attend PE class. . . . You had to know the 10-10-10 program. . . . You had to know the military stuff as well as you knew the political stuff. . . . You must first own and operate a weapon. If you didn't have one, the party would give you one because you had to be under party rules and regulations to have and operate a gun.[31]

Panthers had to know how to handle several different types of weapons, how to break them down and put them back together. They practiced their skills at gun ranges or in secret locales.[32]

Brenda Presley, a Bay Area resident, joined the Panthers in the summer of 1968. In her search for a political organization to get involved in she had explored the Nation of Islam but was uncomfortable with the hierarchical relations between men and women. She was recruited into the Panthers through a chance encounter on the streets of San Francisco: "[I] liked the militancy. I liked the fact that they appeared to be disciplined and they didn't take any mess from anybody. They were really serious."[33]

As the BPP grew, the Oakland office went from being the center of a regional organization to being the national headquarters of a social movement that was erupting all across the country, led by local activists. Although the Panthers posited themselves as a hierarchical national organization, in many ways they were quite decentralized, with committee leadership and multiple leaders.[34] Oakland leaders scrambled to get a handle on the various entities across the country that had declared themselves Panther chapters. They created specific procedures for the admission of new members and chapters and sent field marshals across the country to try to regulate the new chapters.[35]

Oakland Panthers attempted to enforce a uniform structural three-tier organizational model nationwide. The National Central Committee, the highest tier, was made up of the minister of defense, chairman, minister of information, chief of staff, communications secretary, and the field marshals. Other ministerial officers, such as the minister of culture and the minister of education, filled the second tier. Rank-and-file members (privates) and Panthers in Training occupied the lowest levels of this hierarchy. A similar hierarchy was proposed for the state chapters, where the highest

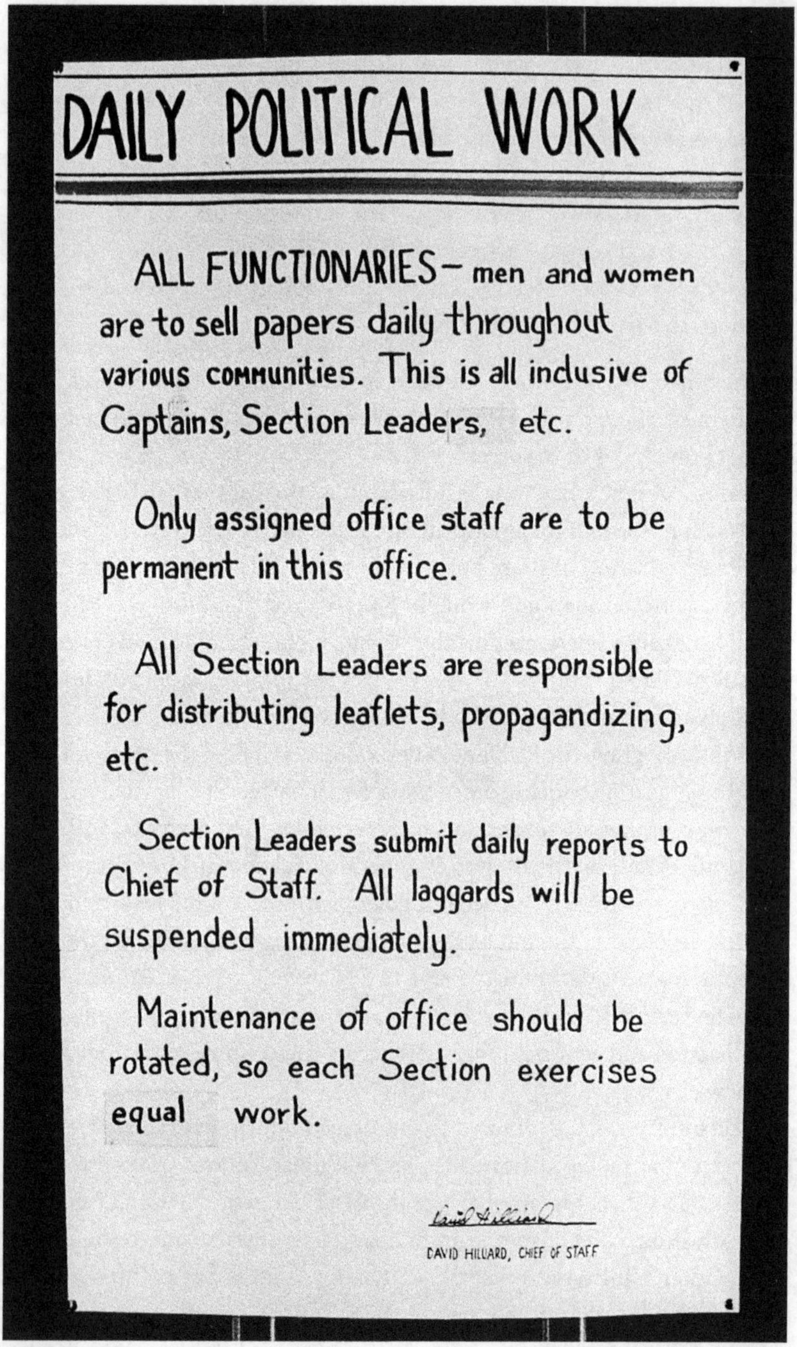

DAILY POLITICAL WORK

ALL FUNCTIONARIES – men and women are to sell papers daily throughout various communities. This is all inclusive of Captains, Section Leaders, etc.

Only assigned office staff are to be permanent in this office.

All Section Leaders are responsible for distributing leaflets, propagandizing, etc.

Section Leaders submit daily reports to Chief of Staff. All laggards will be suspended immediately.

Maintenance of office should be rotated, so each Section exercises equal work.

David Hilliard

DAVID HILLIARD, CHIEF OF STAFF

FIGURE 3.1. "Daily Political Work," Berkeley. No. 102 from the series Black Panthers 1968 by Pirkle Jones, Pirkle Jones Collection © 2014 Marin Community Foundation.

level would be deputy to the minister of defense, and the local chapters, where the highest level would be defense captain. At all three levels advisory cabinets would address issues such as police; jails and courts; brothers and sisters in prison, on probation, or on parole; political and economic analysis; unemployment; housing; publications; communications and media; international relations and the Third World; the draft of black men into the military; education; welfare and health; arming the black community; fund-raising; domestic relations; and the black bourgeoisie.[36]

Although the Panthers were an organization with a presence nationwide, coherence in thought and action among or even within chapters was not a given. Local and regional personalities, political histories, and social conditions structured the actions of Panther chapters and shaped organizational policy. According to Kathleen Cleaver, the models and frameworks that Oakland envisioned did not match conditions on the ground:

> The Panthers were almost like a network of black revolutionaries all calling themselves the Black Panthers, but when you say "national organization" you imply a lot more cohesion and identity than in fact it had. . . . If you go into every chapter nationwide that sprung up, the way the party was structured comes out of some "preexisting set of local relationships." . . . It [the Black Panther Party] became the visions that people had that Black Power and popular rebellion and resistance inspired, became identified with what the Black Panther Party looked like. What's going on here is spontaneous and somewhat organized, but most times quite chaotic, revolutionary change. It's one of those periods of time when people just throw off the bonds and say, "Ready or not, here we come." And young people loved it. That's why the average age of party [members] was once around eighteen, right?[37]

The Black Panther Party's newspaper was a medium of their growth. The front page featured a masthead with a picture of Newton and a picture of a gun. The back page featured Emory Douglas's bold political graphics. The pages in between were packed with articles, speeches, and essays by leadership, articles from chapters and branches all around the country, and reprints of speeches from Malcolm X, Mao, Robert Williams, Che Guevara, and other revolutionary leaders. The newspaper also published updates on Newton's trial and the strategies the Panthers were using to obtain his release. It reported on the growing national Black Student Union movement

FIGURE 3.2. The *Black Panther* newspaper distribution center. Photo from the Archives of It's About Time: Black Panther Party Legacy and Alumni, Sacramento.

and monitored and reported on progressive activism in the United States and abroad. International news stories about African politics and liberation movements and analyses of the Vietnam War were at home in the pages of the *Black Panther*. The newspaper did not just hope to inform; it facilitated readers' political involvement. Protests were chronicled, rallies were announced, and petitions were offered for readers to disseminate.

The paper published "black revolutionary poetry," which celebrated activism, denounced police brutality, and promoted black pride and consciousness. It chronicled police harassment of the Panthers and critiqued government policies. BPP rules, the ten-point platform and program, and a book list with readings on African and African American politics, history, and culture were printed in every issue. Features like "Pocket Lawyer of Legal First Aid" advised people of their legal rights if they were arrested. Douglas's drawings punctuated the articles and brought them to life; his artwork was as central as the articles to defining the Panthers' political vision. According to Douglas, his art "gives people the correct picture of our struggle. . . . All of us . . . from the Christian to the brother on the block, the College student and the high school dropout, the street walker and the Secretary, the pimp and the preacher, the domestic and the gangster; all the elements of the ghetto can understand revolutionary art."[38]

The *Black Panther* was a unifying factor for the BPP nationwide. Hilliard described the newspaper as "the most visible, most constant symbol of the Party, its front page a familiar sight at every demonstration and in every storefront-window organizing project throughout the country."[39] FBI sources noted, "The 'Black Panther' now prints 60,000 issues and even at this figure it is difficult to find extra copies. This is cited to indicate that the BPP receives considerable support from the black community."[40] Chapters and branches learned about each other's activities by reading the paper, and its sales and distribution provided chapters with a common task to complete. The content was often discussed in PE classes. It also provided individual members—who kept a percentage of the price of each copy sold—and the party as a whole with a steady income. Jennings recalled:

> The party was raw. You gotta remember, the party sold weed so we could have money. . . . We was poor brothers, lumpen guys, but what got us over . . . was the Panther newspaper. The paper sold for twenty-five cents. For every paper sold, the seller kept a dime. A person could survive off that. People did come into the party who had apartment[s] and houses before they came into the party, but there were no facilities. You could live off the newspaper. Not only were you getting the word out to the community; you were maintaining yourself.[41]

By April 1968 Panther chapters had formed in several major cities. The first two chapters grew from connections with the Oakland-based leadership. The South California Branch of the Black Panther Party, organized in Los Angeles in January 1968, was the first chapter outside of Oakland. Alprentice "Bunchy" Carter, a close friend of Eldridge Cleaver, had planned to organize a group following the model of Malcolm X's Organization of African American Unity. When Cleaver became the main Panther spokesperson after Newton's arrest, Carter was convinced to organize a Panther chapter in Los Angeles.[42] Aaron Dixon founded the Seattle chapter in April 1968, the first chapter outside of California. A political activist, he had been involved in starting a black student union and a SNCC chapter at the University of Washington. He met Seale while attending a black student union conference at San Francisco State and was inspired to organize locally.[43] Seattle Panthers visited Oakland for support and said that they had been greatly influenced by "constructive suggestions by [Field Marshal] Don Cox and Minister of Education George Murray."[44]

Other chapters were founded when local leaders sought out Oakland leaders' endorsement for organizing efforts already under way. Bobby Rush, a Chicago activist, met with Panther leaders to inform them that he and some others wanted to start a chapter. He was told that a chapter was functioning there already, but he knew that this chapter was defunct. Despite this refusal, Rush organized a chapter. When a crisis arose over Oakland Panthers being arrested in Chicago, the Oakland central committee contacted Rush's group since they were the only viable chapter. Subsequently they received official sanction.[45] The Philadelphia chapter started as an ad hoc group doing community-based work. Travel to the Bay Area increased as networks were formed between other chapters and Oakland. Mary Williams recalled, "A lot of brothers would come here and go through Central and learn the ten-point platform and program with the minister of education. . . . They would tell you about the problems that they were having in different cities where they were from."[46]

Reggie Schell, defense captain of the Philadelphia branch, explained that guidance from Oakland was not always automatic, and local chapters continued to do political work while seeking affiliation:

> When we decided we wanted to be Panthers we called out to California and June Hilliard told us: "Look, you don't got to be no goddamn Panther to struggle." So we went out (this was in 1968) and we were just basically doing our thing because we didn't have any idea what Panther work was. But we set up our first office, right down here on Columbia Avenue. We were doing work around police brutality and situations like that. Police were shooting fifteen-year-old kids, mentally retarded children, and we started calling press conferences and trying to organize the people to do something to fight back. . . . After a period of time we started sending to California for papers; we were selling the Panther Party paper, though we still weren't recognized as a chapter. Then Field Marshal Don Cox came and inspected the branch, put us through a rigid kind of inspection to see if we were qualified to become a branch of the Party.[47]

By the end of 1968 hundreds of African Americans all over the country had been inspired to open Panther branches and chapters in their own communities. In the process Oakland was transformed from the stronghold of a struggling local organization to the headquarters of an unrestrained nationwide movement. The Panthers' growing base in black communities and their anticapitalist rhetoric placed them on the cutting edge of radicalism in the United States and made them a target of the local police forces and the FBI.

UNDER ATTACK

Newton was convicted of voluntary manslaughter on 27 September 1968 and sentenced to two to fifteen years in prison. His lawyer, Charles Garry, had focused his defense on racism and repression aimed at Newton and the Panthers. Prominent social scientists testified to the prevalence of racism in American society and its impact on the jury selection process, that is, the systematic exclusion of black jurors and the prevalence of racist attitudes among potential white jurors. Garry skillfully manipulated the proceedings so that not just Newton but American racism was on trial. Newton's supporters were relieved that he had escaped the death penalty but were disappointed with the verdict and pledged to exhaust all legal means to secure his release. Seale declared that the Panthers would seek power from electoral campaigns: "We will use the guns strategically and in a very organized manner [and] work hard on the political campaign to vote in Huey P. Newton."[48]

On midnight on the day of the verdict, two drunken police officers riddled Panther headquarters with bullets. The office was empty and no one was hurt, and the officers were subsequently arrested, but Panther supporters around the country saw it as a confirmation of the organization's beleaguered state. The visual image of the glass storefront shattered by sixty bullets made national news. According to Seale, "the image of the police outside of the law doing criminal acts" seemed to confirm the Panthers' argument that the police often operated outside of the law. It was a message that "a lot of people wanted to ignore" but couldn't when "that picture [of the shattered glass] was plastered everywhere around the United States."[49]

The Panthers pointed to a pattern of police harassment and misconduct and promptly moved their headquarters to 3106 Shattuck Avenue in Berkeley. Panther offices nationwide were under increasing scrutiny from the FBI and local police. Shootouts, raids, and other altercations between the police and Panthers were breaking out all around the country, especially in Detroit, Los Angeles, Denver, and Newark, New Jersey. The police used petty laws, like unlawful use of a bullhorn and loitering, to harass the Panthers.

Oakland leadership was the focal point of police harassment. Seale was on probation after the Sacramento incident and could be imprisoned at any time. Murray was fired soon after his dual role as San Francisco State educator and Panther member was exposed. Eldridge Cleaver had been arrested in the Hutton incident and was released on parole in June, afterward facing constant parole restrictions. When his parole was revoked in September, he went into exile, believing that he would not receive a fair trial, and later resurfaced in Cuba. Yet another leader who had made an indelible mark on the BPP, overseeing its coalition strategy and bringing his own unique brand of political polemics, was now removed from the organization's day-to-day operations. This crisis of leadership would continue as the Panthers were forced to replace their jailed leaders with members who had to rise to the challenge with little notice or preparation.

Richard Nixon, elected president in 1968 with less than 10 percent of the black vote, pursued the dual strategy of repression and co-optation of black radicalism.[50] He embraced black capitalism and launched economic initiatives aimed at nurturing the black elite and values like "pride, ownership, private enterprise, capital, self-assurance, self-respect."[51] His conservative administration aggressively sought to roll back the gains of the civil rights movement and accelerated the attack on radical activists. The Panthers' critique of capitalism coupled with their mass base made them a target of government harassment and surveillance. Ericka Huggins explained,

> See, they could hear all the buy black, do black, think black, be black, black on, and black power. They could hear that, they didn't care about that part. It was when poor niggers started talking about class struggle that they got frightened. And not just talked about it, but did something. They didn't care about the little coffee clatches in the backs of book stores where people were talking about the Communist Manifesto and happened to be black. No. They were worried about ignorant, poor niggers on the streets with guns talking about the haves and the have nots.[52]

An FBI memo dated 27 September 1968 increased COINTELPRO efforts against the Panthers and classified them as the "most violence-prone organization of all the extremist groups now operating in the United States. . . . [It] is essential that we not only accelerate our investigations of this organization and increase our informants in the organization but that we take action under the counterintelligence program to disrupt the group." The memo offered suggestions "to create factionalism between not only the national leaders but also the local leaders, steps to neutralize all organizational efforts of the BPP as well as create suspicion amongst the leaders as to each others' sources of finances, suspicion concerning their respective spouses and suspicion as to who may be cooperating with law enforcement." It suggested other means for internal destabilization: "Suspicion should be developed as to who may be attempting to gain control of the organization for their own private betterment, as well as suggestions as to the best method of exploiting the foreign visits made by BPP members. We are also soliciting recommendations as to the best method of creating opposition to the BPP on the part of the majority of the residents of the ghetto area."[53]

The FBI tried to undermine the relationship between the Panthers and their supporters, who often functioned as lifelines for the embattled organization. One FBI memo commented on Panther community support: "It is believed true that many older residents of the ghetto fear and dislike the BPP. How true this is among the youth is another matter."[54] The FBI created and mailed letters referring to the Panthers in a condescending manner and signed "Donald Freed," who was a leader of Friends of the Panthers, an organization of mostly white supporters in the Bay Area. They also created false material allegedly written by the Panthers that accused Freed of being an informant. FBI headquarters urged their Los Angeles office to "prepare a specific counterintelligence proposal designed to create a breach between the BPP and [Charles] Garry. Consider such things as anonymous telephone calls as well as cartoons and other logical methods of transporting your idea."[55]

The FBI explored other means to undermine the Panthers, including manipulating tensions between local and national leaders, attacking the organization's financial base, and utilizing informants. One FBI memo noted, "It is realized that the Party is awake to the possibility of 'police spies' in their midst. To date they do not seem to be excessively worried about this, and continue to make their pronouncements over TV, press and before church and school groups. They also put themselves in print in the 'Black Panther,' official publication of the BPP. To date, no 'leak' of significance to the BPP has come to law enforcement agencies which has aroused the Party's animosity. This office will be alert to this possibility." Another memo saw the potential to exploit factionalism: "Primarily this [factionalism] would seem to be on a regional basis, where BPP leaders from the East see no profit in taking orders from provincial leaders like BOBBY SEALE and ELDRIDGE CLEAVER." It noted that "financial records are a possible source of embarrassment to the BPP" and suggested monitoring the Newton Defense Fund. It recommended alerting the IRS in San Francisco to look at the party's taxes and the district attorney to ascertain if "the State can . . . [force] BPP leaders to say where the money from the Defense Fund is being dispersed and provide an accounting of the same." It also suggested that the FBI could manipulate tension between spouses to weaken the BPP.[56]

It was a full-scale attack, and the Panthers' response was to continue to broaden their political base.

THE POLITICS OF COALITION

One of the central strategic decisions the Panthers made to increase their visibility and to gain access to resources was to seek alliances with political organizations in both the white and the black communities. Seeking black allies fell squarely within the dominant Black Power paradigm; seeking white allies did not. Many in the civil rights movement had embraced interracialism, the notion of blacks and whites working together within the same organization for a common cause, focusing on a common identity rather than racial differences. However, many black nationalist organizations emphasized black unity, autonomy, and self-determination and were highly critical of interracialism. The Panthers would have to justify their decision to ally with whites in order to retain the BPP's legitimacy in the black community.

The Panthers' revolutionary nationalist ideology was centered on class analysis rather than blanket condemnation of the white community. They argued that the police were the racist enforcement arm of the state rather than distinguishing between the conduct of white and black officers. When criticism was raised against the Panthers' selection of Charles Garry, a white lawyer based in San Francisco, to represent Newton at his trial,[57] the Panthers responded that Black Power was on trial, not black skin, and that Newton should have the most competent lawyer regardless of race. In addition they cited Garry's commitment to social justice, his record of winning twenty-four capital cases, and his willingness to defend Newton regardless of ability to pay. And they critiqued "Black lawyers, politicians, doctors, teachers and other professionals" who were engaged in a "mad scurry for white power, white values, white acceptance and white hostility to black power."[58]

Like a growing number of Black Power and white radical organizations, the Panthers believed in interracial coalitions based on common political positions with a basis of equality. Part of this was the politics of expedience. Eldridge Cleaver noted that the Panthers "had go inside of closed doors and say how we were going to deal with this" and examine "where we are, where we were, and where we wanted to go, where we [were] willing to go, with whom we were willing to work. We had to look at that in terms of the program of the party and the ideology of the party, and there was nothing there that precluded a working alliance, a coalition with white people."[59]

Cleaver had many contacts in the Bay Area's white left, and the Panthers were able to gain support from hippies, anarchists, and members of the local Communist Party. They sought an alliance with the Peace and Freedom Party (PFP), a majority-white political party based in Berkeley that had been closely involved in the "Stop the Draft Week" protest. Participants at the protest sympathized with the Panthers on the issue of political prisoners and were one of the first groups to hold a press conference in support of the "Free Huey" campaign."[60]

There was an undercurrent of self-interest in the Panther-PFP coalition. The Panthers followed a pragmatic policy of seeking alliances based on established contacts, working relationships, and the possibility of financial support. There was no doubt that they thought they could dominate the coalition with the PFP. On the other hand, the PFP were confident that their alliance with the Panthers would provide them with increased visibility and an entrée into the black community. The PFP gave a donation to the Newton Defense Fund and provided the Panthers with technical equipment, and soon the two organizations began working together.

In December Seale and Cleaver convinced their allies in the PFP to finance a trip to Washington so they could meet with Stokely Carmichael to cement the organizational links between the Panthers and SNCC.[61] They met with Carmichael and others in SNCC and held discussions that prefigured the conflicts that would ultimately undermine their coalition. At this meeting the Panthers were questioned about their position on whites, their coalition with the PFP, and their choice of Garry as Newton's lawyer. The Panthers had most of their contact with SNCC leaders and were not cognizant of internal debates between those who had begun to analyze the African American movement as part of a worldwide class struggle and those who continued to emphasize the racial nature of the African American situation.[62] Despite these differences both organizations felt it was in their interest to move forward with the coalition.

Alliances were a route to resources that were put toward organization building. A week later Seale and Cleaver met with another SNCC leader, James Forman, in Los Angeles. Forman pledged to support the Panthers' efforts to build mass support for Newton's trial. He and other SNCC leaders provided resources and contacts for several "Free Huey" rallies in early 1968.[63] Aided by a donation from the PFP, the Panthers opened a new office in North Oakland, at 4421 Grove Street. The new office gave the party a base in the black community and soon became the focal point of the "Free Huey" campaign.[64]

The Panthers decided that running for political office would give them greater visibility while providing the PFP with viable candidates: "The Black Panther Party for Self Defense views electoral politics as one tool that can be used for the benefit of the black community—if it is not tied to the aims of the power structure."[65] Newton was selected to run for Congress in the 7th Congressional District of Alameda County. Seale ran for the 17th Assembly District, and Kathleen Cleaver ran for the 18th Assembly District.[66]

The focal point of the Panthers' organizational efforts was a "Free Huey" Birthday Rally held on 17 February 1968 at Oakland Auditorium. Thousands of supporters crammed into the venue to listen to Stokely Carmichael, H. Rap Brown, Newton's mother, representatives from the PFP, and other speakers.[67] Panther leaders announced both their alliance with the PFP and their campaigns. They introduced the key SNCC leaders who had been given leadership roles in the BPP: Carmichael as prime minister, Forman as minister of foreign affairs, and Brown as minister of justice. Tensions between allies were evident at the rally. While Eldridge Cleaver heralded the SNCC-Panther "merger" in his speech, Forman used part of his speech to redefine the relationship as an "alliance." Carmichael declared himself a separatist with little tolerance for white allies and white ideologies, such as Marxism. Partly in response, Seale pointedly reiterated that the BPP was not antiwhite.[68] Despite these incidents the rally successfully launched the "Free Huey" movement.

Nationwide the political atmosphere was electric. On 31 January 1968 the Tet Offensive, during which massive losses were inflicted on South

Vietnamese and U.S. forces, had shattered the government-perpetuated myth that the war was being won. More and more people joined the antiwar movement. Partly inspired by black activism, leaders in the Native American, Chicano, and Puerto Rican communities and other communities of color had begun to organize.

This context created fertile ground for the Panthers' message, and "Free Huey" moved from slogan to movement, attracting support in high schools, community centers, and churches in Oakland, throughout California, and across the nation. In the process Newton became a national icon. "Free Huey" became a cause célèbre among the left, and "Free Huey" buttons, stickers, and placards blanketed many communities nationwide. The movement brought together seasoned activists with people who wanted to ally with the black liberation movement for the first time. It incorporated people who staunchly believed that Newton was innocent and had not touched a weapon on that fateful night, as well as those who believed that he had rightfully acted in self-defense. Many of Newton's supporters believed that he was illegitimately imprisoned for his political activity and supported his political ideas regardless of the circumstances behind his arrest.

Cleaver argued that the Panthers were "the vector of communication between the most important vortexes of black and white radicalism in America."[69] The Panthers' connection with SNCC, however, was short-lived; the alliance was unable to overcome ideological differences, lack of communication, and basic mistrust between the two organizations. Ideological points of contention simmered under the surface but were rarely discussed openly. Organizationally SNCC members were divided over the Panther alliance. While some readily joined the Panthers, others were more hesitant. Some insisted that the alliance had been made by individuals and had never been ratified by the entire organization. When Panther leaders demanded that SNCC adopt the Panther ten-point platform and program, some SNCC members balked at this, considering the program reformist rather than revolutionary. The FBI fueled tensions between them with the goal of creating a split.[70] They engineered phone calls to SNCC leaders, warning them that they could be the victim of the Panthers' violence, and worked to create suspicion among the Panthers of SNCC leaders' motives. In July, after a misunderstanding about Forman's scheduling of an important press conference at the United Nations, the relationship disintegrated amid rumor, paranoia, and threats. Shortly thereafter SNCC's central committee voted to end the alliance with the Panthers, and Brown and Forman resigned from the BPP. Carmichael was expelled from SNCC one week after these events; however, he continued his association with the Panthers.[71]

Despite obvious tensions in the alliance, the Panthers and the PFP forged ahead. The PFP helped the Panthers build a bridge between the black and white communities; the growth of the Panthers in the black community was paralleled by a growth in awareness of the Panthers in progressive white communities largely because of this coalition. In a "position paper on coalitions" PFP leaders argued that the white community had a distorted view of the Panthers: "It should also be noted that this is the first coalition between a white radical group and a black radical group. The Black Panther Party for Self-Defense is the healthiest militant black group for us to relate to: it is not racist and it has a program for social change. . . . This coalition can build a way in which blacks and whites can work together and still retain their identity and integrity."[72]

The Panthers and the PFP produced joint propaganda for Newton's and Seale's political campaigns. One PFP campaign poster asked, "Is there anyone worth voting for?" Answering "YES!" the poster elaborated on the PFP's basic platform: "Withdrawal from Vietnam. End draft. Support struggles of working people for full employment at living wage, etc. Revolutionary education in the schools. Community control of police. Lower voting age to 18." A flyer cosponsored by the Panthers and the PFP promoted a joint initiative to "control your local police": "The proposed charter amendments would establish separate and autonomous police departments in Berkeley; one for the Black community; one for campus community; one for the remainder of the city."[73] Another flyer, urging, "Register TODAY in the Peace and Freedom Party," contained instructions on how to write in Newton and Seale as candidates on election day, delineated who was eligible to vote, and summarized PFP demands: freedom for Newton and support of the ten-point platform and program.[74]

The Panthers' involvement in this campaign and their growing base of white supporters helped transform the consciousness of some of their membership who initially saw whites as the enemy. Janice Garrett-Forte recalled, "The money was coming in from whites . . . movie stars . . . doctors. When Black Panthers got shot and couldn't go to a hospital, there was somebody white, a nurse, a doctor that could mend them up. There were wealthy white people who were lending their farms, et cetera so that we could have shooting practice. You could get lost in the United States through white wealthy contacts. . . . So I made a big leap from . . . you know, kill all white people, to understanding that it is a class struggle."[75]

Realizing this, the FBI attacked the alliance between the Panthers and the PFP. A memo dated 14 October 1968 proposed a plan to manipulate tensions between the two organizations:

> It is requested that the Bureau authorize Los Angeles to prepare an anonymous letter, again using street vernacular and appropriate stationary, which will be sent to a selected individual in the PFP, to inform him of statements made by the BPP concerning their association with the PFP. Specifically, the statements will include the fact that the BPP has made the statement in closed Panther meetings, that when the time comes they will "line up the Caucasians in the PFP against the wall with the rest of the whites." The letter will purport to come from an individual who is associated with Panther members and who has heard Panther members boast of what they will do to Caucasians in the PFP when the Panthers finally launch an armed rebellion.[76]

Later the FBI's San Francisco office requested authority for an anonymous letter to be mailed to the PFP by a Mexican close to the Panthers: "He has learned from BPP members that certain whites in the PFP who get in the way of the Panthers will be dealt with in a violent manner."[77]

TACTICAL DIVERSITY

The Panthers realized that defining their political objectives and launching concrete programs were central to their continued development and appeal. They continued to focus on electoral politics as an important part of their strategy, hoping to use it as a platform to publicize their political analyses on the national level. Their initial foray into electoral politics had resulted in Newton receiving twelve thousand votes. But the number of votes was irrelevant to the Panthers: their goal was not to win office but to "educate the people more about the political arena and how it perpetuates racism and exploitation of peoples throughout the community."[78]

In May 1968 the Panthers announced Eldridge Cleaver's presidential bid as a PFP candidate. Cleaver promoted organizational visibility and expansion, hoping that the campaign would "provide us with a very important vehicle for spreading our coalition and projecting our analysis and program on a national scale; and for bringing new people, both black and white, into the coalition." He warned that the Panthers were not going to "get hung up in the illusion of winning power or accomplishing basic change this year or even in the next four years—especially through the electoral process." Instead they would use the campaign to lay the groundwork for a social movement: "We are fighting to win power for the people; this means that our movement must not only speak and act for, but actually involve, millions of ordinary people."[79] He chose Jerry Rubin, leader of the Yippees, as his running mate.

The Panthers moved to follow up on one of Malcolm X's last political initiatives: the idea of African Americans taking their case to a world forum. Inspired by Malcolm, who had drawn up the "Outline for the Petition to the United Nations Charging Genocide against 22 Million Black Americans," the Panthers proposed a UN-supervised plebiscite "in black communities around the nation as a kind of referendum on the future of Black America." The Panthers argued that this would be a way to "answer the question, once and for all: just what the masses of black people want. Do the masses of black people consider themselves a nation? Do they want U.N. membership?"[80]

Internationally they took on imperialism and stood against the Vietnam War. They built on the image of blacks as living in an internal U.S. colony:

> If circumstances are such or the political situation requires that a public demand for protection from the pigs be made, then such demands should be made to the United Nations for U.N. Observer troops to be stationed in the Black community to protect the people from the local power structure's occupying army. By focusing attention upon the situation of Black people as an international issue threatening world peace, in this way we demonstrate our internationalist as well as nationalist position to the people; we simultaneously educate them and put pressure on the U.S. Government in the eyes of the world.[81]

The Panthers modified their ten-point platform and program to incorporate the idea of a UN plebiscite.[82] Point 10 of "What We Want" was originally "We want land, bread, housing, education, clothing, justice and peace." In 1968 Panther leaders added, "And as our major political objective, a United Nations–supervised plebiscite to be held throughout the black colony in which only black colonial subjects will be allowed to participate, for the purpose of determining the will of black people as to their national destiny."[83]

The Panthers took another step toward concretizing their program in the fall of 1968 when they launched the Breakfast for Children Program. According to Seale, upon discovering that teachers at a local high school were thinking about creating a free lunch program for children, he brainstormed with others and came up with the idea of serving breakfast to schoolchildren before school began. Support for the program was not unanimous; Seale recalled justifying the program to Eldridge Cleaver, who feminized the program as "sissy." Seale argued that the program could highlight the government's failure to provide such a crucial social service, as well as add another dimension to their public image and potentially broaden their base of support.[84]

The Panthers appealed to community members to become involved in the program and started the Community Advisory Committee to oversee their survival programs. They drew upon established institutions and longtime activists in the black community. They approached Reverend Earl Neil of St. Augustine's Church to provide facilities to house the program.[85] In November 1968 FBI sources reported that the Panthers were trying to get lists of black elementary school students in West Oakland for their breakfast program and that they were reaching out to parents as well.[86]

Ruth Beckford, a community activist and a member of the Panthers' Advisory Committee who became involved in the planning and implementation of the Breakfast Program, helped plan the logistics of the program: the food, frequency of donations, and staff. She recruited mothers in the Parent Teacher Association to cook for the breakfast program in shifts, and she helped raise money for the program. Beckford recalled that there was a lot of community support. A black dairy owner delivered milk every morning and a local bakery donated donuts. Participating in the program was a lot of hard work; volunteers sometimes arrived at the church at 6 a.m. to cook and lay out the food. Still, Beckford said, despite the rigors of involvement "those women were happy to do it. They felt that this was a very positive program for the Panthers. Where others might have been afraid of any association with the Panthers 'cause they thought that they were violent, . . . this program was their strongest point and was able to rally people from all sections of the community."[87] Brenda Presley recalled, "The Breakfast Program was one of the first free things being done. The whole concept was just so unique in [and] of itself. The response was incredible. The community response was great. People saw that we were not just out here being wild and carrying guns: we were really trying to make a difference. And that was the way I felt we were accepted into the community."[88]

CORRECTING MISTAKEN IDEAS

Tensions between the Panthers' political and military goals, tactics, and strategies emerged, due in part to an open membership policy, weak political education mechanisms, and reckless rhetoric. The Panthers remained uncompromising advocates of self-defense, but they had diversified their tactics and broadened their conception of revolution. Nationwide expansion had brought many competing tendencies inside the BPP, and tensions would erupt around armed self-defense. Some leaders and members had become convinced that the political situation necessitated armed offensives against the state. This core was augmented by those who had been attracted to the BPP only because of its armed stance.

The Panthers hoped to hone and refine their members' military viewpoint and teach them the political theories that lay behind their armed stance, but not all members or leaders were convinced of the utility of the different political paths the party had begun to explore. Seale initially believed, "We could raise the consciousness of the lumpen proletariat. Those are the ones who were participating in a lot of illegitimate activity. And if they had the heart and we could raise the consciousness, we could make a stand in opposition to the power structure while we organized politically the masses of the community."[89] The Panthers had advocated disciplined tactical use of arms and had indirectly and directly endorsed armed actions. Panther leaders saw no contradiction in publishing articles in the *Black Panther* like "Grenades and Bombs: Anti-Property and Anti-Personnel," which explained the mechanics of making grenades and Molotov cocktails and the effectiveness and use of firebombs, while touting their commitment to multiple arenas of action in other contexts.[90]

However, soon the divisions between the Panthers' militaristic activities and rhetoric and their community development and political focus began to cripple the organization. One Panther recognized this growing internal crisis and wrote an article for the *Black Panther* titled "Correcting Mistaken Ideas," which criticized leaders for failing to "wage a concerted and determined struggle against these incorrect ideas to educate (and re-educate) the members in the party's correct ideology—which is also an important cause of their existence and growth." He argued that the "military viewpoint was highly developed" among some members at the expense of the political viewpoint. As a result some party members disregarded the day-to-day organizing, political propaganda, and work among the masses and did not want to distribute flyers or sell newspapers. They measured success only in military terms and "refused to recognize that military affairs are only one means of accomplishing political tasks." The sources of this viewpoint were a lack of political education and "over confidence in military strength and absence of confidence in the strength of the masses of the people." To solve these problems the writer suggested that the BPP renew its emphasis on political education, solicit membership from those who were already politically experienced, and "actively attend to and discuss military work." This would change the nature of the BPP by weakening the influence of those with a purely military viewpoint. His final recommendation was that the party "draw up party rules and regulations which clearly define its tasks, the relationship between its military and its political apparatus, and the relationship between the party and the masses of the people."[91]

Nationwide growth, tactical diversity, and increased political repression characterized the Panthers' second year. They had grown from a self-defense group to a national network of community organizers and political analysts committed to armed struggle. Their embrace of the politics of armed self-defense, a leftist ideology, growing base, successful community programs, and multiracial political alliances was a powerful challenge to the racial status quo. And just as they were poised to address the internal contradictions that threatened the vitality of the organization, state and federal law enforcement worked in concert to uproot, transform, and derail this potential with the use of provocateurs, propaganda, mass arrests, and infiltration.

4

INSIDE POLITICAL REPRESSION,
1969–1971

By 1969 the Black Panther Party was locked in an unequal battle with the state. Many Panther leaders were either imprisoned, in exile, or underground; the FBI was investigating every chapter and all 1,200 members to "obtain evidence of possible violations of federal and local laws"; and the BPP was filled with infiltrators.[1]

In Los Angeles the FBI manipulated the tensions between the Panthers and Us, a cultural nationalist organization led by Ron Karenga, mailing derogatory cartoons and incendiary letters to members of both organizations.[2] The result was a deadly confrontation on 17 January 1969 at the University of California, Los Angeles that left John Huggins and Alprentice "Bunchy" Carter, two well-known Panther leaders, dead.[3] Huggins's home was raided the evening of his death, and Ericka Huggins, his wife and a leading BPP member, along with sixteen other Panthers, was arrested for conspiracy to commit murder. In March, Seale, Jerry Rubin, Tom Hayden, Abbie Hoffman, and four other leading members of the white left were indicted for crossing state lines to incite riots at the 1968 Democratic National Convention in Chicago. In April the police arrested twenty-one leading New York Panthers on a variety of conspiracy charges, accusing them of planning acts of violence and terrorism. According to New York Panther Thomas McCreary, the "Panther 21" became an instant organizational priority, and "New York was flooded with a number of West Coast Panthers" who "came in to fill the void" and helped the chapter continue to function.[4] David Hilliard condemned these arrests as another "heavy handed attempt to cripple the Panthers' leadership structure."[5] Several Panther offices nationwide were raided in June. Ultimately the Panthers became the target of 233 of the total 295 authorized actions that COINTELPRO conducted against "black nationalist" groups.[6] The Panthers claimed that during 1968 and 1969 they suffered 739 arrests and paid $4,890,580 in bail.[7]

This repression occurred at a time when debates about gender and sexuality were reaching a crescendo within the organization. The larger context of the women's liberation movement and the fact that women became the majority of the organization's membership by 1969 shaped how repression and gender intersected.[8] Panther women's experiences of repression were affected by a host of factors, including the composition of their chapter or branch, their position in the organizational hierarchy, their age, and their connections to powerful men. Rank-and-file women, often the Panthers' most visible public presence in local communities, lived the daily reality of surveillance. Brenda Presley was aware that "to some extent letters and things were messed with" and phones were being tapped. But, she realized in retrospect, "what we didn't understand was how infiltrated we were. We suspected some folks but didn't know the extent."[9] For her repression took a toll beyond the litany of raids and high-profile arrests; it involved the slow erosion of relationships, bouts of incarceration, the heightening of internal hierarchies, and an attack on community-based support systems.

Recasting the story of COINTELPRO through the lives of women makes its organizational impact more visible. It reveals that sometimes women provided the foundation that allowed the Panthers to withstand the ravages of repression, but at great personal and political cost. At other times the state and in some instances even their male and female comrades perceived the gender issues that these women would raise as low priority. This vantage point also unmasks the truly nefarious intent of repression. Targeting every external support system and internal fissure, repression didn't just aim to kill; it aimed to shape how the organization lived. It operated as an internal dynamic shaping tactics and influencing how the BPP formulated, justified, and implemented policies, priorities, and reforms. It channeled growth, deepening fissures and putting members in a permanent state of defense. It shaped relationships. Outside of the familiar bonds of comradeship and community, Panther ties had always included the web of family. The BPP was an organization of siblings, spouses, in-laws, and other relatives. As repression increased and the organization became "more of a fortress," these connections were reconfigured and survival mode became daily life.[10]

COMRADE CRITIC

Panther leaders responded to repression by tightening the organizational framework. BPP rules were elaborated to give the national headquarters more control over local chapters and clarify organizational political goals. Members were required to become familiar with the organizing program and spend time doing political work in the community, in addition to attending mandatory physical fitness classes and reading two hours each day. Chapters and branches submitted monthly financial reports, weekly branch reports, and daily work reports.[11] Kathleen Cleaver credited the Panthers' mobilization against counterintelligence efforts to destroy them with this thrust toward "ideological consistency [or] organizational consistency" and "any kind of streamlined procedural military-like structure."[12] Janice Garrett-Forte remembered that lines of authority became much tighter "when the heat started coming down."[13]

Paradoxically, however, the move toward increased centralization unleashed rather than quelled voices of dissent and criticism within the organization. The Panthers began to purge members who were undisciplined, attracted solely to the Panthers' militaristic aspects, or suspected of being spies or agents provocateurs.[14] Panther field marshals "frequently traveled to various cities to organize or reorganize a BPP chapter, administer discipline by demoting leaders to rank and file membership and suspending or expelling other members, [and] close up entire chapters where conditions were not satisfactory to National Headquarters."[15] The names and photographs of purged Panthers, along with the reasons for their expulsion, became a continuing feature in the *Black Panther*; the Oakland branch re-ported the expulsion of thirty-eight members in the 23 March 1969 edition.[16] Many other chapters and branches followed suit.

Accusations of being a government informant became a punitive device used to isolate those who were critical of organizational policies or ques-tioned the Panthers' political direction. In these tumultuous times yester-day's beloved comrade could easily become today's purged "jackanape," and actions that were once permitted or tolerated were now grounds for expul-sion. Adaptability was key to survival, and not everyone wanted to follow the shifting party line. The expulsion of Sherwin Forte, one of the first men to answer the party's call in 1966, is instructive. He and his brother Reginald were strongly influenced by the Panthers' "off the pigs" rhetoric and embraced armed struggle. Sherwin participated in the Panthers' most defining acts: police patrols, selling copies of Mao's *Red Book*, and attend-ing "armed demonstrations." When he was "busted" in connection with alleged police shootings, he was expelled. He recalled that the ouster did not feel like a policy change or ideological evolution; it felt like a "double cross."[17]

Once a person was expelled, there was usually no coming back. In ad-dition to the realities of hurt feelings, anger, and other human emotions, the FBI worked with local police to prevent any reconciliation with ousted members. When Huey Newton's brother attempted to meet with expelled Panthers, the FBI had "the Oakland police inform one of the former Pan-thers that the meeting was a 'set-up.'" The San Francisco FBI office gloated that "such quick dissemination of this type of information may have been instrumental in preventing the various dissidents from rejoining forces with the BPP."[18]

David Hilliard's role as Panther chief of staff and his brother Roosevelt "June" Hilliard's role as assistant chief of staff were dramatically expanded by these changes in the BPP's infrastructure. Both men oversaw the imple-mentation of purges and disciplinary actions for infractions of the rules.[19] Chapters and branches began to call in to national headquarters for infor-mation and permission to issue statements and to receive and give updates on activities.[20] David argued that the BPP would be "stronger, more of a for-tress," after it finally got "rid of all the opportunist elements, the criminal elements." By "work[ing] with the people [who were] left," the BPP would reflect "the very best and the most revolutionary sections of society . . . [those who] definitely . . . want to carry out the desires and aspirations of the oppressed people."[21] In reality, however, purges often undermined morale as they became a mechanism for the expression of internal conflicts and disagreements. David Hilliard, who was perceived as the architect of the "harshly authoritarian policy" that "engendered intense resentment" of "heavy handed treatment," bore the brunt of this criticism.[22]

Despite Mao's oft-quoted teachings on "criticism and self-criticism," there was little room for collective self-criticism or principled political dissent within the ranks of the organization. Candi Robinson, a Panther who had written about the role of revolutionary black women in the *Black Panther*, was called "crazy" by other members for disagreeing with the top-level leadership, "not because they listened to my criticisms or tried to objectively anal[y]ze them but because they (many comrades) have built an attitude, that it is wrong to disagree with members of the Central Committee."[23] Youthful arrogance and political immaturity were further disincentives to criticism and self-criticism. Emory Douglas described Panthers as "young people aged fourteen, fifteen, up to twenty-three" who were "still headstrong, ego-centered, brash, cocky." As a result, "although you acknowledge [criticism and self-criticism] in the framework and context of the party, when you get it coming from a chapter or people . . . if you don't wanna hear it, if you don't like it, then you expel 'em."[24] Bobby Bowen recalled that there was "a lot of arrogance in that we thought of ourselves as revolutionaries. We had that attitude; we projected that attitude to other organizations and people. It was easy to put out criticism, very difficult to accept. And if we did allow it, we only tolerated it up to a point."[25]

Criticism was often used as a punitive measure. Bowen observed that it was "mostly used as a stick rather than something philosophical," a means of punishment or "a weapon that inspired fear when used against another person."[26] Repression raised the stakes for criticism by making speaking out against or even questioning policies tantamount to subversion and grounds for discipline. The Panthers' disciplinary methods, ranging from mandatory exercise, extra duty, confinement, and physical punishment to expulsion, depending on the nature of the infraction, reflected their quasi-militaristic organizational structure. Physical beatings were its ultimate expression.[27] An FBI informant reported, "Anyone holding an official position in a BPP chapter can, and frequently does, arbitrarily hand out punishment for minor rule infractions without fear of recourse."[28] Critics had much to lose, but their number slowly increased as the vise of repression closed around the organization. Among rank-and-file members, repression both stifled and amplified their voices.

Nowhere was this clearer than around the question of money. In 1969 Panther Shirley Hewitt complained, "The BPP is desperately in need of funds as there is a concerted drive to put all their leaders in jail."[29] These arrests highlighted the inequalities in the Panthers' financial infrastructure. Rank-and-file members were full-time organizers, often without pay and with no other financial resources. Garrett-Forte survived on the support she received from the organization in the form of housing, as well as from newspaper sales and donations. That was enough to provide money "to buy food; if you needed some shoes or whatever you got it any way you could." Although "nobody was going without," the standard of living of rank-and-file members contrasted sharply with that of some leaders. She claimed that "central committee members were living pretty good." At the same time, since their high profile made them prime targets for repression, "a lot of money was going for their defense funds and that kind of thing." Rank-and-file members also faced arrest for selling the *Black Panther*, traffic violations, and other minor offenses. These "foot soldiers who were dedicating their lives had to get things the best way they could. There wasn't money filtered down to the ones who were doing the righteous legwork."[30] Garrett-Forte saw the community mobilization that rank-and-file members contributed to the organization and the work done by leaders as equal in value, though they were unevenly rewarded.

Responding to repression was a constant drain on Panther finances, even as their coffers increased from the sale of newspapers and literature and from royalties on books. Noting that the Panthers were desperately trying to solicit speaking engagements to raise funds, FBI headquarters instructed the San Francisco field office to "immediately submit to the Bureau for approval counterintelligence proposal aimed at preventing the activities scheduled." Agents boasted that they had "been successful in the past through contacts with established sources in preventing such speeches in colleges or other institutions."[31]

FBI wiretaps recorded frequent conversations about financial matters.[32] Chapters that called national headquarters requesting money were often advised to juggle expenses to make do. On one occasion June Hilliard told a Panther who called national headquarters to stop calling collect. When the caller complained that his local office only had a pay phone because they did not have money to initiate calls, Hilliard responded that national headquarters could not afford to accept collect calls either.[33] FBI sources noted that the Panthers planned to address some of these issues by calling a retreat to "discuss dissatisfaction on the part of many chapter leaders with regard to amount of authority that the chapter leaders other than Bay Area have" and "financial problems."[34] For unknown reasons this retreat never took place. The discontent that was created by these moves toward centralization remained a crack in the BPP's organizational foundation.

TARGETING PANTHER WOMEN

Law enforcement officials adhered to gendered assumptions about leadership when determining their targets. Ericka Huggins remarked, "When the police arrested and killed, they tended to seek out men, thinking that men were the leaders."[35] By this time Bobby Seale was on trial in Chicago and David Hilliard was embroiled in his own legal battles. In an impassioned speech he had rhetorically threatened the life of Richard Nixon; he was charged with carrying a concealed and loaded weapon and was awaiting trial on assault and attempted murder charges in the incident that had resulted in Hutton's death.[36] In December the FBI, using informants and provocateurs, joined local police to target Panther leadership in two devastating predawn raids on offices in Chicago and Los Angeles. In Chicago the Panther leaders Mark Clark and Fred Hampton were killed in their beds.

Huggins pointed out that the Panthers were able to continue because "behind the scenes women ran almost every program [and] were involved in every level of the party." Because men were being "jailed and killed in greater numbers women rose in the ranks of leadership." Some men "may have had internal unresolved things about women, but about women in leadership, we were in too much danger every day to say no women. It was not like that. We were not an intellectually based organization. We made decisions based on need, and often, too often, we made decisions based on survival."[37] The uncompromising bravery of women in the face of repression belied any chauvinistic notions of women's weakness. Douglas doubtless spoke for many men in the BPP when he acknowledged the impact on his consciousness of "women . . . putting their lives on the line like we were."[38]

Panther women faced frequent police harassment on the streets they called home. Presley recalled, "You would get pulled over. They'd surround the car. . . . A lot of times you'd be followed depending on what you were doing or who you were with."[39] Mary Williams remembered that the police "had the license plates of all the cars. . . . They would stop you and take all your buttons and throw them away."[40] Frequently the FBI contacted Panthers' family members, many of whom were fearful of the implications of their political affiliations. The FBI visited Presley's mother in Alaska and her father in San Francisco. Her mother was "actually freaked out . . . because the FBI went to her job a couple of times and asked her if she knew what her daughter was getting involved with." Agents advised Presley's mother to talk to her, implying that she was "too nice a girl to get mixed up with the Panthers."[41] These incidents were demoralizing for Panther activists, who lived with the daily reality of their own mortality. Garrett-Forte experienced a sense of numbness when she "kinda expect[ed] to get killed" and "expected to die." These were "givens": "The only question was, how was it going to feel when it happened? What kind of situation am I going to be in? It felt inevitable. You didn't think that you were going to get out alive."[42]

Financial pressures coupled with the growing imperative of security led some Panthers to live collectively. Their houses became a combination of living quarters, workspaces, and accommodations for visiting comrades. Collective living, which involved shared responsibilities for cooking and housecleaning, revealed some of the tensions around sexism within the organization.[43] Such domestic labor was a source of contestation and debate. Seale described the ideal situation: "When there's cooking to be done, both brothers and sisters cook. Both wash the dishes. The sisters don't just serve and wait on the brothers."[44] In practice, however, such equality rarely prevailed. While Panther literature promoted internal revolution and provided both men and women with the tools to critique gender discrimination, sexist attitudes persisted and sometimes even thrived within the organization.

Although BPP rhetoric promoted egalitarian gender roles, Panther Roberta Alexander spoke up about gender inequities. She noted that there were many debates on such issues as "women leadership; women being able to be armed, to defend themselves as well as the brothers; on whether or not the women do all the typing or whether or not they also take part in the running of the offices, not just behind the typewriters; and it even goes down to the sexual levels, whether or not the women are supposed to do so and so for the cause of the revolution."[45]

Douglas remarked that despite the "mechanism[s] in place," sometimes even leaders, just like rank-and-file members, resisted taking orders from women "or didn't want to because of their ego." The politicization process central to membership was designed to undermine this attitude: "It's just that the cleansing process was an ongoing thing. We tried to maintain it and not let it get out of control by having rules and regulations and PE classes and sisters in leadership that brothers had to work under. There was adjustment."[46]

The potential of this "cleansing process" probably strengthened the resolve of some women who argued that the Panthers were moving toward the realization that "male chauvinism and all its manifestations are bourgeois and . . . the success of the revolution depends upon the women."[47] Yet these issues were not given priority within the organization. Conflicts about gender were subsumed under the larger category of potentially divisive criticism. Few of the leaders articulated what Alexander dared to say: "We think more . . . about the contradictions . . . between the sisters and the brothers than we do about the pigs."[48] Internal conflicts around gender had the potential to be even more lethal than the bullets of the state.

HUEY'S OPEN LETTER

At this critical juncture the Panthers had an unexpected victory. On 5 August 1970 Huey Newton's conviction for the killing of Oakland police officer John Frey was reversed and he was released on bail while awaiting trial for voluntary manslaughter.

"Free Huey" had been one of the Panthers' major political objectives, and Newton's release was the culmination of years of grassroots organizing and legal appeals. The campaign had adopted the strategy of personalizing Newton, emphasizing his role in founding the BPP, his fearless confrontations with the police in the BPP's first year, and his intellectual acumen. Newton had become an international cause célèbre, a venerated hero, and a notorious legend to many inside and outside the organization. His release put the flesh-and-blood man on a collision course with the symbolic leader that Panthers had so carefully constructed.

The BPP was now a national organization with an international presence that bore only a slight resemblance to the small local group that he had left in 1967. Although he had issued directives, policy statements, and taped messages during his incarceration, he was out of touch with the

FIGURE 4.1. Huey P. Newton walking through Oakland's black neighborhoods after his release from prison. Photo from Black Panther News in the Archives of It's About Time: Black Panther Party Legacy and Alumni, Sacramento.

BPP's day-to-day operations. Being the object of a cult of personality gave him tremendous power in the Panthers' hierarchical organizational structure, yet it also created and reinforced a set of expectations that he could never measure up to.[49] Newton soon became the center of internal debates around centralization, gender politics, and financial hierarchies, even as his ascension to the top leadership position put him in the bull's eye of political repression.

Just ten days after his release from prison, Newton issued an open letter weighing in on gender equality, sexuality, and gay and lesbian rights. Remarkably he pushed the organization to express explicit support for the goals of the women's liberation movement. He argued that "if we feel that the group in spirit means to be revolutionary in practice," the Panthers should not dismiss them. If "they make mistakes in interpretation of the revolutionary philosophy, or they don't understand the dialectics of the social force in operation, we should criticize that and not criticize them because they are women trying to be free."[50] In an interview a week later he elaborated on the applicability of this position within the organization: although it was clear that male chauvinism existed within the party ranks, leaders were "making an honest effort" to fight those "bourgeois attitudes": "We are advancing, we try to keep our ranks open—there are women ministers in the Party. All women are trained, just as the men, with the revolutionary tool. At every level I think that the women should be included."[51] Newton recognized the potential in the BPP's political pronouncements and admitted that the reality did not mirror the rhetoric. While his letter validated the very real struggles going on within the organization, his analysis did not push these debates any further toward resolution.

In the remainder of Newton's letter he provocatively argued that the Panthers should show tolerance to the gay liberation movement. Gay men and women were also oppressed, he acknowledged, and some men, including him, had "hang-ups" about male homosexuality "because of the long conditioning process which builds insecurity in the American male." He urged the Panthers to delete "terms like 'faggot' and 'punk'" from their "vocabulary," especially when describing "men who are enemies of the people, such as Nixon or [Attorney General John] Mitchell." The Panthers were in the process of creating a "revolutionary value system," and such dictates as "a revolutionary must say offensive things towards homosexuals" and "a revolutionary should make sure that women do not speak out about their own particular kind of oppression" were not revolutionary. Instead the Panthers should seek to incorporate the participation of other oppressed groups in their "revolutionary conferences, rallies and demonstrations."[52]

Newton's analysis had the potential to broaden the range of accepted sexual practices within the organization. The Panthers practiced sexual freedom, a philosophy born of the questioning of monogamy in the woman's movement, the widening availability of birth control, and the sense of youthful abandon members brought to their intimate relationships. One female member understood sexuality to be "a very low-key thing" in the party, where members were "sexually allowed whatever was our wish" in a "very open and collective and free realm."[53] In this view same-sex coupling by women was not stigmatized. In practice, however, a person's ability to actualize sexual freedom was shaped by his or her gender and status in the Panther hierarchy; for example, while heterosexual men enjoyed multiple sexual encounters without condemnation, the boundaries of sexuality were more heavily policed when it came to same-sex relationships. Some Panthers equated gayness with weakness, the antithesis of manhood, and branded their enemies with homophobic slurs and insults. Statements like David Hilliard's warning to the Students for a Democratic Society that the Panthers would "beat those little sissies, those little school boy's ass [sic] if they don't try to straighten up their politics" had gone unchallenged.[54]

Newton's open letter created a furor within the party, with much of the debate centering on his support for gay liberation. The political potential of this moment was undermined by the FBI's exploitation of the situation. Newton had become a target of the FBI immediately upon his release. In a letter to the FBI's New York office Hoover wrote, "Newton is the spiritual father of the BPP who is venerated by BPP members along with Mao Tse-tung, Kim Il Sung, Che Guevara, and Fidel Castro. To demythicize Newton, to hold him up to ridicule, and to tarnish his image among BPP members can serve to weaken BPP solidarity and disrupt its revolutionary and violent aims."[55] A memo praised the three-pronged strategy submitted by the New York office to "creat[e] divisiveness among BPP members concerning Newton, treat him in a flippant and irreverent manner, and insinuate that he has been cooperating with police to gain his release from prison."[56]

The FBI seized upon Newton's letter as an opportunity to exploit internal differences to achieve the government's ends. Agents had been advised of "opposition within the Party to a recent stand of HUEY NEWTON in *The Black Panther* newspaper" and its possible relation to "his declaration that Black Panthers should relate to the women's and men's gay liberation league, homosexual organizations."[57] Gays and lesbians had long been targeted by the FBI as deviants and subversives.[58] The FBI's San Francisco office suggested "sending anonymous letters from Panther members, supporters, and sympathizers protesting [the] declaration," hoping that a flood of such critical letters would discredit Newton in the eyes of other Panther leaders.[59] The suggested text for two letters to be sent to David Hilliard reflects the FBI's strategy to create fear of queer men as a political distraction and as emblematic of black men's ongoing rejection of black women as potential partners: "Panthers got enough things to do in 10 point program and fighting for niggers without taking up with the m. . . . . . . f. . . . . . . queers," and "The Panther sisters have to fight to keep the brothers from white chicks. Now what do you want us to do, watch them take up with queers."[60] The FBI sponsored many other letters designed to discredit Newton and increase internal dissention. In this context Newton did not throw his political weight behind the positions he articulated in the letter and made no further comments on controversial issues of gender and sexuality.

The constant barrage of threatening letters and warnings engineered by the FBI, plus the history of attacks on their leadership, led the Panthers to take many precautions regarding Newton's safety and security.[61] Initially he had lived in various houses with other leaders or supporters, but in November 1970 he moved into a penthouse apartment overlooking Lake Merritt and, ironically, the Alameda County Courthouse. According to Newton, the Panther Central Committee decided on that site because of the security offered by the high-rise building and the mostly white neighbors. According to Amar Casey, a Panther who saw things unfold firsthand, "The rank and file felt that it was a necessary and conscious sacrifice in order for the leadership to be able to move around and do the things they needed to be able to do." As "the premier leader . . . some felt that he [Newton] should be able to present himself to the world in a way befitting the head of the Black Panther Party." Making sure that Newton was "looking good" and "able to impress the media or other powerful people he comes in contact with" was important to the BPP's image, at least in some members' eyes.[62] Others did not agree.

The San Francisco FBI office took note of Newton's monthly rent of $650 and speculated that there was "potential counterintelligence value" in this knowledge, especially when juxtaposed with the "ghetto-like" Panther homes and community centers. In February 1971 the FBI leaked this information to the San Francisco Examiner and then distributed the Examiner's exposé to Panther chapters and branches nationwide.[63] The article embarrassed Newton and the party. To many observers his new residence embodied flawed decision making and evidenced the problematic financial hierarchy within the organization. The San Francisco FBI office reported, "BPP Headquarters was beseiged [sic] with inquiries . . . and the people at headquarters refuse to answer the news media or other callers on this question." In one incident "a representative of the Richmond, Virginia BPP contacted headquarters on 2/18/71, stating they had received a xeroxed copy of . . . the article and believed it had been forwarded by the pigs but still wanted to know if it was true."[64] The FBI also leaked the information that BPP leaders had dubbed Newton's penthouse "the Throne," making Newton's assertion that he was forced to live in the apartment for security reasons but wanted "to be back on the streets" seem absurd.[65]

The FBI contemplated using this scandal to drive a wedge between Newton and Cleaver. They drafted a letter to Cleaver purporting to be from a party member and claiming that Newton "picked the place out himself" and that "the high rent" was drawn from Panther funds that could be used for "other party work here and also in Algeria." Stoking the fires of jealousy, the letter closed with the observation "The least Huey could do is furnish you the money and live with the rest of us."[66]

This external campaign fed off and intensified the growing criticism of and disappointment with Newton within the ranks. New York Panther Pam Hannah explained, "He comes in here and the expectation was unbelievable, for a human being. . . . We created a movement that was bigger than life. Could he have lived up to [this]? There was no way he could have lived in those shoes which we had built for him."[67] Many hoped that Newton's presence would revitalize the Black Panther Party. Presley recalled the sense of heightened anticipation: "The expectation was, 'Just mess with us now! Our leader is back! We're going to be a force to be reckoned with for real!' "[68] Bill Jennings said, "We felt like we was whole again. Bobby was in jail but we got Huey back, and with Huey back we'll get Bobby back, and then we'll be . . . back."[69]

The real Newton was quite different from the poster image of the fearless leader posed in a chair wearing a beret, holding a spear in one hand and a rifle in the other. Some members found his demeanor aloof and impersonal compared to Seale's gregarious wit and Cleaver's intense charisma. His decision not to spend much time at party headquarters mirrored the behavior of other Panther leaders but created disappointment as members struggled to reconcile the public figure with the private man. This reality was highlighted by the deluge of phone calls for Newton received at the BPP office. Maintaining personal relationships had been one of the Panthers' defense mechanisms against COINTELPRO. Bobby Bowen recalled, "Folks had been doing a lot of work for a long time, very intense, very hard work, protecting and defending their chapters and branches and their offices, being under attack, being shot at, prosecuted, being harassed by law enforcement."[70] Candi Robinson wrote a poignant letter to Newton reflecting on the "warmth and happiness" Panthers felt when he was first released from jail: "Now we only see you occasionally, I don't expect you to visit us on a day to day basis. But just your presence makes everyone happy. I've noticed that when you do come to the office you are usually just showing someone the office. I wonder do you ever want to be with us."[71]

"COMRADE C"

Newton moved the BPP in an internationalist direction upon his release.[72] At the party's Revolutionary People's Constitutional Convention in November 1970, his keynote speech linked poor communities in the United States to their international counterparts and developed the idea of revolutionary intercommunalism.[73] In an interview with *Sechaba*, the official organ of the African National Congress, Newton pointed to the continuing influence of international revolutionaries on the Black Panther Party.[74] He argued the Panthers believed that "we feel we will never be free until many colonized people are free."[75] He offered troops to the Vietnamese National Liberation Front to fight their common enemy: "the American imperialist who is the leader of international bourgeois domination."[76] He received a response from Nguyen Thi Dinh, deputy commander of South Vietnam's People's Liberation Armed Forces, expressing gratitude for the Panthers' support and criticizing Nixon's continued aggression in Indochina.[77]

In the FBI's efforts to undermine the Panthers' international potential they focused on exiled Panther Eldridge Cleaver, head of the Panthers' international apparatus, who was in a strategic position to ally with other revolutionary movements worldwide. The possibility that the BPP would develop alliances with international liberation movements and with countries considered to be enemies of the United States was particularly threatening. Worried about Cleaver's "close contact with communist nations and Arab guerilla organizations," the FBI monitored his international political activities, noting that in the "fall of 1970, Cleaver made his second trip to North Korea and combined it with stops in Communist China and North Vietnam."[78] Warrantless electronic telephone surveillance of Panther headquarters in 1969 and 1970 was justified by Attorney General Mitchell as a matter of national security.[79]

Newton's relationship with Cleaver was not as close as his relationship with David Hilliard, a childhood friend, and Seale, a trusted political associate. Conflict rooted in their strong personalities and their different ideological visions and tactical priorities for the Black Panther Party had been brewing since Newton's release. The FBI fueled animosity and distrust between the two men. Connie Matthews, a young Jamaican woman who had become the Panthers' international coordinator in Europe in 1969, became the lynchpin of the FBI's campaign.

Matthews had never been to the United States but was deeply influenced by local reverberations of Black Power. She used her contacts and skills to help disseminate the BPP's ideology in Europe and facilitate trips abroad for Panther leaders to meet with supporters. She spoke at rallies and gave many interviews with the European press. By mid-1969 her activities had laid the crucial groundwork for solidarity committees in Germany, France, the Netherlands, Norway, Denmark, and Sweden to support Panther political prisoners. Matthews helped to coordinate the activities of these committees, staging many successful demonstrations and public hearings. Her unprecedented mobility made her a target of the FBI's COINTELPRO, and numerous letters aimed at fomenting dissent between the Panthers' international chapter in Algeria and the national office in Oakland were signed with her forged signature. Although she was a central international Panther operative, her gender made her invisible to the FBI as a leader in her own right. Instead she was used as a pawn in their campaign against Newton, a center of power in Oakland, and Cleaver, who was one of the most highly visible members based in Algeria.

The FBI had begun to foster distrust between Cleaver and the Oakland national headquarters as early as 9 April 1970. It "authorize[d] the mailing of anonymous letters that [were doctored to] appear to be from Eldridge Cleaver to Huey P. Newton," using stationary from Charles Garry, both men's lawyer.[80] The agency speculated that an anonymous letter it sent Cleaver "indicating that BPP leaders in California were undercutting him" led him to expel "five international representatives of the BPP."[81] The FBI gloated, "Newton feels Cleaver is trying to undermine his position and authority in the BPP and accused other BPP leaders . . . of being aligned with Cleaver." The agency increased its efforts, hoping that false letters would "antagonize existing animosities" and disrupt the functioning of the Algiers office.[82]

It is likely that while the FBI manufactured false letters they were actively short-circuiting genuine communication. In December 1970 Cleaver himself wrote a letter to Newton complaining about the distance that was emerging in the relationship between the international section and the Oakland headquarters. He accused Newton of "blocking" the international chapter by his "refusal or failure to communicate with us, to inform us,

and to keep us up to date on developments, particularly on the ideological plane." He intimated that Newton did "not allow anyone else to keep
up communications with us" and urged him to "deal with this soon." The
letter ended on a frustrated note: "Too much time has passed for this to be
kept lagging. So give us that much consideration, Brother Huey, and stop
the blocking."[83]

Suspicion and concern began to grow in the Black Panther Party about
the origin of some of these letters. One FBI memo cautioned, "An Entirely
Anonymous Communication to Cleaver or any BPP functionary or a series
of such letters is believed . . . to be of little value at this time or in the
future. This observation is based on information obtained previously from
BPP sources regarding such communications which have immediately been
branded as coming from the 'pigs.' "[84] The FBI solved this problem by sign-
ing Connie Matthews's name "Comrade C" in several of their forged letters. By this time Matthews had visited the United States, given speeches
at Panther demonstrations, written theoretical pieces for the *Black Panther*,
and worked closely with Newton as his "personal secretary." Now a close
associate of both Cleaver and Newton, she was used by the FBI in their
plan to "create doubts" about people close to Cleaver and foster a "serious breech [*sic*]," leading to "expulsions" or even his return to the United
States.[85] Speculating that it could manipulate her attempts to "solidify her
position with Cleaver," agents forged letters from Matthews casting suspicion on several people, including David Hilliard, Shirley Hewitt, and one
of the first Panther members, Elbert "Big Man" Howard, hoping to "immediately cause great distress to Cleaver." The FBI timed its letters to coin-
cide with Matthews's trips abroad, hoping that "if sufficiently aroused and
angered by that time Cleaver would probably refuse to believe any denial
of authorship on Matthews' part. It should give rise to suspicions."[86] Agents
suggested sending Cleaver a letter implying rampant disorganization and
disunity at Oakland headquarters, written in Matthews's tone and style and
initialed "C." The letter stated, "We must either get rid of the Supreme
Commander or get rid of the Disloyal Members. I know the Brothers mean
well but I fear the only sensible course that the Party can take is to initiate strong and complete action against rebels, exposing their underhanded
tricks to the communities. Huey is really all we have right now and we
can't let him down, regardless of how poorly he is acting, unless you feel
otherwise. Remember he is still able to bring in the bread."[87] Matthews
soon came under suspicion. Probably making the same calculations as the

FBI did about her leadership and the value of her political work, Newton suspended her from the organization.

MILITARISM

Internal debates around sexuality, gender politics, and leadership simmered under the surface because many viewed them as deferrable at a time of political instability. Members and leaders filtered these debates through the prism of loyalty to the organization and to the larger goals of the movement. This loyalty spurred members to make short-term personal and political sacrifices in the hopes of long-term change. Gender conflicts, familiar in daily life outside the organization, were livable and sometimes made invisible, but conflicts about leadership structure and style were not. Debates about militarism, almost always cast as inherently male and top-down rather than bottom-up, were perceived as not just corrosive but combustible. These debates took center stage in internal conflicts.

When Newton was released from prison he supported the forces within the party who centered on moving the Panthers away from armed self-defense. He distrusted Geronimo Pratt, a charismatic, nationally respected Panther leader in Los Angeles who had played a crucial role in organizing the BPP's underground apparatus and its military wing.[88] Pratt had held "vital classes for the Central Committee, especially as to democracy in the military field,"[89] and criticized the suppression of armed struggle within the organization under Hilliard's leadership. He had gone underground and attempted to organize others around the principle of revolutionary violence that was consistently touted as a correct strategy in the Panthers' ideology and rhetoric. After Panther Melvin Cotton Smith made allegations of disloyalty against Pratt, Newton purged him from the organization.[90] He denounced Pratt's creation of what he called "counterrevolutionary, little rebel roving bands" and chastised him for "not adhering to the Party's principles or orders." He argued that, as the masses were the ones who made the revolution possible, underground activity, which involved alienation from the people, was inappropriate.[91] Seale weighed in on this debate from jail, arguing that guerrilla warfare was appropriate only "under the circumstances when the people, the masses, believe and see that guerilla warfare is just."[92]

Now with national content and authorship, the *Black Panther* published the messages the Panthers sent and received on the issue of armed self-defense. It told a different story. While some leaders tried to reduce overt manifestations of militarism, slogans such as "Political power grows out of the barrel of a gun" and "The heirs of Malcolm X have picked up the gun and are moving for their total freedom" continued to be printed. Pictures of guns in the margins were common, often accompanied by such captions as "The Time when People can sit back and view processes of injustice and inequality has come to an end."[93] Political drawings by Douglas and other Panther artists portrayed armed men and women or pigs squealing from violent attacks—sometimes held at gunpoint or with their head in a guillotine—to depict self-defense on a visceral level. In April 1970 the newspaper featured a three-part series on organizing self-defense groups by Field Marshal D.C. that included articles with pictures of different types of guns; information about the specific uses of shotguns, rifles, and handguns; instructions on how to load and unload, disassemble and assemble, and maintain weapons; and how to aim and fire.[94] The final part of this series contained recipes for a self-igniting Molotov cocktail and something called "the People's Hand Grenade," as well as lists of books on weapons and addresses where they could be bought.[95]

The expulsion from the BPP of Pratt, his wife, Saundra Pratt, and all his associates, announced in the 23 January 1971 issue of the *Black Panther*, shocked party members.[96] Panther 21 member Michael Tabor remembered Pratt as "a brother we not only respected and admired and had total faith in but also who had proven himself time and time again as being a true servant of the people." Three months later, Tabor said, his expulsion was the trigger for an intense conflict within the BPP: "I remember the response and reaction of the brothers and sisters, not only in the Party, but in the street when they picked up that edition of the paper, that had in it the purge, the expulsion from the Party of brother Geronimo and his branding as being a pig. This is like the straw that broke the camel's back, and that was the spark that set off the prairie fire. It would not be tolerated any longer."[97]

In the wake of Pratt's expulsion the FBI tried to fuel dissension between national headquarters and the Los Angeles chapter. They sent Cleaver a letter supposedly from someone "close to the BPP in LA": "Eldridge, things are bad enough here in Babylon that we don't need Huey coming back and f____ things up. His pipe dreams ramblings about intercommunalism make me think that nigger is going crazy, and that ain't no bull___. The party can't understand that intercommunalism s___ and the people laugh when we try to explain it. The masses related to the 10 point program but Huey's really on an ego trip this time and everyone is afraid to challenge the fool. Huey went too far in expelling Geronimo from the party too." The letter claimed that even loyal Panthers were now critical of Newton, who acted as if he did not trust anyone. It concluded, "We need some guidance Eldridge or the party is going to fall apart. I don't know what happened to Huey but if you gave the word I think LA would take directions from you, but now we hardly know anything about the international section."[98]

On 19 January 1971 members of the Panther 21 published "Open Letter to the Weathermen Underground" in *East Village Other*, a New York–based underground newspaper, proclaiming solidarity with the Weathermen, which split off from the Students for a Democratic Society in early 1970 and advocated domestic guerrilla warfare. The letter proclaimed the Weathermen "one of the—if not the true vanguard within the confines of the artificial boundaries of the United States of Amerikkka at this time." It suggested that if revolutionary parties "just function—have a newspaper, hold rallies, conventions, congresses etc.," then the "prospects of armed struggle—real revolution, diminish . . . and it [armed struggle] becomes to be looked upon as adventurism." Those who embraced armed struggle would then be "deemed more dangerous" and targeted by the state. Quoting Che Guevara and George Jackson, the letter proclaimed that a revolutionary had to take action "to awaken the revolutionary energy" among the people. Although this letter never mentioned the Black Panther Party by name, it spoke directly to the internal debates raging within the party about armed self-defense.[99]

Newton expelled the seventeen incarcerated members of the Panther 21 who had written the letter from jail. Subsequently Richard "Dhoruba" Moore and Tabor, two members of the Panther 21, jumped bail. The Panthers issued a press release denouncing Moore and Tabor's action, pointing to the fact that the courts had revoked the bail of two other members of the 21 and arguing that Moore and Tabor had jeopardized the Panthers' ability to beat the charges of terrorism and violence. It also criticized Connie Matthews. Now married to Tabor, she was very visible to both Newton and the state. She had left the country right as the Panthers were planning Huey Newton's East Coast tour, an important mobilizing effort to raise support for incarcerated Panthers in New Haven.[100] The press release branded Moore and the Tabors "counterrevolutionary jackanapes" and expelled them from the BPP. They eventually resurfaced in Algiers.

The expulsion of leading members exposed the Panthers' internal fissures to public scrutiny. According to wiretap transcripts, on 9 February 1971 journalists from UPI, AP, and the *New York Times* San Francisco Bureau called Panther national headquarters to find out if reports of the expulsion of nineteen of the Panther 21 were indeed accurate. They were told "No comment" or "Call back tomorrow."[101] After these events the FBI sent a letter to Cleaver allegedly from the Panther 21 in the hopes it "could further aggravate the strained relationship between Newton and Cleaver":

> Brother Eldridge—We of the Panther Twenty one, in true revolutionary spirit, express our complete disbelief over our expulsion by Huey Newton. This action is very bewildering to us. . . . We have never neglected the party. Its needs were always our needs. We witnessed the failure of the Party headquarters to engage in any support for their brothers and inmate[s] involved in the prison insurrection last summer. We know that you have never let us down and have always inspired us through your participation in the vanguard party. . . . You are our remaining hope in our struggle to fight oppression within and without the party.[102]

Another FBI letter upped the ante by threatening Cleaver with violence or death.[103] The situation had reached the crisis stage.

MEN AT WAR?

On 26 February 1971 Newton appeared on the radio program *AM San Francisco* to promote the Panthers' Intercommunal Day of Solidarity, a mobilization aimed at gaining support for political prisoners. Kathleen Cleaver, the Lumpen (the Panthers' singing group), and the Grateful Dead were featured participants in this event. During a scheduled on-air dialogue with Newton, Eldridge Cleaver criticized David Hilliard and called for his expulsion from the Black Panther Party and the reinstatement of Geronimo Pratt and the NY 21. Stung by the unexpected public criticism and challenge to his authority, Newton made an angry phone call to Cleaver fifteen minutes later expelling the entire International Section, including three key members of the Panther Central Committee: Eldridge Cleaver, Kathleen Cleaver, and Don Cox. In response a handful of chapters and branches in New Jersey, New York, and Kentucky left the organization, and individual members of other chapters joined the ranks of the dissident Panthers.

The FBI gleefully took credit: "The chaotic condition of BPP and the split between BPP leaders Huey P. Newton and Eldridge Cleaver [was a] direct result of our intensive counterintelligence efforts aimed at causing dissension between Newton and Cleaver and within the Party." It pledged to "closely scrutinize developments in the BPP to fully exploit through counterintelligence in order to keep BPP off balance."[104] Agents mailed derogatory cartoons from issues of the *Black Panther* to Cleaver and sent him letters suggesting that some of the people who visited him in Algiers had sent negative reports to Oakland.[105]

In its efforts to isolate Cleaver and discredit the Black Panther Party in the international arena, the FBI tried to undo the networks Matthews had built and the agency had previously used for its own destructive purposes. The FBI proposed sending a copy of the newspaper article announcing Cleaver's expulsion to Panthers' solidarity committees in Paris, Belgium, Stockholm, and Copenhagen with a note threatening the committees if they continued to support Cleaver. It would "appear mimeographed or otherwise reproduced for a multiple mailing with the addresses typed in so the lack of a signature will appear natural." The letter would describe Cleaver as "a murderer and a punk without genitals" and warn that "anyone giving any aid or comfort to CLEAVER and his jackanapes will be similarly dealt with no matter where they are located."[106] The FBI's goal was to "divide the allegiance of these groups who have looked to Cleaver for guidance in the past" and "to intimidate these people [the European solidarity committees] to the extent they will not know who to follow and will thus be neutralized by confusion."[107]

The mainstream media followed suit, flattening this complex internal struggle into a conflict between two charismatic male leaders over "reform" versus "revolution." Newspaper headlines across the nation proclaimed: "Black Panther Dispute," "Eldridge and Huey Say," and, most ominously, "Internal Dispute Rends Panthers: Newton-Cleaver Clash Puts Party's Future in Doubt."[108]

Kathleen Cleaver, the primary strategist behind the "Free Huey" campaign and the only woman on the Panther Central Committee at this time, was portrayed as her husband's pawn. Ironically it took an organizational crisis for an issue that had remained largely unacknowledged—the Cleavers' tumultuous marriage—to be addressed publicly, albeit still obliquely. The national organization copyrighted the *Black Panther* and printed an issue whose cover story accused Eldridge Cleaver of holding Kathleen Cleaver hostage, a claim she quickly denied. Accusations of mistreating women became a potent weapon in these factional struggles. The Young Lords, the Panthers' allies and counterparts within the Puerto Rican community, declared, "Both groups are accusing each other of sexism. Yet it seems to us that both sides still have to deal with the chauvinism of the brothers (machismo) and the passivity of the sisters (letting machismo go down). Both factions will have to clean up on this point if they wish to advance."[109]

The expelled Panthers created their own newsletter, *Right On*, and a war of words ensued. Militarism emerged as a key issue, alongside eroding comradeship, financial hierarchies, sexism, and purges. Gender was implied everywhere. In a *Right On* article titled "On the Contradictions within the Black Panther Party," Eldridge Cleaver pointed to the inability to reconcile "people who wanted to move in a purely military fashion" and "those who were too much involved in the political aspect of mass mobilization." As the bureaucracy expanded to deal with "mass demonstrations, around political prisoners, publishing newspapers, getting out leaflets, and all of that mass mobilization apparatus, [and] rallies," Panthers who "didn't fit into that, were kind of shuttled to the side, dropped out of the Party."[110] While there were certainly men who focused on the community programs and campaigns and women who prioritized the politics of armed self-defense, it is clear that the Panthers' shift toward mass mobilization had occurred as its membership swelled with women.

Other authors cast the disagreements in organizational terms. Kathleen Cleaver pointed out the devastating impact that purges had on organizational morale: "Hundreds of beautiful brothers and sisters who had dedicated their lives, dedicated their talents, their hearts, everything they had to the struggle for Black people for their liberation in the US have been forced out of the Party and prevented from joining with their comrades in fighting US fascism. Comrades in jail have been fronted off, shined on. Brothers in exile, brothers underground have been practically ignored." Don Cox said, "The doors within the Black Panther Party are closed to criticism and self-criticism and ideological struggle." Tabor criticized Hilliard for opposing "all military activity" and undermining Panthers who advocated those principles, and he berated Newton for not challenging this stance when he left prison. He pointed out that the party's financial resources were spent on clothing and expensive meals for Hilliard and Newton when "righteous, dedicated revolutionaries who had shed blood and had risked their lives in order to secure the liberation of Black people in particular and all oppressed people in general, were left languishing in penitentiaries throughout Babylon."[111] Sherwin Forte had been expelled while in prison awaiting bail that never came. These dissident Panthers challenged the media's depiction of what was going on as a personality conflict. They called on undecided comrades to voice their criticisms against the current Panther leadership and to "take a principled stand" on the issues rather than on individuals. More chapters broke away from the BPP in the wake of this organizational crisis, reducing the number from forty-five to twenty-eight.[112] At the same time, Panther headquarters in Oakland was flooded with letters of support from other chapters and branches around the country.[113] The lines were clearly drawn.

During Newton and Cleaver's heated telephone exchange, each had warned he had "the guns."[114] Now violence erupted within the ranks. On 8 March 1971 Robert Webb, one of the dissident Panthers, was killed in New York City. The next day New York's Central Headquarters issued a press release, titled "Dep. Field Marshall Robert Webb Murdered by Huey's Assassins," directly tying Webb's murder to the turmoil within the party and accusing Newton of sending assassins to New York.[115] Other murders followed amid repeated denials and denunciations. On 17 April Sam Napier, circulation manager of the *Black Panther*, was brutally murdered in Queens. The death of these beloved comrades created an impassible gulf between party headquarters and the dissident Panthers.

Believing that the breach between Newton and Cleaver was irreconcilable and that the Panthers had been effectively crippled, the FBI identified Hilliard as an "outstanding target."[116] Undermining the Panther leadership structure remained a central FBI priority: "It is felt that the next counterintelligence objective should be to effect a split between Newton and [blackened out] and between Newton and [blackened out] since [blackened out] and [blackened out] are in top leadership positions in the party and if their expulsion could be effected, the party on the west coast would be without effective leadership."[117] Panther lawyers and financial supporters would also be targeted.[118]

OUT OF THE ASHES

As the FBI prepared for a new phase of attack, the Panthers desperately tried to regroup. The dissident Panthers focused on solidifying the Black Liberation Army, an underground revolutionary organization committed

FIGURE 4.2. Sam Napier (seated), Brenda Presley, and John Seale working on the *Black Panther* newspaper. Photo from the Archives of It's About Time: Black Panther Party Legacy and Alumni, Sacramento.

to armed struggle and black liberation. The national organization focused on the future. Newton analyzed the split in the BPP publicly in "On the Defection of Eldridge Cleaver from the Black Panther Party and the Defection of the Black Panther Party from the Black Community." He wrote that Cleaver's leadership had isolated the Panthers from the black community by focusing on the "war between the oppressor and the Black Panther Party, not war between the oppressor and the oppressed community," and he pledged to return the Panthers to the community. This statement simultaneously acknowledged the importance of the grassroots base that rank-and-file members had cultivated and failed to recognize the many internal cracks and fissures that still remained in the BPP's foundation.[119] There was little evidence of collective organizational dialogue within the party about the issues raised by dissenters or departing chapters. Bowen recalled that party members "got the party line, actually we got the mass line. That was all we knew. We proceeded to repeat it and defend what Huey had to say about it. . . . There was not a real effort at self-examination."[120]

This was clearly a turning point in the history of the Black Panther Party. The Panthers had fought a bitter internal war, losing some of their most charismatic members and eroding their base. Fratricide had delegitimized the organization in the eyes of many supporters and critics. State political repression had not just drained organizational resources and demoralized membership; it had shaped organizational development in critical ways. The Panthers' attempts to counter repression and survive as an organization had kept them largely on the defensive, had fostered an internal climate wherein suspicion and mistrust were common, and had eroded internal democracy. Countless news stories and dissident members proclaimed the imminent death of the BPP, but Newton argued that the party was on the cusp of rebirth: "We stood at a cross roads. Would we follow our original Survival Program and live—and if necessary die—for the people, or would we join our potential for nihilism with the State's terrific violence and kill ourselves before the government could exterminate us at their leisure?" Rebuilding the organization would be the Black Panther Party's greatest challenge.[121]

5

"REVOLUTION IS A PROCESS RATHER THAN A CONCLUSION"

Rebuilding the Party, 1971–1974

COMMUNITY CONTROL

In the wake of the BPP's organizational crisis, Seale and Newton worked together to craft a vision for the future. There was still a handful of strong chapters around the country, most notably in Chicago, and interest in the organization was still apparent. In 1971–72 Newton received letters from people who wanted to affiliate with the Panthers in Louisville, Kentucky; Ft. Worth; Portsmouth, Virginia; Milwaukee; Providence, Rhode Island; St. Louis; and Dallas.[1] The Panthers remained influential in prisons. George Jackson, one of their most important field marshals, had been killed by prison guards in an alleged escape attempt from San Quentin on 21 August 1971. His funeral attracted thousands to St. Augustine's Church in Oakland.[2] Attica was one of the many prison rebellions tied to Jackson's death that signaled the rising tide of protest inside prisons.[3] On 9 September 1,300 inmates at Attica State Prison in New York rebelled, took hostages, and demanded religious freedom and free and uncensored access to newspapers. At the request of the prisoners Seale went to Attica to negotiate for them. On 31 October the New York State chapter of the Black Panther Party held a People's Tribunal in Brooklyn that took the form of a mock trial of Nixon, Governor Nelson Rockefeller, and others for their actions at Attica. According to FBI sources, two to three thousand people, the majority of whom were black, attended this four-and-a-half-hour-long event.[4]

Despite these initiatives the Panthers were no longer a viable national organization. Douglas recalled that by 1971 there had been severe attrition in membership: "Some got tired, burnt out. Times had changed [and others were] critical of certain policies."[5] Instead of trying to strengthen the national apparatus, BPP leaders focused on strengthening their ties to local communities and building a mass base. Community control was a dominant theme in black political thought in the 1970s. The radical theoretician James Boggs argued, "All segments of the black community are united in their determination to wrest control of these institutions [education, health, industry, housing, welfare, transportation] from whites. The collective will to struggle for Community Control is thus already far advanced inside the black community. . . . The struggle for Community Control has to be seen as a stepping stone on the road to black control of the major cities of this country and ultimate control by blacks of the national government."[6]

To achieve community control the Panthers aimed to entrench themselves in Oakland and organize black people to demand control over the powerful political institutions in the city. Newton argued that this tactical shift demonstrated the Panthers' political flexibility. "The Black Panther Party did not come down from Mars. The Black Panther movement is a phenomenon born in the crucible of the twentieth century and the American historical reality. It has changed, it will continue to change: we are a part of that process known as the revolution in human rights." He argued that the Panthers had been forced to step back and reassess their strategies and tactics: "We retreated. . . . We had been driven away from our genius: the people. We went home to our great people. We bowed our heads before them, in the churches, the little businesses, the ruins of our ghettoes: the old, the infirm, the young."[7] The challenge was to build an organizational vehicle that would address the disconnect from the black community. Newton had been critical of the majority white attendance at the Panthers' United Front Against Fascism conference in July 1969 and believed the Panthers had to recenter themselves in the black community while staying true to their desire for structural transformation of the United States and class-based politics.

Panther leaders decided to centralize their membership base, skills, and resources in Oakland.[8] Douglas said, "We wanted to consolidate the foundation of the party with the strongest chapters and the central core and begin to build and expand out again."[9] Panthers in Vallejo, California; Chattanooga, Tennessee; Houston; Sacramento; Detroit; Washington, DC; Winston-Salem, NC; Philadelphia; Seattle; and Boston were relocated to Oakland after they closed down their chapters.[10] This was a bittersweet move for many Panthers. Some were leaving behind chapters and branches decimated by COINTELPRO and internal squabbles, but others were dismantling the foundations they had struggled to build in their local community. They left behind family, friends, and the familiarity of home. Douglas noted, "The ones who came [to Oakland] who were the ones who were committed. . . . People stayed because they had invested, and they wanted to continue on and they believed in the ideas. So when they came, they came with the spirit of growth and development."[11] Bobby McCall, who relocated to Oakland from Philadelphia, exemplified this mind-set:

> I had totally dedicated myself to this organization. Regardless of what happened internally, I knew this was what I wanted to do, this was who I wanted to be, this was what I wanted my life to be about: uplifting the black community by any means necessary no matter what it took. And I was determined to do that by any means necessary through this organization, the Black Panther Party. So no matter what contradictions occurred, I just said "Well, that's a part of life," and moved on. Just keep progressing forward. You have the whole community depending on you to show you some hope.[12]

The Panthers made structural adjustments to accommodate relocated members. They implemented orientation procedures, which would entail orientation, skill assessment, and assignment to a work area.[13] Community programs became an organizational priority in this period.

The community programs were the lynchpin of the party's new vision. The Panthers expanded the range and scope of these programs and renamed them "community survival programs." In the Panthers' analysis survival programs were temporary models aimed at alleviating economic distress and teaching self-help and community control. They were supposed to meet the concrete needs of the masses of people as well as highlight the inability of the state to resolve these problems, thus providing mass political education. According to Newton, "Our programs are not a revolutionary program or a reformist program. It is a strategy through which we are organizing people for revolution. [It is] impossible to wage an armed struggle if you don't have the masses organized."[14]

Douglas visually represented the Panthers' new focus in the image of the "survival nurse," a black woman standing near a bus from the People's Free Busing Program holding clothing from the People's Free Clothing Program, shoes from the People's Free Shoes Program, a book from the People's Liberation Schools, and a bag of groceries from the People's Free Food Program. The cap on her head indicates that she works for the People's Free Health Clinic. A gun is in a holster at her side, and she wears a button that proclaims, "I am a Revolutionary."[15] Survival programs also included a free plumbing and maintenance program. The free food program was created to "supplement the groceries of Black and poor people until such time as economic conditions allow them to purchase good food at reasonable prices."[16] The Panthers opened a health clinic in Berkeley to provide free medical attention, medication, referrals, sickle cell testing, immunization, prenatal instruction, first aid kits, and community health surveys. Doctors and other health care professionals volunteered their services.[17] In addition the Panthers created a free ambulance service.[18]

A major community health initiative was raising awareness about sickle cell anemia. The BPP established the Sickle Cell Anemia Research Foundation in 1971 to test people, focus publicity on the disease, and work toward a cure.[19] In December 1972 Seale announced the creation of the Seniors Against a Fearful Environment (SAFE) program in response to an increase in muggings and crime against the elderly. As part of SAFE the Panthers would provide escorts and free transportation to the bank for the elderly at Satellite Senior Homes on the days they cashed their social security checks.[20] Utilizing donated vans the Panthers expanded SAFE to include

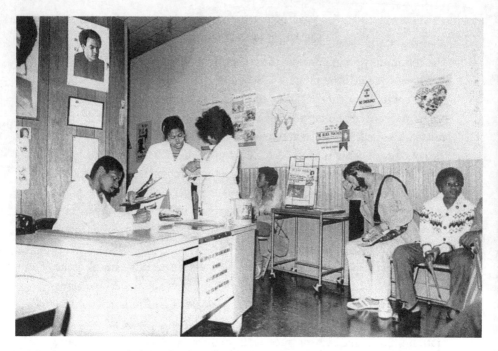

FIGURE 5.1. A Black Panther Party health clinic. Photo from the Archives of It's About Time: Black Panther Party Legacy and Alumni, Sacramento.

rides to grocery and department stores and broadened the transportation service to two other senior housing projects in March 1973. The Panthers would eventually incorporate SAFE as a nonprofit organization with its own board of directors.[21]

The Panthers founded the Son of Man Temple in October 1973. The temple held a community forum every Sunday with guest speakers as well as entertainment. Panther literature described the Son of Man Temple as an "Interdenominational Community Church dedicated to Community Survival."[22] It was a "place where we can come to discover and learn. If we begin the week with this kind of unity and understanding we can carry through each day, our concern, an enthusiastic feeling, about our survival and freedom."[23]

The connection between the Son of Man Temple and the Panthers' survival strategy was evident. The cover of the temple's Sunday program frequently displayed photos taken during survival programs, and "Invitation to Become Survival Workers" was a regular agenda item.[24] During the collection of offerings at a forum on 26 August 1973, a speaker reminded the audience that their contributions would go toward the maintenance of the survival programs: "This congregation is a congregation that meets many days a week to work for the people. We call ourselves soldiers for the people, soldiers for survival. [We're] trying to change the situation of the country for the better."[25]

The Oakland Community Learning Center, which provided a model for community-based education, was one of the BPP's strongest community survival programs. It began as the Intercommunal Youth Institute in 1971, a school program catering to members' children. The Institute taught a variety of subjects, such as math, language arts, science, people's art, environmental studies, and political education. Field experience and critical thinking were central to the Panthers' approach. Oakland parents appreciated the academic rigor and progressive educational philosophy that the Institute provided, and enrollment soon expanded. The Panthers renamed the Institute the Oakland Community Learning Center and moved into a larger building. This building hosted community events, housed the Son of Man Temple, and provided a space for classes and programs on dance, drama, adult education, and music.[26]

The Learning Center allowed the survival programs to reinforce each other for the betterment of the Oakland community and gave more people a vested interest in the party's activities. According to Ericka Huggins, the director of the Center, it embodied the Panthers' holistic intergenerational approach: "A number of new programs have developed just from having the school here. We find out, for instance, that a mother needs certain things otherwise she won't be able to get her child to school. So, we have a welfare rights referral system. There's a senior citizens program functioning here. Quite often, the grandparents and older guardians of the children are involved in the SAFE program. . . . There's a teen program, for the older brothers and sisters of the children. That's how it started."[27]

INSTITUTIONALIZING

The Panthers began to focus on building their organization into a lasting institution. In 1970 they founded Stronghold, a corporation based in New York and directed by Panther lawyers David Lubell and Martin Kenner that would serve as "an entity separate and apart from the Black Panther Party but whose energies and activities are for the purpose of funding the programs of the Party." The corporation ensured that "monies earned by Party leaders and the Party in such matters as books, sales of literary rights, reprints, etc will not be subject to any tax attack if the federal government attempts to go after the Party itself."[28] Stronghold also served as the Panthers' agent and was authorized to enter into contracts and receive money on their behalf and forward it to them.[29] Stronghold received income from Panther speaking engagements and book royalties and advances and in turn paid the Panthers' electric and gas bills, car rental costs, travel expenses, funeral expenses, bail funds and legal costs, rents and mortgages on properties.[30] By December 1972 the corporation owned twenty-one properties, most of them in the Bay Area and used by the Panthers as offices, community program sites, and living spaces where the rank and file lived and worked together collectively.[31]

The Panthers created a collective environment at the Oakland Community Center where students and teachers lived and learned together. Students stayed in dorms and were grouped according to ability rather than age. Panther literature stated:

> Our students participate in determining the policies that govern them. They criticize each other (and their instructors) in order to correct mistakes and mistaken ideas. If they violate the rules that they themselves helped to make, then they are criticized before the collective. All of this is done with the understanding that we criticize with love, never with hatred. Never are children called stupid, dull, or dumb. No one child is forced to make a better grade than another. There are no grades. There is no negative competition. There is only the competition that will produce enthusiasm and prove, through action, that our capabilities are endless.[32]

Funding for the school came from organizational funds and private contributions. In 1973 the Panthers created the nonprofit Educational Opportunities Corporation (EOC) to oversee the Oakland Community School. Its initial trustees were the party supporters Berton Schneider, David Horowitz, and Richard Kaldenbach. The EOC's articles of incorporation described its purpose as "provid[ing] general and vocational educational opportunities to individuals, both adults and minors, at the primary, secondary, and high school grade levels, and . . . offer[ing] adult educational extension services, all of which educational activities shall meet the requirements of Section 214 of the Revenue and Taxation Code."[33]

In March 1974 the EOC received its first grant, from the city of Oakland. By then the Oakland Community School had a staff of nineteen. An EOC annual report dated February 1975 stated that enrollment in the school doubled in January 1974, when a total of 110 students returned or were accepted.[34]

The *Black Panther* newspaper reflected this changed focus. In presenting national and international news, as well as interpretive articles and speeches, the Panthers hoped to win supporters for their organization.[35] In January 1973 the Panthers hired David Du Bois, son of Shirley Graham Du Bois and W. E. B. Du Bois, to edit their newspaper.[36] He immediately made structural changes, which an internal memo described as "report[ing] news with the effect to *inform* rather than just educate." Part of this would involve reducing "unnecessary editorializing within our articles; by presenting the facts, slanted with our line on any event we want to get the message across." The font was changed to accommodate more articles, and a new format divided the newspaper into news, editorial, and entertainment sections.[37] The focus of the paper shifted to national and international news, with fewer articles about the BPP as an organization or movement. The "Program for Survival," however, featured prominently in every issue.

Always masters of rhetorical redefinition, the Panthers described their new survival strategy, with its attendant ideological and structural transformation, as the realization of their "original vision." When asked if their politics had shifted, Newton affirmed that the party's political goals remained socialist: "If there has been any shift, it's in the fact that we have become one of the best organized local parties in the U.S. We have had some change in tactics, but our goal has always been simply one of people gaining control over their community, and we're trying to do that now."[38]

In many ways, however, the Panthers had made a radical departure from their past. The prior focus on the lumpenproletariat was replaced by a commitment to reach out to all ages and classes in the black community. They replaced their Marxist rhetoric with a politics of pragmatism. Armed self-defense was de-emphasized; sarcasm and wit replaced public profanity; and calls to overthrow the "fascist pig power structure" were muted. The focus on mobilizing the community was replaced by a commitment to long-term organizing. The Panthers insisted that these were changes in form, not substance. They proclaimed themselves as revolutionary as ever and argued that their commitment to socialist politics was unwavering. However, they were now committed to working for reform within the system, to politicize people, to educate by example, as the first step toward revolution. Newton stated:

> We are now free to move toward the building of a community structure which will become a true voice of the people, promoting their interests in many ways. We can continue to push our basic survival programs, we can continue to serve the people as advocates of their true interests, we can truly become a political revolutionary vehicle which will lead the people to a higher level of consciousness so that they will know what they must really do in their quest for freedom. Then they will have the courage to adopt any means necessary to seize the time and obtain that freedom.[39]

BLACK POLITICS

To actualize community control the Panthers coupled their survival program strategy with a self-conscious attempt to make connections with black institutions. They moved their headquarters from Berkeley to the heart of the black community in West Oakland, at 1048 Peralta Street. The move from a storefront, which was isolated at night, to a Victorian home on a block surrounded by other homes in a poor black community was transformative. The upper level of the house was used to lay out the newspaper, where staff often worked around the clock. The lower level housed offices readied for security, a waiting room for visitors, living quarters, and a kitchen where Panthers often gathered to eat soul food. With community barbeques and exercise sessions in the backyard, the officer of the day fielding calls from all over the world in the front office, and Sunday political education sessions, the new headquarters became known as "the heartbeat of the party" and the base from which the BPP reached out to the community.[40]

Recognizing that the church played a central social, spiritual, and cultural role in the black community, the Panthers wrote letters to several Bay Area churches explaining their new ideological vision. In the past they had had a close relationship with Father Neil, an activist local preacher who had worked with the civil rights movement. Neil's St. Augustine's Church had hosted one of their Free Breakfast programs as well as funerals for several fallen comrades. However, the Panthers had been very critical of the church, an institution they believed was too conservative. For instance, during a speech to the National Committee of Black Churchmen in Berkeley Hilliard allegedly called the preachers "a bunch of bootlicking pimps and motherfuckers."[41] The BPP's position had changed since then.

In April 1971 the Panthers were invited to meet with Bay Area ministers. Newton spoke to them at the Center for Urban Black Studies in Berkeley, admitting that one of the BPP's prior mistakes was its critique of spirituality as irrelevant. He argued that part of the process of fostering a revolutionary consciousness in the black community was to engage in dialogue with the key community institutions; rather than criticize the church from the sidelines they would try to enact change from within the church, hoping that the contradictions that would arise out of this process would educate the people. The Panthers' vision of their relationship to the church directly paralleled the relationship they saw between themselves and the government. Instead of seeking the overthrow of the system, they would seek to enact change within the system. However, Newton acknowledged that he had little faith in the system's ability to offer more than minor concessions and implied that the BPP's role was to educate people until they came to the same inevitable conclusion: "Until the people feel the same way I feel then I would be rather arrogant to say dump the whole thing, just as we were arrogant to say dump the church. Let's give it a chance, let's work with it in order to squeeze as many contributions and compromises out of all the institutions as possible, and then criticize them after the fact. We'll know when the time comes, when the people tell us so."[42]

The Panthers also took steps to come to terms with black businesses, the other key institution in the black community. In June 1971 Newton proclaimed that the Panthers still adhered to point 3 of their ten-point platform and program, which called for the end of the capitalists' robbery of the black community: "We recognize that capitalism is no solution to the problems we face in our communities. Capitalist exploitation is one of the basic causes of our problem. It is the goal of the Black Panther Party to negate capitalism in our communities and in the oppressed communities throughout the world." However, he acknowledged, many African Americans saw the owners of Laundromats, convenience stores, beauty parlors, and barber shops not as black capitalist oppressors but as fellow struggling community members. He conceded that the Panthers had been hypocritical to engage in blanket condemnation of black capitalists while receiving donations from white capitalists and had not acknowledged the fact that black capitalists were often the victims of white capitalists.[43]

Newton asserted that the Panthers would begin a dialogue with black capitalists about contributing to the party's community survival programs. Such donations would allow the capitalists to give back to the community in a way that would foster the survival and increased politicization of those who lived there. The Panthers announced that they would support the businesses that supported their survival programs and would criticize and mobilize against the businesses that did not. In this process the black community's expectations of black businesses would be radically transformed. According to Newton:

> There is no salvation in capitalism, but through this new approach the Black capitalist will contribute to his own negation by helping to build a strong political vehicle which is guided by revolutionary concepts and serves as a vanguard for the people. . . . So we will heighten the contradiction between the Black community and corporate capitalism, while at the same time reducing the contradiction between the Black capitalist and the Black community. In this way Black capitalism will be transformed from a relationship of exploitation of the community to a relationship of service to the community, which will contribute to the survival of everyone.[44]

Many on the left who believed they had been co-opted and had entered the mainstream criticized the party's ideological transformation.[45] The Panthers replied that they still had the same goals, just different tactics. Huggins defended the new vision:

> Some people say, Well, the Panthers have become pussy cats, the Panthers have become reformist. But, you know, we've found out, each time that we've heard these comments, that usually young, white so-called socialists and communists are saying this. I say, "so-called" because they don't really know beyond the book they've read—or are still reading—what it means to be a socialist. What it means to do hard work. The hard, drudgery, boring, day-to-day, no-reward, you-can't-see-the-future kind of work. They don't know what that means. They don't know what it is to go door to door every day all day long and ask people "Do you . . . ?" and not get to finish the sentence. Or what it is to try to educate people that have no understanding of what you're talking about because they don't have any food, they don't have any shoes, they don't know where their children are going to be in

the next minute, they can't get their welfare check, don't know what their social security number is, don't know where the office is, can't get to the office, and don't want to, anyway. And are having family problems on top of that. So, the point is that we want to do the day to day work with people that will lead to an eventual understanding of why there is a need for alternative institutions.[46]

On the mass level the Panthers' new thrust was welcome. The correspondence that Newton received attested to the fact that he was seen as the leader of a viable organization by many in the black community and some whites. Between 1971 and 1974 hundreds of people from all over the country—the elderly, schoolchildren, prisoners—wrote Newton with criticism, questions about his books, offers to join the organization, and expressions of support.[47] They wrote in response to points he raised in interviews, to ask him to clarify statements he made, or to offer help and advice. In one letter, dated 19 June 1971, the writer stated, "I am writing to express a great admiration for you as the true leader of the American people." Other letters were in the same approving vein: "This letter is written for the baddest nigger who ever came off the set"; "I would like to take this opportunity to thank you for all you have done to help open the eyes of so many blacks in this world such as it is today."[48]

Several writers commented on the BPP's new position on the church. One stated, "I was delighted to read in the *Oakland Tribune* that you were planning to attend church again." The writer extended an invitation to Newton to visit her church, "where blacks and whites together are finding an experience of the living God." This letter was signed "a white neighbor of yours who views Lake Merritt from a much lower prospect."[49] Another wrote, "As a Black Revolutionary woman minister I would like to commend the B.P.P. for joining us in our fight for survival through the church. Years ago, I thought about getting out of the church, but I realized that was where my people were. . . . Young black youth must realize you don't put together a revolution without some institutional base and when you reject the Black church you are rejecting the only institution that Black people have ever controlled."[50] Panthers began attending services in Oakland and, according to Seale, received a warm welcome: "People are re-examining their preconceived opinions. I go to church now every Sunday and elderly black citizens, who used to be scared to be around us . . . keep me there from 10 to 30 minutes afterwards shaking hands."[51]

Newton received a poem on 4 September 1971 titled "Revolution Is the Solution." It is indicative of the mood and spirit of the many people who wrote him:

> An African mind with black
> people at heart;
> my mind is to[o] heavy for
> America to take apart.
> Bobby Seale is free;
> Ericka Huggins is free;
> Huey P. Newton is free;
> Connie Tucker is free;
> Soon Angela Davis will be.
> Now I feel the liberation of me (the masses);
> I can feel the vibration
> of liberation.
> Hey black man you see
> these tears in my eyes.
> Hey black man you see
> these tears rolling down
> my cheeks!!
> It's a cry of black beauty.
> The cry of black beauty is revolution.
> I can feel the vibration
> of liberation!—liberation!—
> liberation!
> Revolution—is—the—solution!!![52]

Yet not all elements of the black community were enthralled with the BPP's new vision. The Panthers' analysis of black capitalism did not differentiate between petty capitalists struggling to survive on "the proletarian periphery" and the economic activity of the black petit bourgeoisie, both of whom were deeply rooted in Oakland's black business establishment.[53] The Panthers' ideological shift put them on the same terrain as Oakland's black middle-class establishment, a group they had vocally condemned in the past. This group had been promoting black capitalism while the Panthers preached revolution, and it viewed the Panthers' new focus with suspicion.

William Boyette, a powerful, established black Oakland businessman, challenged the Panthers' dictate that black capitalists should contribute to the BPP's survival programs. Boyette owned two convenience stores that sold liquor in North Oakland, Bill's Liquor Stores. He was the head of Cal-Pac, the California State Package Store and Tavern Owners Association, a statewide consortium of black liquor stores and clubs. The Panthers had first encountered Cal-Pac during its boycott of Mayfair Supermarket, when it accused Mayfair of stocking liquor sold by companies Cal-Pac believed had discriminatory hiring practices. At Boyette's request the Panthers had contributed to the boycott. But when the Panthers met with Cal-Pac to discuss its support of the survival programs, the organization offered a once-only donation, which the Panthers rejected. Instead the Panthers began a boycott of Boyette's stores on 31 July 1971.[54]

Newton insisted that black businesses should be willing to make a self-determined but continuous contribution to the BPP's survival program: "We see very little difference between Blacks who make profits from the Black community and refuse to contribute to Black survival programs and the white profiteers, such as Mayfair. . . . If they refuse to help the Black community they are parasites that must be forced out of business through economic boycott. Why should the Black community nourish a Black profiteer who has no concern for his brother?"[55]

This boycott aroused a storm of debate in Oakland. Did business owners have responsibility to the communities where their businesses were located? Was black unity a worthwhile goal or an impossible myth given the class stratification in the black community? Should community responsibility take precedence over self-interest and profiteering? Were the Panthers trailblazers committed to acquiring support at all costs for community-based programs or extortionists narrowly focused on the maintenance of their particular solutions to the problems of the black community? Were the Panthers hypocritical by taking aim at vulnerable black capitalists while ignoring the parasitic practices of white-owned businesses?

Boyette mobilized to gain support from Oakland's black business community against the Panthers' boycott. Black small business owners, as well as members of the NAACP, the National Business League, and the United Minority Economic Council, formed the Ad Hoc Committee to Preserve Black Business one month after the boycott began. The committee proclaimed support for some of the Panthers' survival programs but objected to "any forceful measures of donation." They pointed out that Cal-Pac had obtained over two hundred jobs for minorities by picketing wholesale liquor distributors and appealed to people to continue to shop at Bill's Liquor Store.[56]

The Ad Hoc Committee pointed out that Cal-Pac had offered the survival programs a donation of milk, eggs, bread, meat, cereals, and more, which would be repeated at its discretion. It claimed that the Panthers had rejected their offer and instead demanded a financial donation to be continued for as long as the Panthers wished. Newton admitted that Cal-Pac had made this offer, but he justified rejecting it because "a continuing trickle of support is more important to the community than a large, once-only hush mouth gift." He declared, "We will not be paid off; we will not be quiet; we will not go away as long as there is one hungry child, one barefoot person, one medically neglected individual, or one brother or sister without a winter coat."[57] The Ad Hoc committee explained that Cal-Pac refused to make a financial contribution to the Panthers because it believed there would be little accountability for the money. Instead, it argued, contributions should be voluntary and the donor should decide the amount. The committee emphasized that Cal-Pac members were currently supporting other community projects and added, "One-half of the one percent of all business in America are black owned. If this coercive action by the BPP is allowed to continue black businesses will be destroyed. We will be going backwards instead of forward."[58]

The Panthers mobilized on a large scale for these boycotts, which they dubbed "the People's Boycott," to emphasize that the people of Oakland would determine the boycott's success or failure by their actions. The Panthers tirelessly walked the picket lines in front of Boyette's store, handing out flyers and brochures to Oakland residents. One flyer highlighted the demand that capitalists stop robbing the black community and listed the BPP's survival programs. It stated, "The Black Capitalist depends upon the Black community to make his profit. But the Black capitalist can support the Black community by donating to these Free Programs, Survival Programs for the People in our community. In this way the Black Capitalist will become not an exploiter of the Black community, but will help to build the vehicle we need to liberate our communities."[59] Presumably the Black Panther Party was this vehicle.

In a meeting with the Ad Hoc Committee Newton acknowledged that the Panthers had been somewhat insensitive to the constraints on black business: "First of all the black businessman is a victim like all of us. He's discriminated against. It's difficult for us to get loans from the bank, many times we're not dealt with fairly with the wholesale houses and so forth. He's just another victim. Victims have steps, there's some people that are more victimized than others. So what we need, all of us, [is to] unite together."[60] However, he pledged to continue the boycott.

The boycott was tightly organized. The Panthers kept weekly statistics sheets, on which they noted the date and how many people entered the store and purchased something or refused to cross the picket line. They tallied how many customers were kids, regulars, or family and friends of the owner. The boycott slowly gained support and had a devastating impact on Boyette's business. In one week, 22–29 August, 348 people entered the store, and 205 refused to enter. That same month Boyette sought relief through the courts; he issued a complaint against the Panthers and filed for a temporary restraining order and a preliminary injunction, arguing that they were harming his business; intimidating, deterring, and harassing his customers; picketing on his property; and blocking the entrance to his store.[61]

On 6 January 1972 the Panthers extended their picket line to Boyette's other store. Less than two weeks later Oakland's congressman Ron Dellums announced that he had helped negotiate a compromise agreement between the BPP and the Ad Hoc Committee. The boycott, which had lasted eight months, was officially over. Dellums's press release heralded the compromise as a victory for black unity: "The agreement is important because it portends the development of a greater sense of organized unity and purpose than has heretofore existed in the black community. The business and social elements have here pledged to work together in a constructive and purposeful manner so that the fiscal and human resources of that community can be joined in a common effort towards common goals."[62]

Behind closed doors Newton and Boyette signed a private agreement. The first point affirmed the primacy of black unity: "It is most emphatically within the interest of the black community that there be total unity of individuals, organizations and purposes for the improvement and liberation of that community; that all organizations party to this agreement are devoted to the achievement of that unity and to the economic health and well-being of the black community." The Ad Hoc Committee agreed to "implement the principle that for the survival of that community, it is the clear and emphatic social responsibility of all blacks who earn profits from the black community to contribute some portion of such profits to economic, social and survival programs organized by the Black Panther Party within the black community." They resolved to organize other black businesses through their ranks or through another organization to further the goals of the document. The committee agreed to support the BPP survival programs in an ongoing manner in an amount of its own choosing. The Panthers agreed to immediately end the boycott, and as long as the Ad Hoc Committee remained committed to the agreement, they pledged not to boycott or threaten to boycott black businesses.[63]

The Panthers assisted Boyette by distributing leaflets in Oakland to encourage people to shop in his store again.[64] One of their flyers urged, "Support the Businesses that support our community." It listed the addresses of Boyette's stores and stated, "Support Black businessman Brother Bill Boyette Who Contributes To The Community's Free Survival Programs."[65] The Panthers began to provide free advertising in their newspaper for businesses that donated to the survival programs.

STRUCTURING BLACK UNITY

The California state attorney general sent the BPP a letter dated 13 March 1972, explaining that, because the party had solicited money from the public for charitable purposes, by law it had to file "with the Registrar of Charitable Trusts a copy of their articles of incorporation, constitution, or other governing instrument, and also to file yearly reports of income and expenses in connection with their charitable programs."[66] The BPP attorney Garry replied on its behalf that the party was not collecting money for charitable purposes and that all fund-raising was done through St. Augustine Episcopal Church. He did point out that the BPP would be creating a nonprofit corporation to carry out its charitable aims and purposes in the future and agreed to notify the attorney general's office when the nonprofit became official.[67]

The United Black Fund was the name of the nonprofit corporation that the Panthers and the Ad Hoc Committee created to implement their agreement. Its goals were "to raise and distribute funds from black business and other available sources in order to finance the special needs of the black community of California." These needs were enumerated as free breakfast for children, free medical and dental care, free food, free shoes and clothing.[68] The Articles of Incorporation named as directors Reverend Neil; Gwen

Fontaine, Newton's personal secretary; and Newton's brother, Melvin Newton.[69]

The Panthers sent a form letter to supporters announcing that they could now make tax-exempt contributions to the BPP's survival programs through the United Black Fund.[70] By 3 October 1972 the Fund had provided support for the Free Breakfast Program, the People's Free Food Program, the Inter-Communal Youth Institute, the Legal Aid Educational Program, the Free Busing to Prisons Program, the Free Commissary for Prisoners Program, the People's Free Shoe Program, the People's Free Clothing Program, the People's Free Medical Research Health Clinic, the People's Sickle Cell Anemia Research Foundation, the People's Free Ambulance Service, the People's Free Dental Program, the People's Free Optometry Program, the People's Free Plumbing and Maintenance Program, and the Community Cooperative Housing Program.[71]

The United Black Fund made some effort toward putting economic pressure on the white community. When the Ad Hoc Committee asked Newton during the boycott when and if the Panthers were going to boycott the white community, he answered, "Yes, when we all get united then we can really deal with them. When we're all separated to start with how can we fight our real enemy, the real strong man. We always want to go into battle when we're not prepared, first we'll prepare by organizing all the victims and then we'll go against the big corporations."[72] Several months later the BPP drafted a letter to Bay Area white businesses describing the history of the boycott actions against Boyette and the formation of the United Black Fund. The letter stated that the boycott had exemplified the principle of self-help and had brought about greater unity in the black community. Now that the victims were united, they could take aim at the larger target:

> In order for our self-help program to be really effective, we must keep as much of what is ours in our community. In these past months we have been studying large Bay Area businesses, mostly owned by persons not of our Black community. Our studies have concretely proven that the bulk of our money goes to large corporations and, thereby, outside of the community to our dis-interest. . . . It is with these facts in mind that we are calling upon you, as a business presently operating in and draining many of these resources from our Black community, to realistically understand our dilemma. We are

calling upon you to return at least a portion of our resources to us. It's not a helping hand we're requesting, but a reasonable, regular, weekly donation of those resources which keep you "successful" and keep us in poverty.[73]

The letter suggested that donations to the black community could be made through the United Black Fund. It is unclear if this letter was ever approved, signed by the suggested signatories (which included the United Black Fund, Dellums, and Neil), or sent.

Internal reorganization was central to the BPP's survival strategy, and committed cadres were the backbone of the organization. In May 1973 a representative of the Committee to Support the Black Panther Party in Japan visited Oakland and praised the Panthers' dedication to the survival programs. He wrote, "It was not just the scale and the comprehensive span of the programs that impressed me. Seeing the programs actually going on and serving the benefit of the people was really encouraging to us. Many of the groups here learned from your idea and concrete wisdom necessary for such programs, and materialized them in their own programs. In fact, though, what was more impressive was the dedication of the people involved in the program."[74]

The Panthers tried to make the organization a lasting institution to prepare for the long haul. Newton defined a revolutionary vehicle as a "revolutionary concept set into motion by a dedicated cadre through a particular organized structure."[75] As Panther tactics and strategies shifted, so did their inner organizational structure. They had moved from being an organization that applauded revolutionary action against the police to an organization that emphasized day-to-day work. Amar Casey, who had come to Oakland to work at the Panther school in 1973, recalled how impressed he was by the party's infrastructure: "When I arrived in Oakland, there were Panthers coming from all over the country. There must have been 350 to 400 Panthers in Oakland at that time. What they were doing was busy trying to build this big institutional infrastructure. I was amazed at what they owned—it blew me away. They had the school, they had the dormitory for the children, they had a newspaper, they had a restaurant, a medical clinic. They had an amazing infrastructure."[76] Routine paperwork, such as typed memos from meetings, directives, and work reports from chapters and cadres, provide a vantage point into the Panthers' operations. Weekly reports from the different ministries of operation chronicled meetings attended, political work accomplished, financial reports, and interpersonal conflicts.[77] The Panthers created a daily work report form with spaces to fill in hours of field work, numbers of newspapers sold, and hours and subjects of study.[78] To help keep members abreast of current events, the Panthers created memos called "news of the day," which gave brief summaries of the local, national, and international news.[79]

The Panthers also issued innerparty memoranda to facilitate communication. The first, dated 29 July 1972, stated, "The issuance of this memorandum comes as a result of the July 27, 1972, Political Education Class. There, comrades voiced criticisms/self-criticisms regarding the interrelationships of comrades, while suggesting methods of how to best bring about more warmth and love among all comrades." The memorandum included a list of items to be discussed during PE class, such as Mao's "On Contradiction" and "Criticism and Self-Criticism," Newton's Boston College speech on intercommunalism, and books such as *To Die for the People* by Newton, *Seize the Time* by Seale, and *Blood in My Eye* by Jackson. Innerparty memoranda began to appear regularly in 1972. They served as an internal newsletter and provided a place for chronicling arrests, advising about legal defense issues, disseminating mobilization updates, announcing recreational activities and deaths in the family, and reminding parents to pick up their children from school and comrades to write letters to political prisoners.[80]

Central Committee members met on a regular basis, usually bimonthly, at Newton's apartment. There Panther leaders discussed political strategies and organizational procedures and priorities. Members structured the meetings around predetermined agenda items and organizational issues. Due to the party's belief in communalism, politics infused all areas of members' lives, and the borders between workplace and home space, public and private were blurred. The party promoted a collective structure to facilitate the total commitment of its membership; it attempted to meet the needs of members for food, clothing, shelter, and even health care. The job of the health cadre was to keep track of ill comrades and children, as well as epidemics of the flu and other contagious illnesses that could spread quickly in a collective living situation.[81]

The personal and the political had become almost inseparable. Agenda items for Central Committee meetings included comrades' appearance and clothing needs, interpersonal conflict, and the maintenance of cleanliness in work areas.[82] An agenda item for the 21 July 1972 meeting was "Discuss the way *some* party leadership talk to the comrades (rank & file) and the way in which *some* party leadership give instructions to rank & file comrades."[83] The collective distribution of funds to buy shoes and clothing for comrades was discussed at the 2 October 1972 meeting.[84] A memo to central body members dated 16 August 1972 brought up the need for a dialogue on Planned Parenthood, policies for expectant mothers, creation of an infirmary, and teaching remedial reading and math skills.[85]

For many Panthers membership required strict discipline. Free time was often at a minimum. A memo dated 18 October 1972 commented that people had been taking advantage of the recreation time on Sunday to disappear without notice; the memo warned that those people who were not going to the park should inform the office coordinator of their whereabouts.[86] Other memos declared, "All Party members are to attend church every Sunday. There are no exceptions" (8 August 1973); "It is mandatory that comrades go to P.E. class" (29 August 1973); "Comrades who go to school or work should go into the field for a couple of hours each day also. The coordinators are to decide how long each person will stay in the field" (27 September 1973). A memo dated 14 November 1973 directed all comrades to attend PE class on Sunday morning at 8:30, and a memo on 31 January 1974 warned that comrades who were late to the service at Son of Man Temple would have to pay a $5 fine; if they did not attend the service and had no prior permission to be absent they would be fined $10; there would be a sign-in book to monitor attendance.

According to McCall:

> We ate together. We slept together. We lived together. We did everything together like a family, like an organization should. . . . We were a bunch of disciplined, organized young brothers and sisters who were determined to uplift the black community. It wasn't no joke being in the party. It might have been called a party, but it was no party. We had a lot of fun with each other because we loved each other. We had a lot of family affairs. We always celebrated each other's birthdays . . . in a big way. We didn't celebrate holidays, but we did celebrate life with each other.[87]

In 1972 Huggins wrote a poem for Elaine Brown titled "for elaine: on her birthday." In it she reaffirmed the strong feelings that some party members had for each other and their work:

Often we find that life is a
Tremendous cycle of things
good things
oppressive things
hoped-for things
seldom gotten things
not too often joy-full things
each year brings us closer
to victory for the people
—a good thing—and with this victory
a cycle of good things
real things
will follow.
This year on the 3rd month
2nd day
celebrate our progress
from sleep to awakening
from our vision to the manifestation of it
in the people
this year celebrate your life
as a part of this progress
celebrate the future
for our people
our freedom
our liberation.[88]

Huggins wrote another poem, "In Oakland," describing the mixture of hard work and comradeship that framed reality for many Panthers:

east 14th street—
cement,
tar,
blinking traffic lights;
the yellow of yesterday,
the red of today
the green of tomorrow . . .
our lives have never been "normal" . . .
we are part of tomorrow,
our todays and yesterdays

quickly become a vague memory
(so quickly do we move).
Sometimes we can stop to look at ourselves, in motion
and love ourselves and each other.
These are the good times,
the comradely times,
when we can celebrate life.[89]

RE-EDUCATION FOR LIBERATION

As the Panthers redefined revolution, they struggled to separate mass line from party line and to strengthen internal political education apparatuses to prevent tactical shifts from evolving into programmatic ones. One Panther who had been arrested for grand theft auto confirmed the continuing need for PE in a letter to June Hilliard:

> The attempt to transform the criminal mentality into a revolutionary one with me is indeed a crucial struggle. In terms of my rationale, how I equate things and also my guide to action. In many ways I may be considered to be streetwise but my revolutionary maturity has been somewhat slow. One of my problems is I need more study and feel that in the future [comrades] from prison should be sent through a reorientation program so they will have a complete understanding of where we are what we're doing and the exact role of the vanguard party in relation to surface political work as well as infrastructure.[90]

In October 1972 the Panthers held a meeting on the creation of study groups within the organization. Members expressed interest in studying Fanon's *The Wretched of the Earth*, Oakland urban politics, and other subjects.[91] PE classes were used as a forum for discussion of issues. The central body considered a proposal to renew PE efforts, which suggested dividing the collective, approximately a hundred people, into two groups based on skill to study a curriculum that would include "remedial math and English, Party History, Party Ideology and lectures in Sociology (progressive), Psychology (study of the self and others), Biology (the human body, other living things) and advanced math (mathematics in relationship to dialectical materialism)." Instructors would be central body members as well as guest speakers and lecturers. The Panthers laid out a schedule for a year-long program of PE along these lines.[92]

PE classes attempted to make the link between personal shortcomings and politics. One memo from the editing cadre noted, "Following completion of the newspaper, we had a cadre P.E. class on Discipline (from the *Red Book*) and Party Structure. The class was a good one; informative, necessary and well-timed. Certain contradictions arose on the last night's work on this newspaper; tendencies toward laxity, individualism and a disregard of organizational structure. Criticism, self-criticism and a re-education were appropriate methods of correction. It was a class the entire cadre needed."[93]

Innerparty memoranda in 1972 and 1973 indicated that the *Red Book* continued to play a large role in PE classes. Collective reading and discussion of the *Red Book's* "On Contradiction," "Criticism and Self-Criticism," and "Methods of Leadership" appeared on the agenda for several months in 1972.[94]

In 1973 the Panthers created review quizzes to test party members' knowledge of current events, party history, and ideology. The first quiz centered on the relationship between party policies and the ten-point platform and program. Panthers had a fixed time in which to complete the quiz and were encouraged to utilize reference materials. There were short-answer questions, such as "List three major institutions which must be controlled by the people," and analytical and interpretive questions, such as "What is an education relevant to Black people? What does the Public School System have to offer children in the inner-city?" This quiz also tested knowledge of current affairs with questions such as "Where are three major wars of aggression being waged by the United States?" and "What is happening in Rhodesia, Mozambique and Angola?" The second review quiz centered on the history of the black church, the development of black businesses, and the history of the Black Panther Party. Questions on party history asked, "Name 20 fallen comrades (and dates slain)"; "When was the first Black Panther newspaper issued and tell something about the front page story"; and "Name at least two laws that have been created, changed or eliminated because of the activities of the Black Panther Party."[95]

In early 1973 the Panthers developed a survey to determine the skills of their cadres. Although not all members filled it out, the survey provides a peephole into the composition of the party's membership at that time. The survey asked for age, recent employment history, educational background, and job experience. It asked members to indicate if they were on welfare or on probation or parole.[96] The answers reveal that the Panthers at this time were a young, diverse group with a majority working-class membership. Of the 119 Panthers who filled out the survey, 66 were male and 53 were female. Ages ranged from fourteen to thirty-five; the average was twenty and a half. The most common employment histories were factory workers, poverty program workers, clerks, and office workers. Thirty-eight Panthers were high school graduates, and twenty had finished eleventh grade. Thirty-seven Panthers had some college education: sixteen had one year of college, seventeen had between two and two and a half years, two had an associate's degree, two had a bachelor's degree. Thirty-six Panthers were students; eighteen were on welfare; four were on parole; and fourteen were on probation.[97] Using the results of this survey, Panthers were assigned work most appropriate for their skills.

The Panthers created a structure for legal defense. Innerparty memoranda contained updates on legal defense and reminders to write to political prisoners and to send them money, stamps, envelopes, and other supplies if possible. Hilliard's incarceration was a major concern for party members, and they launched a petition campaign to gain support for his release. A memo dated 4 October 1972 asked for volunteers to sort the thousands of petitions they had received in response.[98] The Panthers also supported political prisoners, most notably Johnny Spain, a member of the San Quentin 6, a group of inmates accused in connection with the deaths of three inmates, including George Jackson, and three guards on 21 August 1971. Spain was convicted of conspiracy and the murder of two of the guards.[99]

The Panthers faced arrest and harassment from the police while doing party work, and the Legal Defense Committee kept track of the number of arrests of comrades on petty charges.[100] They instituted bail insurance within the party, beginning at $5 monthly, to cover traffic tickets and arrests.[101] A memo from 19 November 1973 explained, "A monthly premium would cover all traffic tickets received, warrants on file, arrests (bail of $500 or less) and legal services requiring special fees."[102] An article in the 19 January 1974 issue of the *Black Panther* reported that police had harassed Panthers soliciting money for the Sickle Cell Anemia Research Foundation: "The police actions have included arrests, citations, confiscation of donation cans, forced removal from public collection locations and the holding of workers for hours, all clearly illegal acts."[103] The Panthers protested in the courts and won: "As a result of a court decision in San Francisco (Friday, July 28, 1972) comrades can distribute Party newspapers and solit donations in San Francisco without suffering arrest on the charge of 'begging' or 'soliciting' without a license."[104]

CHANGING TIMES

The Panthers revamped their guiding organizational documents. They formed a Rules Committee, which recommended a reexamination of the twenty-six rules that had guided the party. The committee proposed reducing the number of rules to fourteen and creating an implementation plan that would ensure the rules were being enforced. Many of the original rules were made at a time when discipline was a major issue; these would be consolidated and placed near the end of the list. The committee suggested that the first several rules should reflect the party's primary concern: that members understand and follow the ideological principles of the party and the ten-point platform and program. The first rule stated, "All Branches and Chapters must adhere to the philosophical and ideological principles as defined by the Central Committee of the Black Panther Party." This had been the second to last rule in the original version.

The Rules Committee also consolidated the many structural rules in the original version that dealt with issues of communications and finance in the relationship between chapters and branches. The committee included a rule that stated, "No Party member will use, point or fire a weapon unnecessarily or accidentally." However, it chose to delete a rule mandating that all Panthers had to know how to service and operate weapons correctly, arguing, "We think that this should be adhered to but only in light of the Party's internal security requirements in our new and changing situations." The committee suggested that a structured course of PE accompany these new rules. Classes would help party members understand the new rules so they could implement them.

The Panthers also reassessed their most hallowed document, the ten-point platform and program, in light of their new thrust. An article in the Black Panther explained, "The ten point platform and program of the Black Panther Party, like all things, does not stand outside of dialectics. We have recognized that the words written in 1966 do not fully reflect the needs and desires of our people in 1971. Therefore, the platform and program has been temporarily removed from our paper, until such time when words can be arranged and organized into a program and platform which more accurately reflects and defines the present needs and desires of our people."[105] On 29 March 1972 the Panthers unveiled their newly revised guiding principles. The structure of the ten-point platform and program would remain the same: twenty points equally divided between "What We Want" and "What We Believe." However, the content reflected a reordering of priorities and an articulation of new concerns.

The new document contained additions. It took as its subject not just black people but also "oppressed people and people of color." Racially specified oppressors in the original were generalized in the 1972 version. Notably in point 2 "white American businessman" was changed to "American businessman," and in point 4 "white landlords" was changed to "landlords."[106] Free health care, an issue the Panthers had seen as a crucial part of their community survival strategy, was addressed in point 6 of the 1972 version, "We want completely free health care for all black and oppressed people": "We believe that the government must provide, free of charge for the people, health facilities which will also develop preventative medical programs to guarantee our future survival. We believe that mass health education and research programs must be developed to give all Black and oppressed people access to advanced scientific and medical information, so we may provide ourselves with proper medical attention and care."[107]

Issues that the BPP had prioritized in the past were addressed in a new way. The Panthers had always spoken out against U.S. imperialism, and the original ten-point platform and program had demanded that all black men be exempt from military service: "We believe that black people should not be forced to fight in the military service to defend a racist government that does not protect us. We will not fight and kill other people of color in the world who, like black people, are being victimized by the white racist government of America. We will protect ourselves from the force and violence of the racist police and the racist military, by whatever means necessary."[108] The 1972 version took a larger view: "We want an immediate end to all wars of aggression. . . . We believe that the various conflicts which exist around the world stem directly from the aggressive desires of the U.S. ruling circle and government to force its domination upon the oppressed people of the world. We believe that if the U.S. government or its lackeys do not cease these aggressive wars that it is the right of the people to defend themselves by any means necessary against their aggressors."[109]

Police brutality remained a central issue. Point 7 of the original version stated, "We want an immediate end to POLICE BRUTALITY and MURDER of black people. We believe that we can end police brutality in our black community by organizing black self-defense groups that are dedicated to defending our black community from racist police oppression and brutality. The Second Amendment to the Constitution of the United States gives a right to bear arms. We therefore believe that all black people should arm themselves for self-defense."[110] The 1972 version spelled out a more explicit definition of police brutality and a more nuanced advocacy of armed self-defense: "We believe that the racist and fascist government of the United States uses its domestic enforcement agencies to carry out its program of oppression against Black people, other people of color and poor people inside the United States. We believe it is our right, therefore, to defend ourselves against such armed forces and that all blacks and oppressed people should be armed for self-defense of our homes and communities against these fascist police forces."[111]

Point 8 of the original version demanded that all black people be tried by a jury of their peers. The 1972 version focused more on the inherent unfairness of the criminal justice system when applied to blacks and poor oppressed people. Point 9 of the 1972 version stated:

> We want freedom for all Black and poor oppressed people now held in U.S. federal, state, county, city and military prisons and jails. We want trials by a jury of peers for all persons charged with so-called crimes under the laws of this country. . . . We believe that the many Black and poor oppressed people now held in U.S. prisons and jails have not received fair and impartial trials under a racist and fascist judicial system and should be free from incarceration. We believe in the ultimate elimination of all wretched, inhuman penal institutions, because the masses of men and women imprisoned inside the United States or by the U.S. military are the victims of oppressive conditions which are the real cause of their imprisonment. We believe that when persons are brought to trial that they must be guaranteed, by the United States, juries of their peers, attorneys of their choice and freedom from imprisonment while awaiting trials.[112]

Point 10 of the original program stated, "We want land, bread, housing, education, clothing, justice, and peace." It defined the BPP's major political objective as a United Nations–supervised plebiscite in the black "colony" and concluded with wording from the Declaration of Independence justifying the right of people to overthrow the government. The 1972 version contained two important changes: it eliminated the reference to the UN plebiscite and added the "people's community control of modern technology" to the list of wants.[113]

With new organizational priorities, a reinvigorated internal structure, growing acceptance in Oakland's black communities, a brief reprieve from the state, and an uneasy alliance with Oakland's black businessmen, the Black Panther Party was poised to implement the most potent element in its strategy of community control: the quest for local political power.

6

THE POLITICS OF SURVIVAL

Electoral Politics and Organizational Transformation

THE BALLOT

In the 1970s many in the African American community saw electoral politics as a viable avenue to political power and community empowerment. The Voting Rights Act of 1965 and the civil rights movement's focus on voter registration had substantially increased the Black electorate and the number of Black elected officials. In 1964 there were 100 black elected officials; seven years later this number had increased to 1,860.[1] Although Oakland blacks had mobilized to elect Ron Dellums to the U.S. House of Representatives in 1971, local politics remained dominated by conservative whites. By 1972, when more than 25 percent of the city's voting population was black, only 12 percent of members of the Oakland City Council was black.[2] The Panthers were poised to move into this political vacuum.

In 1971 black politicians nationwide came together to form the Congressional Black Caucus to provide a united voice on black political issues and support the election of black candidates. One year later Shirley Chisholm, the first black woman elected to Congress, launched a formidable grassroots campaign for the Democratic Party's presidential nomination. The Congressional Black Caucus and black nationalist leaders discussed the possibility of organizing an independent political convention to encourage discourse among a broad spectrum of black leaders about the black community's political future. These talks culminated in the National Black Political Convention in Gary, Indiana, 11–13 March 1972. Approximately three thousand delegates representing all tendencies of the black liberation movement, from nationalist to integrationist, gathered to discuss the parameters of a unified black political strategy and the creation of independent political institutions.

Newton wrote to Robert N. C. Nix, a Philadelphia congressman, to initiate a closer relationship between the Congressional Black Caucus and the Black Panther Party. He asserted that the party "recognized the role the Black elected official must play, attempting to balance the needs, desires and dignity of our people with the racist and unjust system that prevails over and permeates this society."[3] Newton asked Lloyd Barbee, a Wisconsin congressman, to propose that an invitation to the National Black Political Convention be extended to the Panthers. Barbee complied, writing a letter to conference conveners asserting, "The Black Panther Party is concerned about and will contribute to black political effectiveness."[4] As a result of Barbee's efforts Seale was invited to the convention to represent the BPP. He added his voice to the dialogue about creating a vision for black control of America's major cities.[5]

After a weekend of intense discussion and debate, delegates to the convention agreed to establish the National Black Political Assembly. They created a document that embodied their vision for black politics, the "National Black Political Agenda." Although the Panthers protested that they had been somewhat marginalized at the convention, they reprinted the full text of the document in the *Black Panther* for their readership to analyze.[6]

Attendance at the convention positioned the Panthers as part of the nationwide debate about electoral politics. They began their move to achieve political power in Oakland by organizing two community survival conferences as consciousness-raising events that would combine political speeches with music, food giveaways, and voter registration. According to Newton, these conferences would connect voter registration to community self-determination and serve as the first step in moving toward the political implications of community control. Afterward he said:

> We feel it is necessary to be concerned about the day-to-day needs of our people and survival is a very broad kind of concept. Of course, to eat is to survive to register to vote so we gave away free bags of groceries. And it's a survival tactic because I don't care how many people you feed, you've got to take the fear out of them before they're no longer oppressed. With the [voter] registration, we have developed a block of voters. So we have developed a food program that even the local media applaud. . . . And we want to do more; we want to change the city administration and also the government structure itself. So it's not a revolutionary program, not a reformist program. It's merely a tool for organizing people into a force by which we can transform a decadent system into a system that would be relevant and serve the people.[7]

The conferences were partially funded by advance money for Newton's and Seale's books.[8] The estimated budget for the first conference was more than $10,000 for expenses, including speakers, insurance, rental of a warehouse, sickle cell testing equipment, sound equipment, and the purchase of whole chickens.[9] The Panthers solicited donations of groceries and money through the United Black Fund.[10] They created the Community Committee for Greater Voter Registration, which included representatives of one hundred organizations and churches in the Bay Area, to mobilize community support.[11]

In March 1972 the Panthers held the first three-day Black Community Survival Conference in Oakland and Berkeley. The conference drew a diverse crowd of over sixteen thousand, old and young, gang members and churchgoers. The Panthers gave away ten thousand free bags of groceries, with a whole chicken in every bag, and administered thousands of sickle cell anemia tests, and registered thousands of new voters.[12] Each day of the conference was held at a different venue: Oakland Auditorium on 29 March, Greenman Field in East Oakland on 30 March, and San Pablo Park in Berkeley on 31 March. Johnnie Tillmon, head of the National Welfare Rights Organization, Father Neil, and Elaine Brown, an LA Panther who had become minister of information in the wake of Cleaver's expulsion, rallied the crowd around the theme of community control. The Persuasions, a popular soul group, provided musical entertainment.[13]

Shirley Chisholm's speech was one of the highlights of the conference. She emphasized the importance of black politicians and black voters to transform America:

> On this momentous occasion, both of us are breaking down barriers to black participation in the political system—you, by challenging the stereotype of the unregistered blackman, and I, by challenging the middle-aged white male's monopoly on the highest position in American government—the presidency. Both of our challenges to America are of a new brand: no longer are we hemming and hawing from the sidelines, getting no response because we present no threat. By joining the system, we are hitting white America below the belt, hurting them where they are most vulnerable. Blacks are learning to be sophisticated about power.[14]

On Saturday, 24 June 1972, the Panthers held a second conference, called the Anti-war, African Liberation–Voter Registration Survival Conference. This conference reflected the BPP's continued commitment to internationalist politics. In 1971 Martin Kenner, a leading member of the Committee to Defend the Panthers, had gone to Europe to meet with representatives from the People's Republic of China, the Democratic Republic of Korea, and Cuba. He wrote Newton a letter describing his trip: "The South Viet Namese were far and away the most outspoken in their desire for more help from us. They requested radio programs, leaflets, and drawings—in short propaganda they can use in Nam—as well as Party propaganda here in the paper about US aggression in S.E. Asia. . . . All of the governments wanted to receive the party paper."[15]

Newton led a delegation of over a dozen Panthers to the People's Republic of China in September 1971. Their itinerary included meetings with top officials and visits to sites of historical and cultural significance.[16] Upon his return Newton issued a press release stating that the Panthers had timed their trip "so that we might ask the peace and freedom-loving Chairman Mao Tse-tung to be the chief negotiator to Mr. Nixon for the peace and freedom of the oppressed peoples of the world."[17]

The Panthers had become a source of inspiration and support to oppressed groups around the world. In 1972 Aborigines who had started a branch of the Black Panther Party in Australia wrote to the party's Central

Headquarters to seek affiliation. Brown wrote back to formally welcome the group into the Panther organization and discuss potential areas of future collaboration.[18] The Panthers also provided material aid to Bay Area African liberation support organizations, and the George Jackson Health Clinic periodically sent "free medical supplies to the liberation movements in the African territories of Mozambique, Gineau-Bissau [sic] and Angola, via the African Support Movement."[19]

The Anti-war, African Liberation–Voter Registration Survival Conference made the Panthers' international approach to social change explicit. The conference drew a crowd of approximately five thousand, almost 95 percent black and mostly young.[20] Attendees were encouraged to register to vote and take a test for sickle cell anemia. Fiery speakers, including Seale, Dellums, and Neil, called for the end of the Vietnam War and the total withdrawal of U.S. troops from Vietnam. The speakers also forged a connection between the struggle of blacks in the United States and the struggle of African liberation movements in former Portuguese colonies. A representative of the Provisional Revolutionary Government of South Vietnam addressed the crowd via telephone.[21]

The Panthers circulated a "Survival Petition," which stated, "The struggles being currently waged in Vietnam, in Southern Africa, in the black and poor communities of the U.S. itself, as well as elsewhere, are all our struggles and we are uniting and pledge ourselves to unite ever stronger together for our common survival and complete liberation. This is what we want. This is what we believe."[22] A modest number of conference attendees signed up to contribute to survival programs or become community volunteers. Fifty-three people signed up to be part-time community workers, twenty-one signed up for the People's Free Health Clinic, sixty-three for the People's Free Food Program, nineteen to be sickle cell volunteers, nine to be community volunteers, and fourteen to do voter registration. Twenty-one people expressed interest in membership in the Black Panther Party.[23]

The highlight of this conference was Seale's announcement that the Panthers would seek political office in Oakland as part of a comprehensive long-range plan to achieve political control of the city. He asserted that gaining political power was a tactic to mobilize and organize the black community that would also provide the Panthers with a legitimate voice on Oakland's political scene. Panther candidates would embody the nexus between community organizing and political power, the necessary first step toward revolution. Seale explained, "We are talking about . . . organizing and taking over the whole city of Oakland. . . . [I'm] talking about running for mayor of Oakland, I'm not going to sit up here and promise you that over night all of it is going to be over with, but I'm going to say here we got a three-year plan. We are going to run 4 seats in April, 1973, and use the people to take those seats with the rights of candidates, starting with my-self."[24] Brown later wrote, "With a minor shift in style . . . we had begun a campaign that would turn the vote into a step in the revolutionary process. With a minor change in form, we might transform the content of the hope of black people."[25] Unlike their 1968 electoral foray, the Panthers were not running for office to politicize the electorate and draw attention to their cause; this time they were playing to win.

In May 1972 Ericka Huggins, Herman Smith, Audrea Jones, and William Roberts won four seats on the Berkeley Community Development Council, a twenty-four member antipoverty board with a multimillion-dollar, fed-erally funded budget.[26] The first agenda item at the Black Panther Party's Cen-tral Committee meeting on 29 June 1972 was "the possibility of running Party members in the up-coming Model Cities Board of Directors Election in South Berkeley. To date, two staff members and one board member of the South Berkeley Model Cities have approached us, and expressed a de-sire for members of our Party to run in the up-coming election."[27] Shortly thereafter the Panthers issued a press release stating that they were running candidates for the West Oakland Planning Committee, a committee to fa-cilitate citizen participation in Oakland's $4.9 million budget Model Cit-ies urban renewal project. Model Cities aimed at improving the social and economic conditions in West Oakland, and Panthers ran in order to force it to serve Oakland's poor. The press release proclaimed, "The voting unity is Power of the People: the only means to begin implementing community control."[28] In August 1972 Panther members and supporters John Seale, Earlene Coleman, Emory Douglas, Maurice Powell, Steve McCutchen, Millicent Nelson, Marion Hilliard, Samuel Castle, and Ruth Jones ran for seats on the West Oakland Planning Committee and won six of the eighteen seats.[29]

Of course the Panthers faced opposition. The California State Office of Economic Opportunity questioned the right of the BPP candidates to be seated on the Berkeley Community Development Council, citing a federal regulation that barred membership on community action boards to mem-bers of "subversive" organizations. However, the regulation left the final determination of subversiveness up to the community, and the Panther candidates were ultimately seated.[30]

Seale had taken aim at white businesses in his speech at the Anti-war, African Liberation–Voter Registration Survival Conference, threatening, "We, the people in the community, can boycott every white-owned business [one] by one, shopping at the black owned businesses and, we can run every other white-owned business out of business, or if he don't donate [to the United Black Fund] we will run him out."[31]

This challenge had not gone unnoticed by members of both the black and the white Oakland business establishment, many of whom disagreed with the Panthers' political positions and the very notion of the United Black Fund. Excerpts from Seale's speech were disseminated in "Confidential Memo to Store Managers." While the author of this memo is unnamed, he or she claimed to speak on behalf of Oakland's businesspeople of color. The memo warned that the Panthers planned to "take over political control of the City of Oakland," "boycott every white business that fails to donate to Panther programs," and "drastically reduce the police department": "Obviously, these threats and projections do not reflect the sentiment of tens of thousands of minority business and professional people or of minority businesses and government employees who live and work in Oakland, own their own homes, and rear their families to be self-sufficient, law-abiding and usually community minded. But the unfortunate frequency of this sort of inflammatory barrage, coupled with daily distribution of militant and revolutionary publications throughout the city can only delay the vital evolutionary process of integrating Oakland's citizenry into a prosperous urban society."[32]

The Concerned Citizens Committee, an organization with a self-described membership of "concerned businessmen and businesswomen of both major political parties in your community," disseminated a memo dated 25 September 1972 that queried, "What will your company do if militants take over local governments?" Although the Panthers were not mentioned by name, they were the implied "militants." This memo laid out the "militants'" blueprint of action for community control and suggested that concerned citizens vote for a slate of incumbents instead. It "urge[d] the business community to be aware of what was going on" and "support those local candidates blessed with at least some degree of responsibility, statesmanship and business experience."[33]

Despite this opposition, the Panthers received enough community support to forge ahead optimistically with their plans for political power. They prepared to run Seale for mayor and Brown for City Council on the Democratic ticket. Seale hoped to run a strong campaign against the Democrats John Sutter and Otho Green and the incumbent Republican John Reading. He vowed that the Panthers were going to focus their efforts in a coordinated way and parlay over ten thousand contact names from their survival conferences into a strong political machine.[34]

The BPP crafted a broad political platform designed to reach out to all Oakland's residents. Seale and Brown astutely drew attention to the fact that the current City Council had violated an act that "prohibits a quorum of any governing body from meeting secretly to deliberate or take final action on public affairs." Their stand against secrecy in government won immediate widespread public support.[35] In addition they filed a lawsuit, *Black Panther Party v. Granny Goose Foods et al.*, to ensure that employers were complying with a California law that guaranteed workers up to two hours off with pay in order to vote in specified elections.[36] A poll the Panthers conducted found that most employers did not know about this law, so the Panthers sent letters to over 1,500 businesses informing them of their duty under the law. After several large employers refused to comply, the Panthers turned to the courts. The case was dismissed after the defendants agreed to post notices informing their employees that they were allowed time off with pay to vote.[37]

The Panthers filed another lawsuit, this one concerning the negative impact of urban renewal on local communities. Oakland had launched a city center project that was designed to transform the downtown business district into a large complex containing business offices, retail shops, eateries, and large department stores. The project was supposed to help the city's economy by creating jobs in the short term and by attracting more businesses to the struggling downtown area in the long term.[38] To facilitate easy access, the city was going to construct a system of interconnecting highways. The project, which began in the fall of 1972, resulted in the destruction of approximately fifteen blocks of residential housing downtown occupied by poor people of color.

The BPP and the East Bay Legislative Council of Senior Citizens claimed that Oakland's 1949 housing act, which "requires the construction of decent, quality replacement housing for urban renewal projects in those instances when there is not an adequate supply of low-income housing throughout the city," had been violated. The City Council agreed to create replacement housing for displaced residents after trying to evade the issue and petition the federal government. The agreement required the creation of a nonprofit corporation made up of community groups with collective ownership and policymaking control. In addition the tenants would create a Tenants Union to oversee the project and ensure that rental costs would be kept reasonable.[39]

Seale and Brown unveiled their joint program to rebuild Oakland in a 5 March 1973 press release. Their electoral platform was a fourteen-point program: seven points aimed at raising approximately $20 million in revenue for the city, and the other seven aimed at channeling that revenue toward social programs. The program included a 5 to 10 percent capital gains tax on transfer of property for large corporations; a residency requirement for city police and firemen, 70 percent of whom lived outside of Oakland; ending tax exemptions for public utilities; increasing rental on the Oakland Coliseum; and increasing fees at the city-owned golf courses. The money raised by these measures would be used for social programs such as housing, preventative medical health care, child care, educational improvement, and environmental protection.[40]

RUNNING PANTHER CAMPAIGNS

Brown and Seale adopted an image of respectability and sported sharp professional attire on the campaign trail. Strategically the Panthers sought to emphasize their organic connection to the community. They dubbed their campaign "the People's Campaign" and ran as People's candidates with whom everyone could identify rather than as candidates sponsored by the Black Panther Party. Their purpose was twofold: "educate . . . area residents to the issues and . . . win a seat or position that will increase the people's control in their community."[41] The Central Committee determined, "Titles of Party members should not be used in the newspaper (especially the Chairman's). Also, minimize the use of 'comrade' in newspaper, as well as in contact with the masses of people."[42]

The BPP mobilized their membership of approximately three hundred to coordinate campaign mailings, type and distribute leaflets and other publications, and phone potential constituents.[43] The Community Committee to Elect Bobby Seale and Elaine Brown to City Offices of Oakland sponsored benefit dances, community bazaars, block parties, and rallies,[44] and the Fundraising Committee organized campus speaking engagements, concerts, churches, community art shows, outdoor concerts, and speakers. The party sold books and other propaganda and held ongoing fund-raisers such as bake sales.[45]

The Panthers ran a tightly organized campaign. They mapped out the city; divided it into sections, subsections, and precincts; and assigned a coordinator for each precinct who would become a voter registrar, distribute information, set up block meetings, and organize ten or more precinct workers to make contact with a certain number of voters.[46] Sections reported and assessed their work in section progress reports, and campaign workers tallied areas covered, number of hours worked, and total number of people registered and their ethnic and geographical breakdowns in Daily Precinct Work Sheets.[47]

Voter registration was the lynchpin of the BPP's strategy. Many Panthers became voter registrars and encouraged hundreds of community members to do the same. One memo stated, "Door-to-door registration by precinct is the most important part of the Coalition registration drive. Registration tables reach only a certain percentage of the thousands of people who need to register. Through door-to-door registration, we make a sweep of the community that seeks to reach all those people who probably never would register to vote if we didn't come to their door."[48] Because Panthers trying to register voters encountered apathy from some Oakland residents, an internal memo advised, "Many of the people have been registered already, have no desire to vote or have voted before and have been disillusioned because of the results. Even if people do not register to vote, their initial reaction is to acknowledge the necessity of Bobby Seale running as a candidate for Mayor of Oakland and Elaine Brown running as a candidate for City Councilwoman."[49] The Panthers' efforts paid off. Between 8 November 1972 and 18 March 1973 they registered 14,662 people to vote.[50]

At one Panther mass voter registration meeting at St. Augustine's Church Seale and Brown declared that their campaign meant new hope for Oakland's poor. The city's budget was slated to lose $10 million because of a presidential cut in social programs,[51] unemployment among blacks was as high as 20 percent, and the schools were de facto segregated. Brown stated that in the past poor people did not have a reason to vote, but the Panthers were putting together a people's machine to provide that reason. Seale pledged that one of the goals of the People's Campaign was to take control of the Port of Oakland, with its $93 million budget, and channel the money back into the city. He pointed out that the Port of Oakland, the second largest containerized port in the country, had given the city a preeminent position in world trade. However, despite the fact that the port was a rapidly growing transportation complex, Oakland was gaining little economic benefit from it. The port supplied twenty thousand jobs, but only 30 percent went to blacks and Chicanos, and those were the lower-level jobs.[52] Seale also promised that the Panthers were spearheading a massive community mobilization that would remain intact after the elections and called for people to volunteer to become voter registrars.

The meeting culminated in a campaign song set to the black spiritual "This Little Light of Mine":

> If you want a job, vote for brother Bob.
> Keep unemployment down, vote for Elaine Brown.
> Votin' time, votin' time, votin' time.
> I'm so serious, just you wait and see.
> Votin' time, votin' time, votin' time.
> April 17th, we're going to let it shine.[53]

Another campaign song was "Vote for Survival":

> If you're tired of racist politicians abusing the people's funds,
> Cutting back and talking smack, playing a whole lot of jive,
> Then vote for the man who will see that justice is done.
> Bobby Seale understands our need to survive.
> Vote for Survival.
> Vote for the one who takes the people's stand.
> Vote for Survival ya'll,
> For righteous people's government.
> Chairman Bobby is the man.[54]

The Panthers sought to create a broad alliance of supporters. In February 1973 white supporters formed Whites for Bobby Seale and Elaine Brown. This group's literature assured middle-class whites that Brown and Seale were not radicals to be feared who would arbitrarily raise taxes.[55] Seale and Brown also reached out to Oakland's large Spanish-speaking population. In a 7 March 1973 press release, Seale urged the adoption of bilingual ballots in English and Spanish.[56] Cesar Chavez and the United Farm Workers endorsed Brown and Seale on 29 March.[57]

Panther candidates also received support from the gay and lesbian community. One internal memo noted, "On Wednesday 12-27-72 we had another meeting with a group of gay whites whom we talked to about forming a working coalition. Chairman Bobby was present. He answered their questions and talked to them about the campaign. I think that we will get some workers from their group."[58] The Gay Men's Political Action Group of Oakland endorsed Seale and Brown. One of their flyers proclaimed, "Bobby Seale and Elaine Brown, people's candidates for Oakland city offices have announced their support of Gay rights for Oakland and have pledged themselves to work for an end to the oppression of Gay people as part of their campaign to serve all the people of the city." It stated that Brown and Seale were committed to a progressive program that included ending job discrimination and police harassment of gay people and other issues of importance to gay people in Oakland.[59]

Seale argued, "Most Black politicians who have been elected to office in the past . . . lack the real organized forces that they really need, brothers and sisters dedicated to the liberation struggle." He saw students as a pool of politicized and skilled people who could potentially fill the local government bureaucracy.[60] Twenty-four Panthers and two community workers who had registered at local colleges under the Economic Opportunity Program were the catalyst for the creation of several campus-based organizations to support Seale's and Brown's campaigns.[61] Merritt College students and faculty formed the Merritt Bobby Seale and Elaine Brown Landslide Election Committee.[62] Black students at Laney College, Merritt Hills, Grove Street, the College of Alameda, uc Berkeley Health Students, Cal State Hayward, and Mills College formed the Black Student Alliance as "an outlet through which Black, as well as other concerned students involved in technical as well as academic studies can apply their skills in meaningful practice in the community."[63] The Black Student Alliance served as a conduit through which black students became involved in local elections and the Panthers' survival programs; its chairman and cochair were Panthers.[64]

The pace of the campaign increased as Election Day drew near. When Seale was recognized as one of the front-runners, the incumbent, John Reading, responded by distributing literature warning of the possibility of the Panthers taking over Oakland. A last-minute mailer was titled "The Radicals Will Vote, Will You?"[65] The BPP used parks and school auditoriums to hold food giveaways to create positive publicity.[66] Seale explained, "We don't give bags of groceries away for the sake of giving bags of groceries away. We give them away to remind the people of the unemployment, to remind them of what's got to be done and to remind them of the necessity of organizing and unifying around the objectives, around the programs we were talking about."[67] On election day, 17 April 1973, the Panthers provided everything from transportation to babysitting to facilitate voters' access to the polls.

When the votes were tallied, Brown had won over 34,000 votes but lost her bid for City Council. Seale received 45,000 votes, 37 percent of the total. It was enough to put him in a run-off election with Reading.[68]

The Panthers felt triumphant. Brown recalled, "We won the votes of approximately 40% of the electorate. We won the solid support of Black people in Oakland. The Panther constituency had indeed expanded. We had planted our ideas a little deeper. We had established a foundation."[69]

International supporters, such as the Japanese Committee to Support the Black Panther Party, sent congratulatory letters.[70] A supporter from Denmark wrote, "The high percentage of votes he [Seale] got really was a tremendous step forward. I guess you really have showed now, that the party has a significant base in the community. Funny to think that Bobby alone in the city of Oakland got more than the CP [Communist Party] have been getting in all of the country. Here in Denmark we have a saying: 'Rome was not built in a day'—but the election result showed that it is not far away."[71] Seale issued a statement:

> The thousands of people, Black people, other people of color, working and poor people who voted for Bobby Seale for Mayor of Oakland, have set the victorious wheels into motion for the realization of true freedom for all Americans and people all over the world. . . .
>
> Black people, enslaved and powerless for these many centuries, along with working and progressive people, organized into a mighty political thrust, a thrust for more than an elective office. We organized to make our power known and felt. . . . For, this election has made an historic decision, here in the midst of this most powerful country: Black people, especially, as well as the majority of people have decided that together we can move mountains and turn the tide of reaction, so that we all may live and be free from exploitation, slavery and the many ills we have faced.
>
> It is a new day in Oakland, a new day in the world, a day history shall declare was a day of reckoning for humankind, an ending and

a beginning. Upon this victory, we shall move to implement, in concrete ways, a people's program for the people of this city, and then in other cities and counties and states. We shall build upon this firm foundation, and go from victory to victory across this entire nation, until the principles of freedom and justice for all shall be delivered to all by the power of all, the power of the people.[72]

Although Seale captured 20,000 votes in the run-off election, Reading won with 55,342.[73] Despite the loss, the election proved that the Panthers were a formidable local political force. According to Brown, the context of declining state repression gave them the opportunity to build "the revolution without being directly confronted by police attacks and arrests, heavy bails, or funerals" for the first time.[74] The BPP seemed poised for a new phase of development. The mobilization process for the elections, however, created a new set of organizational and financial challenges that precluded the party's ability to build political momentum.

ATTRITION

Despite their pledge to utilize the campaign as an organizing tool, the resources that the Panthers had marshalled for the elections were quickly spent. The volunteers that they had organized drifted away in the days leading up to the run-off election. A July 1973 section progress report warned, "Most area offices have lost touch with the people who once worked on the campaign."[75] Dwindling financial resources were the source of anxious internal dialogue and section progress reports frequently referred to the lack of adequate office equipment and funds.[76] One report characterized finances as "very, very, very bad," pointing out that the organization had "$546.00 worth of bills; House, P.G.&E [Pacific Gas and Electric Company], and telephone from last month, which we don't have any money to pay."[77] Another report noted the impact of the financial deficit on their political work: "Because of the financial situation we haven't been able to do any consistent door to door work around the subscription drive, voter registration or any of the other activities that are done to hold the previously established and to build new face to face relationships with the people on the precinct level."[78] These financial challenges prompted the Panthers to move their central office from a house in the heart of the Black community to an East Oakland storefront on 85th Avenue.

FIGURE 6.1. The Black Panther Party's Central Headquarters at 85th Avenue and East 14th Street in East Oakland, 1977. A community meeting is being held in the office and a free Christmas tree giveaway is outside. Photo from Black Panther News from the Archives of It's About Time: Black Panther Party Legacy and Alumni, Sacramento.

Party members had made many personal sacrifices to keep the campaigns alive. Panther Veronica Hagopian had worked tirelessly on the campaign. She recalled, "For a while during the campaign, we didn't see much of our children. It wasn't until the campaign ended that we started a weekend program where the kids would come home for the weekend."[79] According to Emory Douglas, "The campaign was almost a twenty-four-hour thing. We had to close down a lot of the other operations or keep them going on a smaller scale because we had to focus people to take on leadership in the different levels to make sure voters got out, our literature got out. All those things took a drain on people. [This led to] burnout."[80] By 1974 membership in the Black Panthers had whittled down to less than one hundred people.

Membership in the Black Student Union and other Panther-created organizations also declined. Back on 3 May 1973 Panther Johnny Stake had written a letter to the Central Committee requesting that members of the

Black Student Union who were "working in the campaign to elect Elaine Brown and Bobby Seale to Oakland City offices" be allowed to return to Merritt College. He feared that the weakened club would not be able to implement programs and might be shut down.[81]

Reduced membership affected the viability of the BPP's survival programs. The Elections Committee noted the connection between overwork and diminished focus on community programs: "At times, this [pace of the campaign] puts a tremendous strain on on the facilities, committees and party survival programs. However, this was expected, when the elections committee first expanded."[82] The Panthers touted their survival programs as a strategic measure; however, they failed to actively engage in community-based political education to teach Oakland residents about the politics behind these programs. As a result, though these programs achieved many successes, they were rarely a catalyst for community political action.

The history of the BPP's health clinic is instructive. The Panthers believed that by showing the community that "it is possible to receive professional, competent and, above all, preventative, medical help without paying any money for it," they were teaching "the people . . . to understand that as taxpayers they do not have to stand for the lackadaisical treatment given to them by county hospitals and other public health facilities."[83] A January 1973 memo noted that doctors were available at the clinic four days a week for approximately sixteen hours total. In one week sixty-five patients, many of whom were white, received medical attention. Although the memo pointed out that more doctors and more supplies were needed, it was clear that the clinic was serving community needs.[84]

However, in order for the clinic to be successful according to the Panthers' conceptualization of the survival programs, community members had to "begin to ask questions and to organize themselves to change existing health services so that they truly serve the people."[85] The clinic had little success meshing an overt political agenda with the provision of social service, especially when the diversion of organizational resources to the elections further reduced staff. The January 1973 memo noted, "Outside of the Saturday paper sales, still no work is being done outside of the infirmary and the clinic." A few weeks later another memo complained, "Again this week, no community work was done because of the great amount of work required to maintain the infirmary and the clinic with such a minimal staff. The health cadre implemented plans for forming community outreach teams to bridge this gap.[86] However, by April the cadre reported that outreach efforts were at a low, and the clinic was attracting fewer patients: "During the period between March 27 and April 5, 56 people were seen at the clinic. The patient load has dropped considerably over the last six months. This is due to the shortage of doctors available at the clinic. . . . The clinic's participation in community affairs and functions (such as the outreach program) is non-existent, because of the staff's inability to get out due to the school, and things to be done in order to catch up. (Situation will worsen as a result of going into the field on Friday and Saturday.)"[87] Health cadre reports warned that low staff, inadequate funding, and inability to do community work would eventually lead to the clinic's decline.

As financial problems grew and the survival programs faltered, party members played a larger role in sustaining the organization. Memos directed "comrades to buy collectively, an item at a time, for the Child Development Center and the Institute" and to "give $10 to the Institute for food and transportation each month. . . . The above-mentioned $10 is not to be confused with the $10 due each week from each cadre for field trips."[88] In addition, Panthers were ordered to "bring fifty cents ($.50) with them to Son of Man Temple Services every Sunday to contribute to the fund to buy lunch for the children during services."[89] Some Panthers took jobs and donated all or part of their salary to the organization.

The Panthers' political faltering after the run-off election was fueled by internal tensions that attacked the spirit of party members, their faith in the organization, and ultimately their will to continue to belong. Newton was at the center of many of these tensions. COINTELPRO had left him distrustful, insecure, and introverted at the same time that he was struggling to come to terms with the implications of the cult of personality around him. It was a formula for unchecked abuse of power.

SUPREME SERVANT OF THE PEOPLE

Soon after Newton's release he ordered rank-and-file members to disarm and centralized the party's military apparatus under his direct control. Later he said, "I started to have bodyguards in 1970, because the Party decided I should have, uh, security and I should have chauffeurs so that I will be once removed from any police harassment." These bodyguards formed the core of an armed security cadre that provided personal security for Newton and other leadership.[90] Bobby Bowen recalled:

There was a directive that all party members should go and see *The Godfather*. And so we all trooped down to the movie theater, and the explanation was that we needed to see how the godfather was protected. So we sat in this movie theater and watched the gangsters and mafiosos and their character and demeanor and attitude and dress and style . . . protect the godfather. And shortly after that we had the development of what we called the Goon Squad and we had these Panthers dressed up in big hats and overcoats, the whole thing, and they were, you know, strapped [armed]. . . . These were party members recruited and trained and developed in various forms of self-defense and martial arts and firearms [and] weapons techniques.[91]

Newton remained a charismatic and functional leader despite rumors of misconduct that began to swirl around him. In March 1973 he traveled to Denmark, where he met members of the Danish Socialist Party, Parliament, labor unions, the Socialist People's Party, and the Communist Party and addressed 1,600 people in a public forum that was hailed as one of the largest meetings of the left in Denmark in recent history. He spoke to a crowd of seven hundred at Aarhus University and met with representatives from Amnesty International and David Hilliard's support committee. He spent one day in Sweden meeting with representatives from the Swedish Communist Party and various unions and workers' movements.[92] In April he traveled the United States promoting his autobiography, *Revolutionary Suicide*. He enrolled in the History of Consciousness PhD program at the University of California, Santa Cruz, where he wrote papers titled "Energy and Aggression," "Oakland, an All American Example," "Eve, the Mother of All Living," "The Dialectics of Nature," "Genesis according to Science," and "Intercommunalism."[93]

However, Newton divorced himself from much of the party's day-to-day operations, spending little time at party offices and allowing only a handful of people to visit him in his apartment. McCutchen described Newton's growing insularity: "Huey very seldomly visits Central Headquarters. He made more visits to the Oakland Community School. . . . The emphasis on gathering locations had shifted from the central headquarters to the school because the school actually became the center of the party, became the beacon of the programs by then. . . . Huey would only be there, on occasion, as needed or if there was something special."[94] Instead Newton surrounded himself with a close circle of trusted people, including his bodyguards and other members of the party leadership. He frequented Oakland clubs and after-hours joints, most notably the Lamp Post, a nightclub and restaurant he purchased from his cousin to earn funds for the party that was staffed and run by Panthers. In April 1972 Newton and one of his bodyguards, Robert Bay, were arrested, accused of assaulting a local disk jockey, Marlon Scott. The trial resulted in a hung jury in August 1973.[95]

The Panthers had become more enmeshed in Oakland's poor communities at the same time that illegal drugs were saturating these communities, and Newton's leadership ability was compromised by his growing addiction to alcohol and cocaine. Seale recalled, "Two or three months after Huey got out of jail, he's snorting cocaine. The next thing I know when I get out jail, after a month, I realize that Huey is trying to absolutize himself, like he's the only founder of the Black Panther Party."[96] Although the Panthers had rules of conduct about substance abuse, casual alcohol consumption and marijuana use had historically been tolerated. An internal memo dated 28 February 1973 reminded party members that drinking in public and being drunk at parties and functions were prohibited: "We are never sure of what we will be called upon to do nor do we know who may be watching us. We always, 24 hours of the day, represent our Party." It specified that carrying marijuana was a risk and that transporting it in party-owned vehicles was not allowed, and it warned that marijuana and alcohol should not be consumed before night duty.[97] In contrast an FBI memo noted, "HUEY P. NEWTON has been observed on frequent occasions and appears to be under the influence of narcotics, probably cocaine. He has been most recently observed entering or leaving his apartment house at 1200 Lakeshore with his eyes set in a glassy stare."[98]

The party did not have mechanisms to hold leadership accountable, though it set up a Board of Methods of Corrections to deal with internal problems and maintain discipline by punishing, or "correcting," members who broke the rules. Brenda Bay, a member of this board, wrote a memo to the central body arguing for preventative measures to rid the party of the frequent offenses that sent people to the board for punishment:

> All of the comrades who have come before this board have displayed one or more of the problems: lack of understanding of Party ideology and principles, lack of ideological self-cultivation and honesty. These basic problems have led to the tendency to be dishonest, inability to be objective, selfishness, and irrational behavior. We must view these

shortcomings from both sides—the individual's shortcomings and the Party's. We are all aware and this I reiterate only for emphasis the following: We must be aware that our structure, life style and ideology play a role in the individual shortcomings and individual shortcomings in turn influence our Party (note that order is not suggested). We must all act to correct these shortcomings. My suggestion is there is a meeting to discuss this problem and recommend concrete methods of correction, concrete actions and new policies and or enforcement of old ones. I feel that it is incumbent on the duty of the leadership to be most instrumental in helping to solve this very pressing problem as our Party and struggle are at stake. There is a lot of focus on making the struggle forward at this time, but we must take a close look at our internal problem, for it is a threat to that movement.[99]

Newton's security cadre, who were untouched by most party rules and regulations, played a major role on this board. As such they were relatively immune to punishment for their own acts and well positioned to reward criticism with retribution. Darron Perkins's story is instructive. Perkins, who had once endured five lashes with a bullwhip without flinching when he was brought up in front of the Board of Corrections, believed that physical punishment was a viable method of maintaining "iron discipline" to deal with the "hardheaded." His resilience made him notorious within the organization. This fact, coupled with his military training and gangbanger background, elevated him in the ranks until he became part of the Panther security cadre and the Board of Methods of Corrections.[100]

Most party members accepted the discipline of the organization in all of its forms, including the physical. They sacrificed their individual rights to the collective structure, believing that "the reactionary forces against change were so strong, we had to use a closed fist to break through."[101] Thomas McCreary argued, "The Black Panther Party only functioned because people submitted themselves to that type of leadership. And without that type of submission to leadership, not necessarily physical, to discipline, the party would not have been able to grow like it did."[102] Bobby McCall remembered receiving physical discipline after repeated lateness to open the Lamp Post: "It just made me a stronger person and it made my will more stronger and more determined to do what I wanted to do, and that was to be in the Black Panther Party. . . . I survived it. It made me get to the Lamp Post on time. . . . Some people couldn't handle that. They get disciplined, and next thing you know, they gone 'cause they just couldn't handle it. . . . It was no joke."[103] Amar Casey described an occasion when he received physical discipline:

> So I got ten lashes on my back, tear the skin off my back, but I didn't have to go through that and I didn't have to withstand that kind of discipline, but that was the level of our dedication. So we're talking about a collective that is exploited, but they were the cream of the resistance of the sixties and the seventies because these are people who came from all over the country and the cream of that black consciousness movement and the cream of that core resistance that was in the Panther Party, that came out of SNCC and so forth. A lot of those people were here and were extremely dedicated, so you didn't have to use any coercion.[104]

However, some party members began to object when discipline was used in a punitive and arbitrary manner to silence critical voices and to buttress the authority of the leadership. Bowen recalled the internal impact of the security cadre: "We began to see that they were being used a lot inside the party, as opposed to just external aggression. They were being used to control and contain party members who, for whatever reason, the leadership felt was being disrespectful or not performing in a manner considered appropriate for whatever leadership was looking [for]. So if you were disrespecting somebody in the Central Committee you could get a knock on your door one night and it could be the Goon Squad telling you that they didn't like that or the Central Committee didn't like that. It could get nasty."[105]

A 31 March 1973 memo clarified the BPP's policy on internal discipline:

> This statement is to make it clear to all comrades that our Party can not function without organizational discipline, discipline within the collective and the attainment of self-discipline within each one of us. We stand firm on our decision from long ago to suggest different forms of correction for particular and specific violations of policy and principle. There is no way, however, that any comrade may arbitrarily receive any restriction or method of correction without having violated a policy, directive or principle that we adhere to as members of the revolutionary organization, the Black Panther Party. The more serious and consistent the violation, the more stern the correction.

It is expected that this will clarify much of the confusion about organizational discipline and its necessity.[106]

This memo assiduously avoided mentioning some of the abuses that had begun to plague the organization. It also served as a mechanism to silence critics of the security cadre's actions while simultaneously delimiting the bounds of discipline. Without a system of accountability, however, this memo was advisory, not prescriptive.

The Panthers had not fostered an environment that legitimized questioning of leadership. According to Brown, "There was no doubt that some Panthers conformed to the discipline as a result of blind faith in the leadership. There were some who accepted our internal scheme because their personal agendas coincided with the party's. There were those afraid to act alone. There were those with gang mentalities. The bases of individual adherence to the party's centralized structure were as varied as the members."[107] Hagopian explained, "We just accepted the party's leadership, some of us dogmatically. I know for myself, I didn't question. I was very young and full of dreams."[108] Terry Cotton said, "Rank-and-file members were sometimes intimidated by leadership. They were afraid to even speak sometimes to leadership. They feared being eliminated from the party or either they were gonna get some kinda harsh reaction. They were afraid to even approach the leadership. . . . Some did approach the leadership. Whether they were receptive to it or not, I don't know."[109]

The dependency of cadres on the party to meet their material needs and, in effect, provide a family structure often reduced their ability or desire to dissent from party policies. Bowen compared the cycle of denial and blame that accompanied Newton's abuse of power to the ways domestic violence impacts most families: "By this point we're all in the cult of personality. We want to be in denial. We don't want to believe. We want to think we are revolutionary . . . and all the glorification we put on being Panthers. And to some extent there was quite a bit of arrogance that went into that denial."[110]

PURGING DISSENT

David Horowitz, at the time a BPP supporter and leading New Left intellectual, wrote a memo on the party's inner structure criticizing the fact that the party's three distinct elements—the political unit, the living unit, and the survival programs and community unit—were combined: "At present, these are all part of a single structure, with a single membership requirement, a single command hierarchy and a single code of discipline."[111] Horowitz suggested the party needed to differentiate the different structural forms and specifically focus on the growth and development of the political apparatus:

> The Party must strive to maintain its discipline by active political education among its members, by struggle over political lines and by the force of its moral authority, rather than by administrative acts of expulsion. The resort to administrative discipline, particularly when administered by above, has historically been disastrous to vanguard parties, since it is so open to abuse by inept or unscrupulous leadership which seeks to cover its mistakes, enhance its power and destroy its critics by expelling its opposition from the Party ranks. A party that depends on administrative discipline to maintain its unity of action soon loses its high caliber cadres and degenerates into an impotent sect. By intimidating all opposition within its ranks, it suppresses its own dialectic and loses the capacity to think.[112]

Horowitz's words were prophetic. Rank-and-file members had always interpreted, implemented, and influenced party policies. Whether initiating a dialogue about gender, highlighting the ambiguities of the BPP's armed stance, or criticizing organizational priorities, they played a crucial role in the Panthers' development. According to Cotton, "The rank and file were the foundation of that party. They couldn't exist without us. We were the one who kept the party up. The disruption, the corruption, that came from the leadership."[113] Douglas acknowledged the same thing, noting that the success of the party was in the parts that made up the whole.[114] This dynamic interaction between leadership and rank and file that had been compromised because of policies Hilliard adopted to battle COINTELPRO was further eroded under Newton's leadership.

As a result some Panthers began to leave the organization, and expulsions were reinstituted as a retaliatory or punitive mechanism. Between 5 April 1973 and 24 January 1974 over twenty-eight people were expelled from the Black Panther Party.[115] Douglas claimed that despite the diminishing membership and the personal bonds that were broken in the departure process, many members remained dedicated to the organization: "You had people in the party who had been friends, who had come from the same chapter; they were relatives, cousins who had been expelled from the party, and they stayed in the party even though their family members had been expelled. So people were committed. They may have felt remorse, or were glad, but they stayed on as long as they could."[116]

Nevertheless dwindling membership led to demoralization, especially when major leaders were expelled. Ray Masai Hewitt's expulsion in 1973 was emblematic. Hewitt, minister of education from 1969 to 1973, was a well-respected party member whose expulsion caused shock and surprise.[117] According to Brown, Hewitt had criticized how power was being wielded in the organization and the lack of organizational democracy:

> In a central committee meeting I did not attend, Masai brazenly stated, like the boy who announced the emperor was nude, that the Party operated on the basis of Huey's will. The Central Committee had become no more than a rubber stamp for it. The party had to address that weakness, to allow for a true consensus of will, at least the will of the Central Committee under the principles of democratic centralism. Huey had reduced the governing body of the party to little more than glorified members of the rank and file, Masai added. He concluded claiming that he was not in truth, therefore, a member of the Central Committee, as were none of the rest.[118]

None of the other Central Committee members agreed with him, and Newton responded by demoting Hewitt to the level of rank and file. Brown justified Newton's actions and tried to convince Hewitt "to see that while Huey had indeed assumed absolute leadership and was capable of brutal abuses, he was the same man who had invented the Black Panther Party, who had developed the theory of intercommunalism, and had challenged our common oppressor—with his own life." This image of Newton was central to Brown's self-perception: "If I did not believe in the ultimate rightness of our goals and our party, then what we did, what Huey was doing, what he was, what I was, was horrible. If the party had no humane or lasting value, that would nullify the loss of so many precious lives: of John [Huggins], Bunchy [Carter] and George [Jackson] and Jonathan [Jackson] and Fred [Hampton]. It would mean a disastrous mistake had been made in a Faustian bargain."[119] A few weeks later Hewitt left the party.

David Hilliard, who was still in jail, was targeted next. A 24 February 1974 memo announced that he had resigned from the BPP and subsequently had been expelled. Hilliard's close associates, including his brother, June Hilliard, assistant chief of staff and head of security, and his wife, Pat Hilliard, who had worked on the party's finances, were also expelled.[120] Rumors flew within the party that his "resignation" had occurred because Newton believed that he was engineering a coup against him and was plotting with his supporters to take over the organization. Although the party had mobilized for Hilliard's release from prison, the personal relationship of these two childhood friends had become distant and strained. Newton did not visit or contact Hilliard very often while he was prison. Perhaps seeking a litmus test of acquiescence to his authority, Newton had insisted that Hilliard end his long-standing relationship with Brenda Presley.[121] Newton's request came on the heels of heightened tensions with Presley, who had an intimate relationship with Newton, over her relationships with other men.[122] Hilliard wrote Newton a poignant letter from jail in response to his expulsion, arguing that if he wanted to take over the party he would have done so when Newton was in prison: "You have taught me well: suffering is no stranger to me. 'I will ride the Whirlwinds of Change While You direct the Storm.' You have full control of your organization and I bear no ill will against you. I am not your enemy and you know it. I want to be your friend, Huey, not because I fear you, but because I love you."[123]

Hilliard's expulsion created further confusion within the ranks of the organization. Bill Jennings recalled the announcement: "One night they called a meeting after everybody had come from the field at the Oakland Learning Center, and how it was done is they passed these sheets of paper out and it says David Hilliard is expelled from the Black Panther Party and June Hilliard and Brenda Presley are also expelled. . . . And Bobby stood up in the class and says 'Anybody got any questions about this?' Of course nobody had any questions."[124] Like Jennings, some members left the party after Hilliard's expulsion.

Jennings had served as security for Hilliard and had come to respect him, but his criticisms of the party went beyond personal loyalty. During the postelection fiscal crisis in the organization, Jennings had devised creative ways to survive financially, whether that meant sharing with other comrades funds he received from state assistance or student loans or keeping part of the money he collected from newspaper sales or the donation can. He had become critical of the financial hierarchy and the allocation of funds: "You would see some people in leathers . . . and other comrades with one pair of shoes. . . . I am twenty-three at that time. I'm hip. I can see what's going on in the organization. If I give them the money, that don't mean that my rent going to get paid, that don't mean the eight people in my cadre are going to get dressed." The unfairness, coupled with Hilliard's dismissal, pushed Jennings out of the organization. He observed wryly, "You didn't announce it [your departure] at that time, unless you were looking to get your head beat in."[125]

A few months later Seale left the party. After the elections he had put much of his energy into the creation of a system for ensuring cleanliness, personal discipline, and efficiency in the Panther collective. Under his guidance the Panthers created an "Inspection Check List" of items that comrades had to have on their person at all times. These included a watch, a key ring, a valid ID, and tissues. At meetings and PE classes comrades had to be armed with several more items: two issues of the party newspaper; one copy of the "Program for Survival," which listed all twenty-two survival programs; and twenty Son of Man Temple guest cards. Comrades had to carry a toothbrush, deodorant, and a shoe shine kit; offensive body odors and sloppy appearance would not be tolerated. White-glove inspection teams were formed to ensure that comrades adhered to these rules.[126]

Seale began to express overt disapproval of Newton's actions when Newton suggested selling drugs to raise funds for the party:

> In January Huey brought a brick of drugs over the Santa Rosa house, where I used to stay. . . . I came in there . . . and he's in there talking with other party members around him, with his special little group of bodyguards around him, and this brick of drugs. So I said to him, "Huey, what is this, man?" I said, "Huey, come on man, let's step out on the back patio deck, let's talk." And Huey says, "You don't understand. I'm going to raise some money," and I said, "No you're not. 'Cause this is not where it's at. Plus, you're snorting it up." [Newton replied,] "Ah, I'll talk to you later, let's talk about this later. Just don't say anything in front of the other party members." I said, "Okay, okay." It was May when I found out that he was trying to take over the [Oakland drug] trade. It was January with the brick. The brick made me start thinking: sooner or later I'm going to leave here. . . . I knew I was gone.[127]

Shortly after this incident Seale left the party. Cotton recalled, "Bobby was the one most closest to the rank and file. We could talk to him when we had problems. [He was] patient and understanding. His departure had a negative impact. Bobby was more of an organizer than Huey."[128] Seale's departure precipitated the exodus of other party members, including his family members and closest associates.

Rumors about Newton's drug use and connection to Oakland's drug trade began to pervade the organization. According to Casey, "What began to seep down and disturb a lot of people was the corruption. It was not that he lived in a nice apartment or nice house—it was the corruption, it was the repeated examples of money that was supposed to go to the programs, used to buy cocaine or personal comforts. For the collective to make sacrifices to buy Huey a nice secure house, no one had a problem with that, but people did grumble about . . . people buying cocaine, drugs."[129] Bowen elaborated:

> So we started to see these things happening, and there was always the concern about drugs and the rumors that were going around. Well, first of all the party members, from early on, most of us smoked marijuana and drunk wine . . . Bitter Dog or Panther Piss, but then as time moved on it became more serious, and we began to be aware that leadership was very heavily involved in the consumption of drugs and it became a very serious problem in the organization, to the extent that there was some antagonisms between party members and community folks, drug dealers particularly, that evolved and that resulted in some violence. At one point, my understanding—I was never a part of it, but I know that some of the speakeasies that were in operation in Oakland, that Huey was involved in some conflicts in trying to control those speakeasies in terms of what they were doing, the drugs. And I don't know what that was in details, but I heard.[130]

In November 1973 the FBI began to investigate allegations that Newton and unidentified associates were trying to extort money from black social clubs in Oakland. They had been informed that "NEWTON is currently attempting to 'organize' all private social clubs in Berkeley–Oakland, California area and that NEWTON is requesting weekly payments of $150 to $200 from each club. Refusal to make these payments results in physical force on the part of NEWTON and his men or closure of the club."[131] Seven months later one FBI agent reported that "he had conducted several interviews with known prostitutes and narcotics violators, but no information was developed to substantiate NEWTON's reported activities."[132]

Some members of the Central Committee justified these actions as a means of acquiring funds for the party's legitimate operations, analogous to the justification for the Boyette boycott: forcing businesses that exploited the community to give something back. According to Brown, the Panthers approached local black businessmen for donations to the United Black Fund. She hinted that force was used against businesses that refused to donate, writing that Newton "instructed men from the special security squads to begin visiting Oakland's 'after-hours' clubs." Brown remained the public face of Panther respectability, outwardly oblivious to "the kicked-in doors or shot-up facilities of reluctant after-hours contributors": "It had been a mistake of the ultraleft *and* the right to presume that the 'legitimacy' we had exhibited in our recent electoral campaign characterized our party. We had no respect for the laws of the United States, a cloak of fork-tongued legal idiom that disguised the most iniquitous acts." She heralded the party's two arms, "the militant, dark side and the more moderate reformist side," as the achievement of "a state of perfection."[133]

A few months later this precarious balance was toppled. On 17 August 1974 Newton was accused of pistol-whipping Preston Callins, an Oakland tailor, in his Lakeshore apartment. He was arrested and booked for assault with a deadly weapon. He was also charged in the 6 August 1974 shooting of seventeen-year-old Kathleen Smith, who died several months later.[134]

COINTELPRO CONTINUITIES

The Panthers alleged that the government played a role in these incidents and took the public position that Newton was innocent. Historically state political repression had precluded the Panthers' ability to effectively address internal corruption. Bowen offered this example: "Sometimes you would have community members come by and say, 'Hey man, I see Huey is in Vegas. Sure is spending him up and having a great time.' And we would say, 'No man, that must be a provocateur agent.'"[135]

Governmental wrongdoing was not simply a convenient excuse for the Panthers. It was a reality. The Nixon administration was under increased criticism at this time. In March 1971 activists had broken into FBI headquarters and taken files that proved the existence of COINTELPRO. The arrest on 18 June 1972 of administration-sponsored burglars at the Democratic National Convention offices at the Watergate was the first thread in the unraveling of the many misdeeds and illegal acts of the Nixon administration. The scandal and subsequent loss of public confidence culminated in Nixon's resignation in 1974. The Panthers issued a position paper advocating the elimination of the American presidency, arguing that Watergate was the latest manifestation of the historical trend of authoritative chief executives and that the power of government should be restored to the legislative branch: "A conspiratorial coup d'etat intended to secure for Richard M. Nixon the divine right of kings has been revealed through the hearing of the Senate Select Committee on Presidential Campaign Activities. This conspiracy undermines our country's republican form of government, jeopardizes our country's potential for good in the world and constitutes a serious threat to peace and progress for all humankind."[136]

Nixon's downfall confirmed the Panthers' belief that the government was capable of using backhanded methods against perceived enemies. The FBI campaign against the BPP had changed in nature and scope as the Panthers' activities evolved; the raids on party offices nationwide in the late 1960s had been replaced by surveillance and harassment in the early 1970s. In April 1973 the FBI contemplated using midlevel Panthers and returning Vietnam veterans as informants within the organization.[137] The FBI rented the apartment next to Newton's, tapped his telephone, and bugged his home. When Newton began to hold meetings in his kitchen to avoid being overheard, the transcribers grew frustrated that Newton and his guests were often "too far away to be intelligible."[138] One of the BPP's internal memos warned members, "Remember, our phones are 'bugged.' Limit gossip and eliminate any conversations that will, in any way, violate our security (collective or individual). Limit conversation about Party business. Do not solve internal Party contradictions by phone, unless in a case of extreme or real emergency."[139]

Since 1973, according to Joan Kelley, the coordinator of legal defense for the BPP, the police had arrested Panthers who were soliciting donations for their Sickle Cell Anemia Foundation. The number of arrests increased dramatically in 1974, even after the law that required solicitors to obtain a permit was ruled unconstitutional in January 1974. Warrants for overdue traffic violations were consistently served on party members.[140] Oakland police officers burst into the Oakland Community Learning Center facilities claiming to be in "hot pursuit" of criminals on several occasions in 1974.[141] On 16 April the police raided the Oakland headquarters and arrested fourteen occupants for possession of illegal weapons and drugs and conspiracy. They were later released for lack of evidence, but the Panthers claimed that key organizing material had been seized by the police during this raid and never returned.[142] The headline of the 11 May issue of the *Black Panther* was "Police Attack on B.P.P. Members Continues." Articles inside condemned police for arriving minutes after a robbery at the Lamp Post restaurant and arresting Panther employees instead of the thieves. McCutchen remembered, "[You had to] always be aware of where you were and what might happen. I think that's something most Party members carried with them, just as a soldier in battle is always aware where they are, even though they may be on leave."[143]

The Panthers alleged that the government conspiracy against them involved the FBI, the IRS, which assigned six agents to scrutinize Newton's tax returns and to inquire into the financial records of contributors to the Panthers in early 1974, and the Alcohol, Tobacco, and Firearms Division of the IRS.[144] In 1974 the BPP filed suit against the IRS, claiming that these agencies were attempting to destroy them by intimidating potential contributors. The complaint in *Black Panther Party v. Internal Revenue Service et al.* asserted, "This action seeks to prevent the Internal Revenue Service from issuing and serving blanket summonses upon third parties in order to obtain records divulging the names of contributors, and subscribers to, and members of, the Black Panther Party for the purpose and with the effect of destroying financial and membership support for the Party."[145]

According to the suit, the IRS had inquired about BPP accounts at the Bank of America in Oakland and attempted to gain information about the party from publishing companies and *Playboy* magazine, which had interviewed Newton. The IRS countered that its investigation into Newton's activities was legitimate.[146] The judges agreed and dismissed the suit but ruled that the Panthers could file an amended complaint alleging collusion between the IRS and the FBI.[147] The two agencies were indeed cooperating: according to FBI records, "IRS officials stated that although they have NEWTON under a continuous type of investigation with reference to tax matters, nothing has been substantiated to date to verify tax evasion or other criminal activities. IRS officials stated that if information is developed which might be of interest to the FBI, they will immediately make that information available."[148]

Doubtful of his chances of receiving a fair trial, Newton skipped his court hearing on 23 August and fled into exile in Cuba. Although the police did not uncover "information to corroborate the reported criminal activities of HUEY P. NEWTON as they have to do with the organizing of private social clubs in the East Bay area of San Francisco,"[149] after Kathleen Smith's death in November the charges against Newton included murder. The fate of the Black Panther Party once again seemed uncertain.

Newton's abrupt departure threw the organization into turmoil. The FBI noted, "NEWTON's disappearance has somewhat tainted any possible legitimate posture that the BPP may have attained . . . with its community programs. . . . The BPP appears to be in financial straits as evidenced by a dwindling BPP newspaper circulation, a noticeable amount of support from other extremist groups that have turned away from the BPP, a possible loss of several pieces of BPP real estate used as collateral for seven Deeds of Trust, each valued at $20,000 security bond for NEWTON which NEWTON forfeited at the time of his disappearance."[150]

THE ELAINE BROWN ERA

Brown stepped into the leadership vacuum created by Newton's absence. Ericka Huggins described that period:

> Before the time of Huey going to Cuba, women were in leadership. And that again was organic. Because of the male-predominant society we live in, when the police arrested and killed they tended to seek out men, thinking that men were the leaders. They didn't know that behind the scenes women ran almost every program, were involved in every level of the party. . . . The greater numbers of men were taken away from leadership, [the more] women rose in the ranks of leadership. And it became apparent at one point that women should become a really viable part of the Central Committee. And some of that had to do with women asking for it, and some of it had to do with the fact that women were the ones who were running everything anyway. Huey and David were well aware of that, and Bobby Seale. There wasn't much resistance about that. . . . They may have had internal unresolved things about women, but about women in leadership, we were in too much danger every day to say no women. It was not like that. We were not an intellectually based organization. We made decisions based on need, and often, too often, we made decisions based on survival.[151]

Once in power, however, Brown discovered that her intimate relationship with Newton and her nondeferential attitude toward male members angered some Panthers, who began to complain that women had taken over the organization.[152] The FBI reported, "BROWN does not appear to attract support or adhesiveness of members as NEWTON did in the past."[153]

Brown believed that power in the BPP had traditionally been wielded as either a "scepter of terror or a sword of freedom."[154] She chose to employ both. She relied upon Chief of Staff Larry Henson, one of Newton's most notorious bodyguards, to silence her critics and assert authority over the ranks in the wake of Newton's departure. At the same time Brown crafted a public image of respectability and advocated electoral politics and local community organizing. She declared, "The majority of people in this country believe in the concept of electoral politics and bourgeois democracy. They just think they haven't had the right people to vote for. . . . You have to operate at twenty levels constantly. And this includes everything from what people call violent to non-violent activity. You have to put together a survival program for the immediate needs of people and for their education. This is a mass revolution, not just the Panthers vs. the police. This is the people vs. the oppressors."[155]

Under Brown's leadership the BPP became a powerful force within California's Democratic Party. The Panthers supported the liberal gubernatorial candidate Jerry Brown in his winning campaign in 1974, and in April 1975 Brown ran for a seat on Oakland's City Council. Though her bid was unsuccessful, she garnered over 40 percent of the vote, despite the fact that in the last few months of her campaign she was accused of being a conspirator or accomplice to the murder of Betty Van Patter, a Panther bookkeeper Brown had fired, and that shortly afterward she was found carrying cocaine during a routine security check on a visit to an incarcerated Panther. Brown insisted that the drugs were not hers, but she pleaded guilty to a simple possession charge to avoid trial. The murder allegations were later dropped.[156] These accusations created a flurry of rumors and speculation, but Brown's hands-on style, political savvy, and personal charisma allowed her to maintain a precarious balance that had eluded Newton.

The BPP's political muscle in the city continued to grow. In 1976 the Panthers supported John George in his successful bid for election as the first black county supervisor in Alameda County. A Panther representative was selected to serve on an advisory committee to the Genetic Disease Control Unit of the Department of Maternal/Child Health, a division of the state health department.[157] Brown served as a Democratic delegate when Governor Brown ran for president, reasoning that he had won Panther support "because we thought he was representative enough of a liberal kind of philosophy that at least the world would remain intact for the next four years, so we could put *our* struggle together."[158] In December 1976 Brown was appointed to the Oakland Council for Economic Development (OCED), a board the Panthers had criticized in the past as elitist because eleven of its fifteen members were Republicans who lived outside of Oakland. The Panthers had worked with other local black organizations, such as the Oakland Black Caucus, to push for a more representative OCED.[159] Brown viewed her seat on the Council as a way to represent the interests of Oakland's poor communities of color, and she pledged to push for jobs and open access to the Council's activities.[160]

Although the OCED approved the construction of an extension to the Grove-Shafter Freeway that would cut right through the heart of the black community to ensure easier access to the new City Center, Brown and other local activists opposed it.[161] After the Legal Aid Society of Alameda County and the West Oakland Planning Committee filed a lawsuit, the city was forced to agree to build low-cost housing to replace housing demolished during freeway construction, and the state was ordered to allocate $5 million to relocate residents who would be affected by the highway.[162]

After the lawsuit was settled the Panthers reversed their position, embracing the freeway as the key to the success of the City Center project, which in turn meant jobs for Oakland. Brown and other activists pressured the governor to move up the start date for the project, and he acceded after gaining assurances that "at least half the freeway construction jobs and 30 percent of the permanent jobs in the City Center would go to minorities."[163]

In 1977 the Panthers campaigned for Lionel Wilson, a longtime ally, for mayor of Oakland and played an important role in voter registration, mobilization, and "get out the vote" actions. Wilson's campaign built on Seale's successful showing in 1974. He won, becoming the first Democratic mayor of Oakland in thirty years and the first black mayor of Oakland ever. Upon his election Wilson appointed Brown to his transition team.[164]

Reflecting on the history of the Black Panther Party on its tenth anniversary in 1976, Brown declared that the Panthers were achieving their goal of community control. Their next step would be to control the city's economy by controlling the Port of Oakland and to overhaul the educational system.[165] Casey recalled, "Elaine was very, very serious. . . . Elaine was focused on her mission as chair of the Black Panther Party. I often say that I felt she was our best military leader we ever had. She knew how to apply that power of that collective so that you could, you know,

[see] results. . . . The [BPP] school became a much respected school, our children were well taken care of, our facilities got cleaned up, our bills got paid, the money was used effectively to hire lawyers, and so forth."[166] By 1977 the BPP had regrouped and regained public respectability and the confidence of its small but dedicated membership. At this pivotal moment Huey Newton returned from exile.

"I AM WE"

The Demise of the Black Panther Party, 1977–1982

NEWTON'S RETURN

The Black Panther Party began to pave the way for Newton's return from Cuba almost immediately after his departure. In August 1974 they created the Committee for Justice for Huey P. Newton and the Black Panther Party (CFJ) to mobilize grassroots support for his case.[1] By 1976 CFJ offices had sprung up in Los Angeles; Detroit; Washington, DC; Norfolk, Virginia; and Harrisburg, Pennsylvania, and veteran activists and politicians such as Julian Bond, Noam Chomsky, Ossie Davis, Jane Fonda, Tom Hayden, and Congressmen Ronald Dellums, Charles Diggs, Parren Mitchell, and Charles Rangell had signed on as sponsors.[2]

The CFJ published "Justice for Huey and the Black Panther Party," a short news bulletin with time-sensitive updates, as well as *I Am We*, a newsletter that provided more in-depth analysis. "I am We" was a phrase that Newton coined in his autobiography to describe the oneness of the human experience, to suggest that repression was aimed at all activists, not just the Panthers.[3] "Justice for Huey" printed a chronology of repression against the Black Panther Party in the 1970s, claiming that 312 Panthers had been arrested in the Oakland area between late 1973 and mid-1976: "In the spring and summer of 1974, several federal agencies in conjunction with the Oakland police intensified these attacks in a concerted effort to discredit, imprison and kill him [Newton]. He was shot at; a 'contract' was put on his life; the IRS used the pretext of investigating his tax returns to get information on Party contributors; his apartment was wiretapped and burglarized; he was arrested on false and discrediting charges; and finally he was forced to leave the country under the threat of being framed and murdered in or outside of prison."[4] The news bulletin argued that the BPP's focus on community activism, such as grocery giveaways, voter registration, survival programs, and election campaigns, had posed a strong ideological challenge to the state. The Panthers claimed that they now faced a "new and more sophisticated version" of what had happened in the past.[5]

The Panthers fought back in new and sophisticated ways. They used the Freedom of Information Act to make public thousands of pages of FBI and CIA documents detailing government repression against them.[6] In 1976 they launched *Black Panther Party v. Levi et al.*, a federal civil rights action against officials in the Justice Department, the CIA, the FBI, the Departments of the Army, Treasury, and Justice, the IRS, the U.S. Postal Service, and other agencies for conspiring to destroy their organization financially and politically. The BPP, Newton, Father Neil, parents of the slain Panther John Huggins, and party supporters such as John George, an attorney and member of the Alameda County Board of Supervisors, were among the plaintiffs in this case. They accused the defendants of burglaries, raids, unlawful opening of mail, false arrests, auditing Newton's tax returns, placing an undercover agent in the apartment next to Newton in 1971, conspiring with Us members to kill Bunchy Carter and John Huggins in January 1969, sending false letters, infiltrating the BPP with provocateurs, murdering the Chicago Panther Fred Hampton, sabotaging and discrediting BPP programs, suppressing the party's right to free expression, and other acts of general harassment.[7] In the summer of 1977 the FBI conceded that it had between 1.5 and 2 million pages documenting the Panthers.[8]

By using the courts and political propaganda the Panthers succeeded in freeing Newton once again. He returned to Oakland on 3 July 1977 to face the murder charges that he had fled from years before. The Central Committee channeled organizational resources toward his upcoming trial. They discussed strategies to expand the CFJ and vowed to commit several comrades per day to solicit donations for bail and legal defense. They planned to sell CFJ T-shirts, pamphlets of Newton's speech "On the Original Vision of Black Panther Party," and even advertising space in the *Black Panther*.[9] In September 1977 they accelerated the distribution of CFJ material and sent newsletters and stickers to chapters and branches.[10] They identified corporations and other wealthy individuals to approach for donations.[11]

The CFJ aggressively sought recruits in the white community to assist with fund-raising and education. They created interracial fund-raising teams and literature that emphasized that governmental harassment and surveillance crossed class and racial lines, hoping to counteract the reality that "many white liberals in Oakland (and Berkeley) don't know about the School, the Survival Programs, or the Party's consistent involvement in electoral politics. Most have a pre-1971 image of the Party (violence, rhetoric, anti-white)."[12] By the end of the year the Panthers had mailed *I Am We* to two thousand people and received nineteen $106-a-month pledges.[13]

Newton's return would prove cataclysmic. He was the embodiment of the BPP for many inside and outside the party, and few had problematized his relationship to the organization. *I Am We* metaphorically reflected the fundamental unity the Panthers sought to craft between the group and the individual. The juxtaposition between the "I" that was Newton and the "We" that encompassed the Black Panther Party became more and more detrimental to the viability of the party as Newton continued his involvement with drugs and illegal activities. His actions undermined the legitimacy and vitality of the survival programs, especially after the Panthers strategically identified him with the programs to bolster his public image. Although the Panthers struggled valiantly to reform the party from the bottom up, the growing collision between Newton's decline and the party's ability to carry out its mission foreshadowed the demise of the Black Panther Party.

Soon after Newton's return, allegations by some members that the party had become "weak" and "female" began to surface. Newton moved quickly to reassert his leadership, installing macho security squads, establishing circles of brotherhood, and challenging alternative sources of influence.

Huggins remembered, "There was a decline because he came back in, I feel, and was envious of the work that Elaine had done. So he started changing things back to a kinda point that was easier for him to handle. . . . After he came back he was always at the Central Committee meetings. Even when he wasn't there, he was on top of everything, though. He was charismatic. So people made their decisions based on 'What would Huey do? If Huey was here, what would he say?' And a lot of that was fear and intimidation."[14]

One month after his return Newton issued a directive: "1. All members are hereby notified that the official title of Huey P. Newton is President of the Black Panther Party. He is also and may be referred to as the Founder, Leader and Chief Theoretician of the Party. 2. Elaine Brown is hereby designated as Vice-President and Chairperson of the Party."[15] The message was clear. A few months later Brown resigned from the BPP. On 18 October 1977 she scrawled a brief letter of resignation to Newton: "I'm sorry—which is sorry—for which you may hate me forever—But it seemed too much of [a] man's world for me. After ten years of everything—that this could stop me (us).—I love you, anyway."[16] According to Brown, the precipitating event that led to her departure was the beating of a Panther woman as punishment for an angry statement she made to a Panther man. Brown strenuously opposed Newton's decision to order this beating, but he refused to acquiesce. When Newton called a Central Committee meeting to discuss the matter, she declined to attend and fled from Oakland with her daughter, fearing that she might become a "sacrifice" in Newton's attempt to reassert control over party ranks.[17]

A few days later violence erupted. On 23 October, the day before the preliminary hearing in Newton's trial, three men attempted to break into the home of Mary Matthews in Richmond. She fired her revolver at them. One man, Louis T. Johnson, a Panther, was killed. Physical evidence led the police to believe that Flores Forbes, a Panther who had been one of Newton's bodyguards, was one of the other assailants. Matthews lived next to a key prosecution witness against Newton who was going to testify at the preliminary hearing. Newton denied having any knowledge of the incident, which became known as the Richmond Incident. However, the press insinuated that the shootout was a botched attempt to kill the witness and that Newton's assassins had mistakenly ended up at the wrong address. The local press was filled with damaging headlines: "Newton Witness Slaying Target," "Newton Aide in Death Plot?," "Newton Links to Suspect," and

"Newton Link to Death Plot—Accomplice Killed Gunman Police Say."[18] This incident undermined the party's legitimacy and eroded public support.

Brown's departure from the party was made public a few weeks later. Her typewritten letter of resignation, dated 16 November 1977, differed greatly from the earlier, handwritten version. This letter framed her sudden departure in terms of personal crisis: "Without injecting too much philosophy, let me say there comes a time in each life that is kind of a turning point. . . . Day-to-day life in a struggle to change the odds in favor of the People is excruciatingly difficult as it is. My mental and physical strength, after 10 years, were waning, in fact nearly collapsing. I suppose, then, I felt incapable of going on. It is difficult to say in light of those who have sacrificed so much and continue to. I can only honor and support them and make note of my own weaknesses." Brown wrote that Newton's return allowed her to relinquish her duties, focus on her personal issues, and return to her songwriting career. She expressed love and admiration for Newton, continued commitment to the BPP's goals, and respect and friendship for members: "The ideas upon which it [the BPP] was founded are a part of me. Its goals for total human freedom and dignity and peace are my goals. Yet, I have come to know that I must be at peace with myself in order to reach out to others. Perhaps I will find it." She concluded the letter by pointing out that although people might speculate about other motives behind her departure, her letter contained the entire story.[19]

THE BEGINNING OF THE END

Many key leaders in the Panther hierarchy left the party at this time, including Phyllis Jackson, who had served as treasurer for the Educational Opportunities Corporation (EOC) and chief administrative officer.[20] According to McCutchen, these resignations transformed the organization: "Elaine resigned from the party and the party was ineffective. The party didn't have an administrator. Huey was not an administrator. He was a theoretician. Ericka [Huggins] was director of the school; she could not administrate the party. So without Elaine there, the party had no effective administrator. The party lost much of its success after Elaine left."[21]

Brown's resignation was widely quoted in Bay Area publications, and the full text was reprinted in an article in the 22 November 1977 *San Francisco Examiner*. This article pointed out that despite the growing suspicions of tensions between Brown and Newton, both had confirmed that her departure had occurred on friendly terms. The reporter lauded Brown for her contribution to the BPP's development: "And although Newton has remained the party's guiding force and chief theoretician, it was the eloquent and attractive Brown who mingled well with local Democratic Party leaders and implemented programs that transformed the Party's image from that of a gun-brandishing revolutionary cadre to a politically influential, community-based organization."[22] Local black liberals called Brown's departure a loss for the BPP and for the Oakland political community.

A strong undercurrent of apprehension accompanied Brown's departure as many people began to speculate on the direction that Newton would take the BPP. These concerns came from traditional Panther critics such as the *Oakland Tribune*, which titled an article on 27 November "Black Panther Party Falters: Leadership Crisis."[23] But even Panther supporters expressed concern. One wrote in December saying that he would stop contributing monthly to the BPP due to Brown's departure and what he called the "cult of personality" around Newton: "Unless the party can broaden its roots in the community, unless it can retain the support of its own membership without cults and purges, etc., it cannot hope to achieve its goals."[24]

A new twist on the violent Richmond Incident was revealed in December, when Nelson Malloy, a Panther who had helped Forbes make his escape after the incident, was found buried and left for dead in Las Vegas. Two other Panthers were sought in his assault. Many observers believed that the attack on Malloy was ordered by Panther hierarchy to silence Forbes.[25] Critics compared the Panthers to a street gang or an organized crime family. In an article titled "Bay Area Left Backs Away from Black Panther Party," the *Berkeley Barb* pointed out that accusations of illegal activities against the party had whittled away its support in progressive circles. The writer argued that these new charges gave "new life" to older allegations of extortion against local businesses and speculated, "The apparent cooling of East Bay Progressives towards the Panthers seems to stem from recent press reports linking some members of the Party to a variety of illegal and unethical activities, including extortion, murder and conspiracy." Stalwart Panther allies like Congressman Dellums and Alameda County Supervisor George, elected with Panther support and mobilization, had begun to distance themselves from the party. Oakland's mayor and longtime Panther ally Lionel Wilson withdrew from the Oakland Community School board of directors.[26]

Although private speculation abounded within the party, this new wave of accusations was met with denial that was shaped by both commitment to the BPP's goals and fear of voicing criticism. The Panthers publicly maintained that the charges against them were a result of a renewed COINTEL-PRO, asking in their news bulletin, "After 11 years of intense attacks and harassments, who among us is so naïve as to believe the federal police are not involved in what is happening now."[27] Once again allegations of repression supplanted critical self-assessment.

Newton insisted that he had no choice but to leave the country because he had been watched, recorded, and followed.[28] As part of this "conspiracy" "law enforcement officials have . . . enlisted the assistance of private citizens to pose as victims of, and witness to, the alleged offenses."[29] Signed legal declarations made by party members, lawyers, and supporters buttressed his case. Panther Joan Kelley, head of internal legal defense, chronicled a pattern of false arrest and detention of Panthers, raids, burglaries at the homes of Panthers, and attempts to foster disruptive behavior at the Lamp Post. She claimed the police had engaged in "a pattern of conduct designed to provoke Black Panther Party members to violence and to enlist the services of private citizens as agents to commit acts of violence against Black Panther Party members."[30] Brown attested to a conspiracy against the Panthers by law enforcement officials, who burglarized BPP property in collusion with private citizens. She reported that she frequently heard a clicking sound when using the phone and accused the government of using illegal electronic surveillance to monitor party members. Panther cars and apartments had been broken into, and FBI officials frequently came to her apartment and recorded all of her visitors from the security guard's log. According to Brown, this government conspiracy included auditing the BPP's financial records and attempting to maximize its tax burden.[31] Many of Newton's lawyers testified that they believed their phones were being tapped. Fred Hiestand stated, "From the time I began to represent Huey P. Newton and the Black Panther Party up to the present [1977], I am informed and believe that my phone conversations were and are intercepted, monitored, and/or recorded by agents of the government."[32]

OAKLAND COMMUNITY SCHOOL

Although the Panthers were able to mobilize some public support for these claims, the stigma of criminality hovered around Newton and tarnished the party's image. The furor over the Richmond Incident and the

FIGURE 7.1. Staff of the Oakland Community School, 1970s. Photo from the Archives of It's About Time: Black Panther Party Legacy and Alumni, Sacramento.

subsequent allegations of wrongdoing created a backlash against the Panthers' survival programs.

The Oakland Community School (OCS), the Panthers' most visible and successful survival program, faced the harshest repercussions. The OCS had earned a nationwide reputation for excellence in community-based education. In February 1976 it was featured on the cover of one of the most popular magazines in black America, *Jet*. Students at OCS ranged in age from two to eleven. They lived in dorms and received full tuition, free health care, three nutritious meals a day, and individualized attention in classes that rarely exceeded ten students per teacher.[33] Twenty-seven full-time accredited teachers taught art, music, science, Spanish, environmental studies, and physical education.[34] In the summer students participated in a structured program of trips, classes, and recreational activities.[35] By 12 May 1976 approximately 125 children attended the OCS.[36]

The school's approach to learning was holistic. According to Huggins, director of the OCS, the goal was to "provide discipline with freedom, to allow flexibility and creativity. A basic tenet of our school philosophy is to show children how and not what to think. Meditation is one way of developing that skill. It is a method, a technique for learning about the inner self by turning the mind within."[37] In addition to daily meditation students participated actively in school administration through the Youth Committee, which planned activities and administered discipline among students. Parents could join a Parents Advisory Board, created in 1976 as a medium through which parents could be involved in the school administration and activities as well as contribute to OCS fund-raising efforts.[38]

The OCS was housed in the party's Oakland Community Learning Center (OCLC), the central terminus for many Panther activities and community events. The OCLC was the site of the Legal and Educational Program, which offered legal counseling, free transportation to prisons for visits, a free commissary for prisoners, food stamps, and welfare counseling. Drama workshops, party fund-raisers, lectures on African politics, debates on police brutality, forums on the rights of the handicapped and disabled, sports programs, GED and consumer education classes, plays, and films were offered there.[39] It also provided teen and youth service programs such Teen Counseling, Junior High and High School Tutorial Program, Martial Arts Program, and Youth Training and Development. The OCS held events at the Center that combined the Panthers' community service mission with their goal of community education. In November 1976 the OCS sponsored an event that included African speakers lecturing on politics and liberation, a performance by OCS students, and a giveaway of five hundred bags of groceries. Through the OCLC the Panthers were able to create a core group of community supporters, anchored by the parents of the children who attended the OCS.[40]

The school was administered by the Educational Opportunities Corporation, the nonprofit 501(c)(3) corporation that was the employer of two of the men suspected of being involved in the Richmond Incident. Although there was no evidence to challenge the integrity of the agency, an audit of its youth service programs was launched at the end of 1977.[41] The EOC did not pass the audit; according to the Office of the City Auditor, its financial statements did "not present fairly, in conformity with generally accepted accounting principles, the financial position of [Seniors Against a Fearful Environment program, Coordinated Youth Services, and Summer Employment for Disadvantaged Youth] programs as of October 31, 1977." Accounting records had not been well maintained; they contained misstatements and bookkeeping and calculation errors and lacked documentation to support the validity of expenditures.[42] In response Joan Kelley, chief administrative officer of the EOC, outlined a plan to take corrective action and committed to attending follow-up meetings with the Office of the City Auditor.

The EOC's ability to get grants, an important source of the party's income, was compromised after the audit. In the past it had been included in a $450,000 federal grant administered to five youth service corporations and was awarded $88,000 from the City Council to hire eight Oakland residents to work at EOC Service Corporation for one year. In addition it had received three grants for child care, the meal program, and the Berkeley Comprehensive Employment and Training Agency.[43] The EOC channeled financial support to the OCS from foundations like the James R. Dougherty, Jr. Foundation, state agencies such as the State Department of Education, and private individuals.[44]

In the wake of the Richmond Incident and the resignation of key Panthers, the OCS was thrown into a financial crisis. For the first time parents were asked to contribute $35 a month or whatever they could afford in tuition to the school.[45]

ISOLATING THE COLLECTIVE

The Richmond Incident was part of a larger tapestry of organizational crises. Collective living and rigorous work routines bred an insularity that left many rank-and-file Panthers with feelings of isolation. Although Newton's inner thoughts are largely absent from the historical record, a poem Huggins wrote after meeting with him at this time suggests that he felt the same loneliness:

> in the end
> when all is history
> and we are wherever
> fate has taken us
> what will it all look like
> how will it be summed up
> how will you have become—and all of us . . .
> who will have betrayed whom
> i see you sitting somewhere
> so very alone,
> as you are now,

with all of us around you
i see you there but history
can not take the turn
that causes me to be
the cause of any part
of your loneliness.
whenever you are, I am
not too far away.
i will be the one, perhaps, who, in the end,
can share a portion
of your pain—Some of which i feel
now.[46]

After the topic of loneliness was broached at a political education class, Newton invited comment on the party's unspoken policy of Panther women dating solely within the organization.[47] This policy was rooted in the chauvinistic assumption that women were more likely to let emotions weaken their political commitment and allow men outside of the party influence them to leave. Although this policy was not uniformly applied, some women bought into the notion that party members could best understand and support each other's unorthodox lifestyle and strong political commitments. For them politics had a role in the choice of a partner. In this equation male Panthers had access to Panther women and also to women outside the party on the assumption that the men could influence the women to join the organization.[48]

Party members responded to Newton's invitation with an outpouring of emotions, opinions, and grievances that reflected deep dissatisfaction with the organization's gender dynamics, internal structure, and relationship to the Oakland community. One Panther woman wrote:

> I feel that the great sense of loneliness which I feel and know that others feel can be greatly helped with the coming of people in the community being able to spend time with us. . . . But, let us consider the amount of people who have left out of reasons of loneliness. No animosity, or breech of party policy just sheer loneliness and the desire to feel needed has chased many a person away. Apart from the accepted and obvious feelings of alienation of being a party member and all those stigmas attached to that and the very real sense of family separation, we must also undergo a type of alienation from

our sex. We Black Panther women who don't like to go out, who don't like to receive flowers, who don't want to spend time alone with a person unless we are in bed, or who are suppose to be available for those late night runs, can become lost. Now I really don't think that any individual in the streets holds the answer to a more enjoyable life and wholesome self yet the attention is needed, and wanted. Also I believe that there would be an eventual end to the feelings of sexual oppression and jealousy. More equal grounds could be gained and this would promote more male appreciation of the female and more female appreciation of herself.[49]

This writer went on to say that women had played a major educative role in many revolutions, but due to the lifestyle of some Party workers, "we barely see the masses much less have a chance to educate them." Consequently, she argued, myths of Panther women as "robots or some type of Black humanoid" abounded both inside and outside the party. Women often faced "abuse and misuse" at the hands of their male comrades: "Within the past months a comrade slopped into bed with me and began to disrobe me and have sex, to which I firmly objected and he did finally give up. But this same comrade barely speaks to me or tries to take me out or anything like that. It's not as if this happens daily, but it happens too much. Incidents like this that don't get reported and are just thought of casually perpetuate all of the terrible misconceptions of the Black Panther woman."[50]

JoNina Abron, editor of the Black Panther newspaper, wrote, "Throughout the 29 years of my life, I have experienced the dual pain of being a Black woman in America. When I joined the Party five years ago, I was thrilled about becoming part of an organization that believes in the equality of men and women. However, I have since learned that my comrades and I have yet to overcome many of our backward ideas." Abron argued that all party members should be free to choose partners outside of the organization if they chose people

who have ideals and goals common to us. . . . My concern about male-female relationships extends beyond the sexual aspect. Ultimately it will take a new and humane society to alter the ways in which men and women in America treat each other. Within our Party, it bothers me that there are a couple of comrade brothers who still view women as sexual objects. We should have *no* men in the Black Panther Party who feel this way or women for that matter. It bothers me that there are a few brothers who seem unable to carry on a conversation with me once I explain that I am not interested in going to bed with them. It makes me feel that they feel I have no value beyond my body. . . . I would like to see the Party seriously begin to deal with this issue. While we have a number of women in leadership positions in our Party, they are respected by the men *because* they are in the leadership.[51]

Women, she conceded, were sometimes guilty of the same attitude toward men who are not in leadership. "I know we are all products of this society, but we should expect more from each other because we are members of the Black Panther Party. Why can't we love and respect each other as human beings instead of males and female?"[52]

Veronica Hagopian suggested that external relationships could root the party more deeply in the community: "If the sister has been around for a good while and her practice has proven her to be a responsible person, I think this can be a positive thing for the Party and for the particular man we may see. It may not even be with the intention of bringing him in as a member, but bringing us closer as friends and allies."[53]

Amar Casey and Melvin Dickson, rank-and-file Panthers who had staffed the community programs in various capacities, argued that men and women should be bound by the same guidelines and principles: "We all, we are sure, can personally remember past instances when brothers who left the Party or their work suffered as a result of their relationships with a community sister. With both brothers and sisters adhering to such policies as have been mentioned, perhaps a sense of personal equality would prevail among comrades' internal relationships."[54]

Another woman wrote that she agreed with the policy of women not dating outside the BPP because she believed that men from outside would have a hard time understanding the rigors of a Panther woman's life and might become jealous or influence the woman to leave. She did protest, however, that the collective structure limited individual choice about pregnancy: "I think a sister who don't have any children should be able to have one. I hated to write this one down because I know it is selfish feeling this way. If 10 women got pregnant it would really slow down the work, but maybe if two got pregnant at a time?"[55]

The outcome of this dialogue, which largely took the form of memos to Newton, is uncertain. It created a space, however, for rank-and-file members to seek inner organizational reform in response to obvious decline. Their proclivity to work in partnership with leadership blunted the critical edge of their efforts. Rather than explicitly define Newton's activities as problematic, members petitioned him to seek solutions or to join them in reform efforts.[56]

Innerparty memoranda chronicled many attempts to reform the political education structure and reach out to the community in 1977–78. One memo called for more meetings and dialogue among the central body to carry out work and pursue better communications: "We have lost our balance: our cadres function in isolation, our political education has been neither consistent nor strong enough (though recent improvement has been made), our tasks are often carried out in a non-structural manner, *and* our children (who follow our example) suffer in their overall educational development. We cannot and do not deny external pressures, harrassment and forces which work against us. We are a revolutionary Party! But, because criticism and self-criticism are essential to an organization which functions through democratic centralism, we must place and accept blame."[57]

On 31 March 1978 Abron wrote a memo to Newton requesting that central body members address PE classes on a regular basis "about the development of Party programs, the trial and other internal matters."[58] A few weeks later she pointed out that PE classes were plagued by lateness and low attendance despite the fact that the Ministry cadre was changing the structure of the classes to include weekly quizzes and other interactive mechanisms such as films, guest speakers, and member presentations.[59] In another memo she warned that members needed to "improve our overall attitude towards PE classes."[60]

Panthers recognized that community political education was central to their survival as an organization. In another memo to Newton, Abron noted that the Panthers had not held regular community PE classes for three years and advised, "We need to be doing more to inform the people who work with us and others who just want general information about the Party and current events. This is particularly important now because of the upcoming [Smith] murder trial."[61] The Ministry cadre wrote Newton recommending that community members be allowed to attend Panther PE classes: "There are a few non-Party members who attend regularly now, but there are many others who would like to."[62] Casey wrote Newton in July to ask him to speak at one of the PE sessions for teens working at the OCS over the summer.[63]

Weak PE classes and social isolation taxed members' commitment to the collective structure. In April 1978 the Panthers held a meeting to discuss the children's collective. James Abron, who attended that meeting, recalled, "The party basically took care of you from dusk to dawn if you had kids. The people who worked at the school, those were the ones who were basically in charge of your kids. You were basically given your kids on the weekends, but Monday through Friday we would teach 'em, feed 'em, take 'em to our dormitories and wash 'em, help them with their homework, put 'em to bed, clean their clothes, wipe their butts, and then [laughter] the process would start over again. And we had three or four dorms plus the Child Development Center."[64] Some Panther parents viewed the dorms as a temporary measure rather than a political program, questioned the need for the children's collective, and argued that they could teach their children themselves. Huggins explained that the dorms were a socialist program born out of the desire to expose children to a collective experience and the need to distribute parental responsibilities. She suggested that the Central Committee create new dorms that would appeal to parents and disseminate a statement of purpose for the children's collective. She also advised that leaders should meet with collective parents more often.[65]

FINANCIAL CRISIS

The decline of public support in the wake of the Richmond Incident exacerbated the Panthers' financial crisis. They had not developed a sustained method for channeling community support. Instead, going out in the community to solicit donations was the dominant method of acquiring funds for the running of programs and maintaining the cadre. Casey described his experience:

> I was able to see, you know, how we were basically living off the donations that you collected when you went out in the field. You see, every weekend you'd go out into the field to collect donations for sickle cell anemia, ostensibly. It was really for the Black Panther Party. Very little, if any, went to that particular research. Very little if any went to the medical clinic. So you got a percentage, sometimes 30 percent, sometimes 50 percent, it depends. And that's what you had to live on. And it worked a bit because you were supported, you got food and housing, but you were pretty dirt poor for the most part.[66]

When publication of the *Black Panther* was jeopardized due to lack of funds, Panthers devised creative fund-raising strategies. Two wrote to Newton arguing that the BPP should expand its focus from small, local fund-raisers with limited returns to elaborate stage performances so they could not only earn more money but also develop a skill to be used in the future.[67] In May 1978 a memo from JoNina Abron revealed that morale was low due to the fact that the *Black Panther* had gone to press only three times in the previous six weeks. She suggested that the Panthers publish on a biweekly schedule and volunteered to work as a freelance writer under a pen name to raise funds. She pointed out that the estimated cost of printing 5,500 copies of the sixteen-page newspaper was $402 and suggested that the Panthers focus on fund-raising this amount.[68] Austin Allen wrote to Newton suggesting that the BPP improve the content of the paper by augmenting local news coverage with more visuals. He suggested selling advertisements, giving away old issues, and offering free trial subscriptions to boost community interest in the newspaper. He also suggested that the Panthers create a glossy magazine, which would provide more flexibility than a newspaper.[69]

In January 1979 members of the newspaper cadre warned Newton that new methods of fund-raising for the newspaper would have to be adopted. Organizational resources could no longer be relied on to distribute the newspaper in LA, Chicago, Detroit, and Milwaukee. In support JoNina Abron sent another memo: "If we are to continue publishing the paper, I feel strongly that we are going to have to move in the direction of having individuals or distributing companies handle sales for us in the major cities." She suggested adopting aggressive fund-raising activities, such as renting out Panther films, selling ad space in the newspaper to progressive businesses, and booking speaking engagements for members. She ended on a dire note: "I do not mean to be redundant, but unless we take action immediately, the publication of our newspaper will again be in jeopardy, even on a biweekly basis."[70] At the end of January production of the *Black Panther* was halted due to lack of funds. A memo to Newton suggested printing the paper on Monday instead of Thursday: "What few checks we get in these days normally come at the end of the week. Also, the comrades who sell the paper in Compton, Detroit, Chicago, Milwaukee and Richmond, Virginia would have a couple of days extra if we changed to a Monday printing day."[71]

Declining resources eventually affected all of the programs, and by June 1979 members were juggling their limited funds to meet the organization's various needs and discontinuing programs such as Seniors Against a Fearful Environment.[72] JoNina Abron wrote Newton suggesting that money the Panthers were expecting from the sale of their printing equipment be used to pay the printing bill. When they received newspaper subscription renewals from institutions in September, they would use this money to pay utility bills at Central Headquarters. This would ease the burden of the EOC and the OCLC, which was currently paying these bills which "drain[ed] the school finances."[73]

The Panthers sold their assets to raise funds. This had begun in 1977, when the vast majority of the BPP's ten properties were transferred from Stronghold to the EOC.[74] A memo dated 1 September 1979 announced the sale of property and the relocation of members: "The incomes of comrades living in Party facilities that will be sold must be increased so that they will have enough money to pay rent where they relocate and other living expenses."[75]

McCall's account of this period revealed the unwavering loyalty that some Panthers felt toward the party:

> The newspaper was our major source of income. The collection of donations for sickle cell anemia, the Lamp Post, grants for the school—those are the things that kept the programs going for years and years and years. There were people who supported us financially who kept giving us money until they couldn't give anymore. . . . [By 1979] the funds were drying up. It wasn't that we didn't have support in the community; it was that we didn't have the funds, like [for] the Lamp Post. The IRS was constantly harassing us about taxes. The Oakland Community School was constantly harassed about the grants we were getting. Huey was constantly being harassed about anything they could harass him about. Court costs were costing us an arm and a leg, and funds were just drying up. As soon as we could raise some money, they would figure out a way to take it away from us. My source for being able to stay in the Party so long was the Lamp Post. We were thriving. Then we started losing business at the Lamp Post because of all this that was being blamed on Huey. So funds start drying up at the Lamp Post. Funds start drying up at the school. I had

to go out and get a job, which I did and gave all my money back to the party.[76]

Others chose to leave, citing exhaustion, loneliness, or the desire to attend school, spend more time with their children, or achieve some measure of financial stability. By 1979 the Black Panther Party had been reduced to approximately fifty-seven members, whose areas of work were the central body, Oakland Community School, the EOC and programs, the Ministry of Information, and the Lamp Post.[77]

The OCS, the Panthers' most visible and viable program, was best equipped to struggle for its own survival. Financial problems were a major topic of discussion at OCS meetings in early 1979.[78] The OCS cadre discussed grant proposal writing and the possibility of holding benefits, candy sales, and radiothons to raise money. They computed a per child cost ($98 per month from 148 children) in anticipation of having to charge for the various services they provided for students. They reactivated the Each-One-Teach-One pledge club, which they had begun in 1973, to generate funds for tuition and devised a flexible plan that would require parents to pay 10 percent of their income to tuition regardless of how many of their children were enrolled in the school. They grappled with the reality that these new funding requirements would probably mean a drop in enrollment.[79] However, they were aware that an overhaul of their financial strategy was needed to "develop alternate plans for surviving, not counting the childcare $."[80] A weekly report in early February suggested hiring a grant writer or finding a volunteer to write a minimum of one funding proposal a month.[81]

The OCS also drew on community resources for support. Parents of the children who attended the school had become deeply invested in its continued success and supported its vision. When the school reached out to the community for financial support, the response was overwhelmingly positive. The Parental Advisory Board was very active in fund-raising for the school. It sponsored discos, organized a school memory book, sold candy, and even paid instructors' salaries when it was able.[82]

The OCS cadre created a newsletter to update the community about the school's activities, announce fund-raising events, and advertise services offered by members, such as Emory's Printing and Graphics company and Donald Cunningham's photography services.[83] The newsletter highlighted the school's continuing success and featured student testimonials about how the school had impacted their lives. In March 1979, however, the OCS had to borrow money to meet its payroll.[84]

The Black Panther Party could no longer sustain its survival programs or the material needs of full-time members. Members were asked to fill out questionnaires about their income and expenses and their interest in participating in collective buying with Amway, a bulk sales company.[85] Their field operation was discontinued because they didn't have enough personnel to secure permits to collect donations. Instead members were instructed to get part-time jobs on the weekends to supplement the $100 they would now receive monthly.[86] A memo from the Central Body dated 15 September 1979 announced, "Every comrade, regardless of stature, will be getting money, according to need."[87]

RESIGNATIONS

Ideologically weakened and no longer a financially self-sustaining close-knit unit, the Panthers could not recover from this downward spiral. Internal contradictions and the fundamental need for individual self-actualization drove the last remaining members from the party. Casey recalled how the total commitment of the membership made their potential exploitation total as well:

> It was a system based upon sometimes brutal exploitation of the collective. Okay, so you have these people who are committed one hundred percent, twenty-four hours a day, seven days a week to the Black Panther Party, and . . . the system basically would exploit that collective until a person would get tired and just leave. That's basically what it was. . . . We're talking about from when you get up at five o'clock in the morning because you're working in the dormitory with the children and you have to bathe them and get them dressed and ready for school. You ride in the van and come to school; you teach school all day. Either when the kids leave at the end of the day at five o'clock, either you ride in the van and go to the dormitory and clean up and bathe them and get them ready for bed and go through that whole process again, or you stayed in the school and you cleaned the whole school, you see. Which could mean you don't leave that school until twelve midnight, and then you go home and you got to be back there by eight the next morning. . . . Now when you went through

that five days a week and then on Saturday you went into the field [collecting donations], okay, and then Sundays you usually had some sort of meetings to go to. So you end up having half a day on Sunday really to yourself. That was pretty much it. That's what exploitation of the collective means. Now you're doing this week after week after week after week after week after year after year, you're doing this. No holidays, ain't none of that, ain't no break. Constant. . . . There was very little balance in terms of the development of the individual, the development of the capacity of the individual to be able to maintain themselves.[88]

Many Panthers wrote to the leadership expressing similar views; they found it increasingly difficult to subvert individual needs to the collective, especially when they believed that the collective was flawed. One member requested time to complete a graduate degree and go to law school.[89] Another pleaded for his own apartment "rather than being a grasshopper and staying any and everywhere." He complained, "I can't even keep my own child because of me not having my own place."[90] Another recounted a bitter story about being arrested on traffic ticket violations and bailed out for $65. Upon her release she was hurt to discover that despite the many financial sacrifices she had borne and her contributions to the organization in the role of legal defense coordinator, some of her comrades had whispered that she should have spent the weekend in jail. She questioned the financial priorities that could allow someone who worked ten hours a day, five days a week to be denied money and basic moral support, arguing that comrades were being treated "unlike anyone campaigning for humanity should treat another human being." The final straw came when her desire to attend law school was greeted with veiled accusations of individualism. Ironically, when she called to resign, she discovered that she had been expelled.[91]

Tommye Williams wrote, "[I have] come to a crossroads in my life—one path is the Party and the other path is my personal happiness." She pointed out that the BPP was rife with inequities: "Some comrades have to struggle each month to pay rent, bills, food, and to buy necessities for their children, and some comrades don't have a source of income at all. Other comrades do not have to worry about their financial necessities." She criticized the collective parenting system, arguing that Panther parents needed to spend more individual time with their children: "Our children are growing up—half the children don't know their parents or their parents don't know their children. They need a sense of security, to know who they are. At the present, the children still do not receive enough time with their own parents." This affected her relationship with her son: "As it stands now, I spend Sundays (when there is not a meeting) with him and a couple of hours . . . three nights a week with my son. I would like to spend Saturdays with him also and participate with him in different activities, which interest him. I spoke with Ericka about this particular issue. It was worked out that I go home early a couple of days of the week. This might work temporarily for me but it is still an issue which affects most of the mothers in the Party."[92]

McCutchen had faith in the BPP's ideology, but "the human error . . . caused me to move away, to withdraw. What was left of the party could not produce, could not encourage those ideas, those dreams, those products. . . . What was left was a shell. I did not want to be part of a shell and call myself a revolutionary. I stayed for as long as I thought feasible."[93] He argued that financial problems were a major factor in the party's decline:

> We weren't attracting new party members because of economics. We lost members because of economics. Party members had to weigh the advantages and disadvantages of twenty-four-hour commitment and were being forced to find their own places and pool resources. How were they going to pool resources without having access to funds? We were losing members for that reason. Other party members wanted to go to school or return to school. So those who have to have a choice between staying in the party and going to school, then they were gone. Community workers would come in, primarily a lot of the parents from the school and other members of the youth, the teens. . . . Those were primarily the workers who supported the party during this time period.[94]

Austin Allen offered a bittersweet blend of criticism of the organization and homage to the impact of membership on his life:

> I think I've had things I've agreed with and disagreed with over the years like any other comrade, but a lot of it is I guess I've lost the desire to struggle hard to bring up my points of view. I've learned a tremendous amount of things about myself and the world by being in the Party for the past 7½ years, and I owe this to my comrades that have been understanding when I needed it. I don't take any of the

experiences I've gained while in the Party lightly at all. And I doubt I could have learned as much as I have anywhere else.[95]

Casey's letter of resignation, addressed to Newton, contained a systematic organizational critique:

You once said that personal problems can be expressed through politics. This is true. However, it is also true that personal problems can be expressed politically. The line seperating the two is thin indeed. But many people that are still with us have personal problems which are the result of a political policy or line. They are unable to express their personal problems as they relate to the rules, policys and guidelines of the Party. Consequently they just leave or "hang in" as many comrades say these days. What they don't realize is that this Party, the peoples and that it is what we make it. That Huey Newton is not a god or prophet, as you constantly remind people all the time.[96]

He pointed out, "So many comrades have left and so many are on the verge of leaving because we suffer from lonliness, the lack of personal lives, extreme poverty and the lack of personal development. These problems are often expressed in contradictions, between the leadership and the lead [sic], parents and their children, men and women and comrades and the community." Internal development had been "negligible." "Party members don't socialize, don't transfer skills in an organized manner, don't study party ideology or revolutionary theory, [there is a] lack of physical development, weapons training, medical education." They faced the "personal indignity" of going into the field to solicit donations while their basic needs were not being met. "How can we as revolutionaries hope to administer thousands perhaps millions one day through the city, state or federal governments when we don't have the financial self-reliance to manage our personal money?" He suggested that the party adopt socialism: "Free medical care, education, food, etc. A guaranteed income and a revolutionary spirit. Perhaps in this way we could overcome our selfishness and become true Communists."[97]

THE FINAL CRITIQUE

In May 1979 cadres made their final collective attempt at internal reform. They issued a report pointing to the lack of political education for the BPP's decline:

One of the primary reasons why ideological deterioration has occurred and unprincipled maladies such as bossism, obscurantism,
arrogance and liberalism is rampant throughout our party is due to
the fact that there is no serious study of party ideology. This is in spite
of the rich traditions of organizers and experience. Without being
ideologically armed, our comrades, especially the rank and file, are
left defenseless against the subversion of our party principles. . . .
Our party must firmly embrace the principle of criticism and self-
criticism. Without this our leadership becomes separated from our
party body as is the case now, consequently isolating the party from
the people. Our party must be a microcosm of the kind of society we
want to create to replace the old.[98]

For the first time the leadership was clearly implicated. The report sharply
criticized leaders'

elitist attitude that leadership knows what's best for the rank and file
without consulting them, not accepting criticisms and suggestions
from them and not helping them with their difficulties. . . . The un-
written policy of running people's lives instead of giving direction to
their lives must come to an end. The basis of loyalty is not regimenta-
tion, threats and orders but guidance, concern, understanding, and
love. . . . The party cannot grow and develop its structure if its membership is technically and intellectually backward. Every attempt by
every comrade to grow and develop is blocked by the structure. The
structure should encourage the development of cadres, including objective independent thought, leadership, initiative, etc. in all areas
of work. Unfortunately, the structure has been manipulated to effectively isolate any individual showing the above qualities.[99]

The report suggested holding an emergency party congress where members
could voice criticism "without fear of retribution" and partake in a vote of
confidence or no confidence for the current leadership. It concluded with
the prediction that if drastic measures were not taken, the Black Panther
Party would deteriorate in approximately six months.[100]

There is no record of an emergency party congress ever taking place. Indeed the repetition of the same themes in memos and letters of resignation
from 1978 to 1980 suggests that few reforms were made. Despite the fact
that Newton had managed to complete a PhD program in the History of

Consciousness from the University of California and lead a Panther delegation to Beirut, he was in the throes of his addictions. According to Huggins,
Newton's addiction "permeated everything, and the people around him
knew as well. And there was a lot of internal energy spent on it, and other
resources, cars. . . . Everybody knew. But people were in denial about it,
and I couldn't be in denial about it after a while. . . . And although I was
coming out of denial about speaking up, I was in denial about how dangerous it could be to my own well-being." When she spoke to him about
his addiction she received an "unbelievable" response: anger and hurt that
someone who had been so close to him for so long would reproach him.[101]

Only twenty-seven Panthers were left by the fourteenth anniversary in
October 1980. One third were over thirty-five years old and had taken
part-time jobs to sustain themselves.[102] The party had been reduced to
the OCS, where the vast majority of members worked, and a legal defense
structure centered on Newton. The inexorable dialectic between the two
would sound the final death knell for the organization.

The Panthers' financial problems had taken a heavy toll on the OCS. By
early 1979 the school had 146 students, six salaried staff, fifteen cadres,
three volunteers, and a waiting list of over 450 students.[103] One year later
enrollment was down to 94 students.[104] Unable to rely on community fund-
raising and limited grants, the Panthers unsuccessfully attempted to raise
$113,000 to cover the OCS deficit.[105]

Newton's legal battles had kept the Committee for Justice active. He
had been tried three times since 1977. His two murder trials had ended in
hung juries, and the charges were subsequently dropped. In 1978 he had
been convicted of being an ex-felon in possession of a weapon and sentenced to two and half years in prison. He appealed this conviction, and his
sentence was stayed. The BPP framed his lawsuit as "an important action
toward ending illegal government harassment of organizations and individuals who actively organize against oppression in America."[106] Panthers
mobilized for Newton's retrial, launching petition campaigns, press conferences, and door-to-door advocacy.[107] The petition drive of the Committee
to Stop the Retrial of Huey P. Newton collected 1,600 signatures and 650
postcards.[108] This community support was testimony to the BPP's continued political currency. In August 1980 the Committee solicited funds from
over sixty individuals and organizations and issued several press releases
to generate public support for a new hearing on Newton's gun conviction
charges.[109]

New allegations against Newton surfaced in 1982. The government claimed that from 8 March through 21 April Newton and his associate William Shuford conspired to gain OCS money by false pretense. Newton was accused of obtaining a payroll advance from the EOC's bank account using false information that implied that replacement funds would subsequently be deposited into the account. Those funds never appeared. Newton and three others were accused of using state funds paid to the OCS for their own purposes. They were also charged with padding enrollment figures to get more money from the state between 1980 and 1982.[110] Other Panthers were accused of conspiracy to conceal and destroy public records in the face of impending audits. In total Newton was charged with thirteen criminal counts.[111] The integrity of the OCS and its ability to get funding were severely compromised.[112] The last few members of the Black Panther Party slowly drifted away, and the Oakland Community School officially closed its doors in 1982.[113]

The centralization of authority and the inability of rank-and-file members to hold leadership accountable severely circumscribed democracy in the Black Panther Party. The organization that had managed to empower black men and women to challenge so many institutions and fight for structural change in the world had disempowered them from believing that they could take the reins from one of their own party's founders. Because criticism was unwelcome or resulted in only small reforms rather than a change of course, departure became the only recourse for disaffected members. In the end Newton would be the only Panther left standing in the wreckage.

Conclusion

On 22 August 1989 Huey Newton was killed on one of the same violent West Oakland street corners that the Black Panther Party had tried to transform. His death pushed the party to the front pages of newspapers and launched countless retrospectives on the organization's legacy. Despite the fact that he was imprisoned (1967–71) or in exile (1974–77) for key years in the BPP's development, Newton's death was used as a portal into the past of the party. Entering graduate school at that time, I was more intrigued with the organization that Newton had helped build. I want readers of this book to come away with an understanding that the Black Panther Party was a vehicle for social change, a sum greater than its parts. The structure of this vehicle has remained largely invisible as the BPP's history has largely been told through the lives of leaders, the evolution of places, the intractability of state violence, or as a series of moments and flashpoints on a timeline rather than through the lens of organizational history. The constant during the party's evolution over sixteen years was its organizational structure. The party provided an operational apparatus—hierarchy, meetings, rules, fund-raising mechanisms, and other formal and informal structures—that was a direct reflection of its ideological framework and its analysis of the material conditions in the United States at the time. The dialectic between these dynamics—structure, ideas, possibilities—has formed the engine of this book. The memos, minutes from meetings, letters, artwork, photographs, wiretap transcripts, poems, trial documents, speeches, flyers, directives, press releases, daily work reports, manuscripts, audiotapes, and videotapes that the Panthers generated form a rich repository of struggle that I have mined to tell the narrative history of the Black Panther Party from the inside out.

I want readers to know what it meant to live inside an organization that considered itself revolutionary—to experience comradeship, to feel the joy that came with a deep political commitment, and to feel the agony of betrayal by people, ideas, and the very organization they were committed to. People formed bonds of friendship in, came to political awareness within the context of, and grew up in the BPP. For many members it was their source of income, source of habitat, and source of friendship and family. But the inequities evident in U.S. society were brought into the organization and became part of its foundation. Much of the Panthers' history reflects the attempt to grapple with sexism, classism, individualism, and materialism and create alternative structures, institutions, and lifestyles. The Panthers took issues that were traditionally defined in gendered terms, such as child rearing, birth control, and housework, and made them organizational issues. They grappled with the theory and practice of sexual freedom within the organization. They did this partly because of ideological dictates but mostly because members, usually women, demanded it. The fact remains, however, that the Panthers' story starts with women demanding equality, respect, and dignity in the party and ends years later with most of the demands unmet. This does not negate the party's growth over time but underscores the need for an unrelenting, creative, and self-renewing struggle against misogyny within black liberation organizations.

This is a needed history. While the lament of "needing a leader" seems to periodically emerge from communities seeking change, the need for organizations is heard more rarely. In particular, Black Power organizations are assumed to be nihilistic at their core and irreconcilably different from their counterparts earlier in the timeline of the black freedom movement. Often this is explained as a byproduct of the vicious state political repression faced by these organizations or the challenging urban environment where they originated. The legacies of these organizations are usually either framed as cautionary tales, such as Newton's death, or valorized without much attention to detail or nuance. There is much to learn about the organizations at the helm of the black freedom movement in the 1960s. The nuts and bolts of the BPP's organizational history reveal the human strivings and failings of young people bent on transforming the world and themselves with the tools they had at hand as they ran election campaigns and conferences, staffed community programs, and stood up to the police. It is a story that is both heart-wrenching and beautiful and, at times, heartbreakingly ugly. It is our history to examine and learn from.

In 2016 a new generation of activists have joined movement veterans to mobilize around issues such as police violence, mass incarceration, political prisoners, poverty, workers' rights, justice in the Middle East, and intimate partner violence. They continue to be inspired by the Black Panther Party.

Huey Newton was asked in an interview if he thought the ten-point platform and program would be realized in his lifetime. His response was optimistic:

> No, it doesn't depress me, because the Black Panther Party and its ten-point program are immediate demands, and they're demands that could be satisfied now, but I feel they will not be satisfied now because of the oppressive conditions. But later, even after those demands are satisfied, there'll be more battle cries, and new reasons for people to protest, and to right wrongs. Revolution is a law of nature; contradiction is the ruling principle of the universe. And that brings about development, of course. So, if it's not the Party, then it's some other organization that will attempt to make more freedom for man. This is a permanent process, to my understanding at this time. Of course, we know that laws are subject to change. We'll all have to analyze it to see what we'll be struggling for the next time. If you stop struggling, then you stop life.[1]

Notes

INTRODUCTION

1 Black Panther Party, "What We Want–What We Believe," October 1966, carton 18, folder 4a, Social Protest Collection, BANC MSS 86/157 c, Bancroft Library, University of California, Berkeley; Black Lives Matter, accessed 24 May 2016, http://blacklivesmatter.com/.

1. SEIZE THE TIME

1 Donald Hausler, "Blacks in Oakland: 1852–1987," Public History Room, Oakland Public Library, Lakeshore Branch, 120.

2 Marilynn S. Johnson, *The Second Gold Rush: Oakland and the East Bay in World War II* (Berkeley: University of California Press, 1993), 52.

3 Hausler, "Blacks in Oakland," 122; Willie R. Collins, "Jazzing Up Seventh Street: Musicians, Venues, and Their Social Implications," in *Sights and Sounds: Essays in Celebration of West Oakland*, edited by Suzanne Stewart and Marty Praetzellis, the Results of a Focused Research Program to Augment Cultural Resources Investigations for the I-880 Cypress Replacement Project, Alameda County, Oakland Public Library, 322.

4 Hausler, "Blacks in Oakland," 99, 141.

5 Hausler, "Blacks in Oakland," 142. See also Gretchen Lemke-Santangelo, *Abiding Courage: African American Migrant Women and the East Bay Community* (Chapel Hill: University of North Carolina Press, 1996); Gretchen Lemke-Santangelo, "Deindustrialization, Urban Poverty, and African American Community Mobilization in Oakland, 1945 through the 1990s," in *Seeking El Dorado: African Americans in California*, edited by Lawrence Brooks De Graaf, Kevin Mulroy, and Quintard Taylor (Los Angeles: Autry Museum of Western Heritage, 2001), 346–48.

6 Robert O. Self, *American Babylon: Race and the Struggle for Postwar Oakland* (Princeton, NJ: Princeton University Press, 2003), 160–64.

7 Editorial, *Flatlands*, 12 March 1966.

8 Johnson, *The Second Gold Rush*, 215.

9   Hausler, "Blacks in Oakland," 117. See "Oakland, Institute on Human Relations November 13, 1946," folder, "Blacks, Social Conditions," and Seminar report, "What Tensions Exist between Groups in the Local Community?," folder, "Chronicle Housing and Employment Discrimination," Oakland Public Library.

10   Johnson, *The Second Gold Rush*, 214.

11   Edward Hayes, *Power Structure and Urban Policy: Who Rules in Oakland?* (New York: McGraw-Hill, 1972), 62; Douglas Massey and Nancy Denton, *American Apartheid: Segregation and the Making of the Underclass* (Cambridge, MA: Harvard University Press, 1993), 58; Eric Brown, "Black Ghetto Formation in Oakland, 1852–1965: Social Closure and African American Community Development," *Research in Community Sociology* 8 (1998): 255–74.

12   Hayes, *Power Structure and Urban Policy*, 108.

13   The total net population loss was minimal. In April 1960 there were 367,548 Oakland residents, and in the summer of 1966 there were 365,127. Mich Kunitani, district supervisor, Oakland Department of Employment, to Huey Newton, 21 February 1967, enclosure p. 2, folder, "Department of Employment Information, 1967," box 47, Huey P. Newton Foundation Papers, Special Collections, Green Library, Stanford University (hereafter HPN Papers). I accessed the HPN Papers at Stanford University in 1996, when the archival recording process was just beginning; box numbers, folder titles, contents, and so on may have changed during processing.

14   Scholars of urban economics have argued that the economic and social segregation of African Americans in the 1960s was "the direct result of an unprecedented collaboration between local and national government" (Massey and Denton, *American Apartheid*, 57–58).

15   Lemke-Santangelo, "Deindustrialization," 349.

16   Hausler, "Blacks in Oakland," 125–26.

17   Brown, "Black Ghetto Formation in Oakland"; Self, *American Babylon*, 137–42.

18   Hayes, *Power Structure and Urban Policy*, 57, 79, 61; "The Poor Speak Out," *Flatlands*, 9 April 1966; "Bulldozing the Poor," *Flatlands*, 26 March 1966.

19   "Bulldozing the Poor."

20   "The Poor Speak Out." There is a rich literature on urban renewal, including Massey and Denton, *American Apartheid*, esp. 55–57. They conclude that "urban renewal almost always destroyed more housing than it replaced" (56). See also Arnold R. Hirsch, *Making the Second Ghetto: Race and Housing in Chicago 1940–1960* (Chicago: University of Chicago Press, 1998).

21   "Flatlands Says," editorial, *Flatlands*, 12 March 1966.

22   Hayes, *Power Structure and Urban Policy*, 48–49.

23   Lemke-Santangelo, "Deindustrialization," 348–49.

24   Mich Kunitani, district supervisor, Oakland Department of Employment, to Huey Newton, 21 February 1967, enclosure p. 1, folder, "Department of Employment Information, 1967," box 47, HPN Papers.

25   Norman Melnick, "Negro Attitudes on the War on Poverty," *San Francisco Examiner*, 24 August 1966.

26 Hayes, *Power Structure and Urban Policy*, 149. In contrast an alternative poverty program budget designed by the East Oakland Parish of Community Involved Priests and rejected by the federal Office of Economic Opportunity suggested a budget of $15 million, of which $3.5 million was to go to new public housing, $1.5 million to organizing the poor, and only $500,000 to staff and direction. See Hayes, *Power Structure and Urban Policy*, 147–60, for an assessment of the War on Poverty in Oakland; Melnick, "Negro Attitudes on the War on Poverty."

27 Mich Kunitani, district supervisor, Oakland Department of Employment, to Huey Newton, 21 February 1967, enclosure p. 2, folder, "Department of Employment Information, 1967," box 47, HPN Papers; Melnick, "Negro Attitudes on the War on Poverty."

28 Melnick, "Negro Attitudes on the War on Poverty."

29 "Flatlands Says."

30 See Donna Murch, *Living for the City: Migration, Education, and the Rise of the Black Panther Party in Oakland, California* (Chapel Hill: University of North Carolina Press, 2010).

31 Phil McArdle, "Oakland Police Department History 1955–1993," part 7, Public History Room, Oakland Public Library.

32 Hayes, *Power Structure and Urban Policy*, 36–39.

33 "Crime Commission Reveals Local Cops Brute Methods," *California Voice*, 13 January 1950, cover.

34 Collins, "Jazzing Up Seventh Street," 302.

35 "Brutality Charge to Be Probed," *Oakland Post-Enquirer*, 6 June 1947.

36 "Report Claims Oakland Cops Beat Negro," *San Francisco Chronicle*, 31 December 1949.

37 Donna Murch, "The Campus and the Street: Race, Migration, and the Origins of the Black Panther Party in Oakland, CA," *souls* 9, no. 4 (2007): 336–37. See also Judith May, "Struggle for Authority: A Comparison of Four Social Change Programs in Oakland, California," PhD diss., University of California, Berkeley, 1973; Laura Mihailoff, "Protecting Our Children: The History of the California Youth Authority and Juvenile Justice, 1938–68," PhD diss., University of California, Berkeley, 2006.

38 "Investigation Finds Oakland Police Dept. Guilty of Brutality," *California Voice*, 27 January 1950.

39 "Oakland Police Inquiry," *San Francisco Chronicle*, 5 January 1950.

40 "Crime Commission Reveals Local Cops' Brute Methods," *California Voice*, 13 January 1950. The police chief at the time did not acknowledge that a problem existed, and few reforms were made. See Hausler, "Blacks in Oakland," 122.

41 "Oakland Police Inquiry." Oakland's black newspapers continued to chronicle accounts of police brutality against African Americans in the 1950s. The *Sun-Reporter* was at the forefront of this reporting. See "Police Brutality, Old Story," editorial, *Sun-Reporter*, 26 February 1955; "What's Wrong with Our Police Department," *Sun-Reporter*, 7 June 1958; "New Police Brutality Cases Anger Parents: Ask Police Chief and Mayor 'Stop Brutality,'" *Sun-Reporter*, 14 November 1959; "Victim of Police Brutality?," *Sun-Reporter*, 4 March 1961.

42　"Police Brutality, Old Story."

43　"Police Brutality Review," *Flatlands*, 5–18 June 1966.

44　"Analysis. Oakland: Crisis Next Door," 30, carton 3:37, Social Protest Collection, BANC MSS 86/157 c, Bancroft Library, University of California, Berkeley (hereafter SPC).

45　Gerald Horne, *Fire This Time: The Watts Uprising and the 1960s* (Charlottesville: University Press of Virginia, 1995), 3.

46　Caption for cover photo, Alameda County Weekender, *Alameda Times-Star*, 4 September 1965.

47　Carton 2, "Anti–Vietnam War," folder 2:2, "Scheer for Congress," SPC.

48　"Flatlands Says," *Flatlands*, 12 March 1966.

49　"Flatlands Profiles," *Flatlands*, 12 March 1966.

50　See Daniel Edward Crowe, *Prophets of Rage: The Black Freedom Struggle in San Francisco, 1945–1969* (New York: Garland, 2000), 208–13.

51　"Recent Trends in the Local Civil Rights Movement," 23–24, carton 3, folder 3:37, SPC.

52　See Jo Freeman, "From Freedom Now! to Free Speech: The FSM's Roots in the Bay Area Civil Rights Movement," in *The Free Speech Movement: Reflections on Berkeley in the 1960s*, edited by Robert Cohen and Reginald E. Zelnik (Berkeley: University of California Press, 2002), 74.

53　"Transcript of a Recorded Interview with Mark Comfort," Robert Wright, Interviewer, Oakland, CA, 16 November 1968, 1–4, 16, Civil Rights Documentation Project, Moorland Spingarn Research Center, Howard University.

54　"Bomb Victims Mourned Here," *Oakland Tribune*, 19 September 1963.

55　"Flatlands Profiles."

56　"Meeting at Tech High on Attacks," *Oakland Tribune*, 22 September 1963; "Tension at Oakland Tech Hi," *San Francisco Chronicle*, 22 September 1963; "5 Arrested in Tech High Strife," *Oakland Tribune*, 24 September 1963.

57　Quote from Freeman, "From Freedom Now! to Free Speech," 78. Newspapers were describing the Sheraton sit-ins. See "Sit-in at Cadillac—107 Go to Jail," *San Francisco Chronicle*, 17 March 1964; Paul T. Miller, *The Postwar Struggle for Civil Rights: African Americans in San Francisco 1945–1975* (New York: Routledge, 2009); Crowe, *Prophets of Rage*. For a critique of the lack of black involvement on a mass level, see "Who Is Running Rights Sit-ins?," *San Francisco Examiner*, 16 May 1964; "Call for Moderation," *San Francisco Chronicle*, 12 March 1964; "Cadillac Sit-in: 107 Go to Jail," *Golden Gater* (San Francisco State College newspaper).

58　Waldo Martin, "Holding One Another: Mario Savio and the Freedom Struggle in Mississippi and Berkeley," in *The Free Speech Movement*, edited by Robert Cohen and Reginald E. Zelnik (Berkeley: University of California Press, 2002), 86–89.

59　See David Lance Goines, "The Free Speech Movement: Coming of Age in the 1960s" (Berkeley: Ten Speed Press, 1993). Also see Martin, "Holding One Another."

60　"Recent Trends in the Local Civil Rights Movement," 23–24.

61 "The Core Restaurant Project," carton 3, folder 3:26d, and "CORE Moves Downtown," folder 3.26, SPC.

62 "Put an End to Discrimination at the Oakland Tribune," flyer, box 18:22, SPC.

63 "Ad Hoc Committee Gets Unanimous Endorsement," *East Bay Labor Journal*, 18 September 1964; "Ad Hoc Committee Gets Unanimous Endorsement," box 18:37, SPC.

64 "No Comfort for Knowland," *Flatlands*, 18 June–1 July 1966.

65 Hausler, "Blacks in Oakland," 177; "Flatlands Profiles"; "Police Pressure Building Up in Oakland," *Movement*, September 1966.

66 "The Negro's Stake in Oakland," *Oakland Tribune*, 5 September 1966, reprinted from the *Post*, California's largest black paper.

67 "Flatlands Profiles."

68 "Interview with Mark Comfort," *Spider Magazine*, 24 May 1965, http://www.oac.cdlib.org/view?docId=kt8489n9b1;NAAN=13030&doc.view=frames&chunk.id=doe125&toc.depth=1&toc.id=&brand=oac4.

69 See Amory Bradford, *Oakland's Not for Burning* (New York: David McKay, 1968), 4–5, 148.

70 "Interview with Mark Comfort."

71 "A Night with the Watts Community Alert Patrol," *Movement*, August 1966.

72 "Freedom Now Headquarters," flyer, box 18:22, SPC; "Interview with Mark Comfort."

73 "Oakland Direct Action Committee," pamphlet, 2, box 18:22, SPC.

74 "We Want Freedom in Oakland," box 3:44, SPC.

75 "A Few Words about SNCC," carton 4, folder 31, SPC.

76 "Support the Lowndes County Freedom Organization," carton 3, folder 3:55, SPC. For the history of origins of this symbol, see Jeffrey Ogbonna Green Ogbar, *Black Power: Radical Politics and African American Identity* (Baltimore: Johns Hopkins University Press, 2004), 76. For a full history of this period, see Hasan Kwame Jeffries, *Bloody Lowndes: Civil Rights and Black Power in Alabama's Black Belt* (New York: New York University Press, 2009).

77 "Comfort and ODAC Return from Alabama," *Flatlands*, 20 September–3 October 1967.

78 "Interview with Mark Comfort."

79 For instance, *Flatlands*, 18 June–1 July 1966.

80 "Support the Black Panther Party," carton 3, folder 55, SPC.

81 "Support the Lowndes County Freedom Organization," box 3:55, and "A New Freedom Party Has Formed," carton 3, folder 55, SPC.

82 "A Report: A Summary of the First State-wide Convention of the Poor—Oakland, California, Feb 26–27, 1966 with attached resolutions," 3, folder 5:25, SPC; "Convention of the Poor," *Flatlands*, 26 March 1966; "Proceedings and Summary: First Statewide Convention of the Poor," folder 5:25, SPC.

83 "The Poor Meet, Form Statewide Federation," *Movement*, March 1966; "Convention of the Poor," *Flatlands*.

84 Hayes, *Power Structure and Urban Policy*, 146–48; folder, "Oakland Anti-poverty Program," Oakland Public Library; *Flatlands*, 12 March 1966.

85 Folder, "Oakland Schools, Racial Problems, Other Than Clippings," Oakland Public Library.

86 "Oakland: Crisis Next Door," box 3.37, SPC.

87 Folder, "Oakland Schools, Racial Problems, Other Than Clippings."

88 "Ad Hoc Committee on Education," *Flatlands*, 23 April–6 May 1966; John P. Spencer, *In the Crossfire: Marcus Foster and the Troubled History of American School Reform* (Philadelphia: University of Pennsylvania Press, 2012), 195–99.

89 "Report on Castlemont Violence Clears Ad Hoc Committee," *Montclarion*, 26 July 1967; "Inside an Oakland Boycott Freedom School," *Movement*, November 1966; "Boycott Baby Boycott," *Flatlands*, 8–21 October 1966.

90 "Trouble at Castlemont" and "East Oakland Erupts," *Flatlands*, 22 October–4 November 1966.

91 "Oppose the Drafting of Black Men," flyer, 26 April 1966, sponsored by the Soul Students Advisory Committee, carton 18, folder 18:37, SPC. Mark Comfort, identified as a candidate for the 15th Assembly District, is listed as a speaker.

92 "Comfort Wins a Stay," *Flatlands*, 21 May–4 June 1966.

93 "Flatlands Says," editorial, *Flatlands*, 18 June–1 July 1966.

94 "What Black Power Means," *Flatlands*, 13–27 August 1966.

95 Michael Thelwell, *Ready for Revolution: The Life and Struggles of Stokely Carmichael (Kwame Ture)* (New York: Scribner, 2003), 475.

96 Bobby Seale, *A Lonely Rage: The Autobiography of Bobby Seale* (New York: Times Book, 1978), 19; Bobby Seale, *Seize the Time: The Story of the Black Panther Party and Huey P. Newton* (Baltimore: Black Classic Press, 1991), 4; Huey Newton, *Revolutionary Suicide* (New York: Writers and Readers, 1973), 13–15.

97 Newton, *Revolutionary Suicide*, 19–28.

98 Seale, *Seize the Time*, 3–12.

99 Seale, *Seize the Time*, 13.

100 Bobby Seale, interview by author, 13 October 1997, tape recording, Oakland.

101 George Breitman, ed., *Malcolm X Speaks* (New York: Grove Press, 1965), 22.

102 Ogbar, *Black Power*, 81–82.

103 Newton, *Revolutionary Suicide*, 71–72.

104 Folder, "Bobby Seale–Herman Blake Manuscript," p. 14, box 7, HPN Papers.

105 Bobby Seale, interview by author.

106 See Seale, *Seize the Time*, 24.

107 Ogbar, *Black Power*; folder, "Newsletter: 'Black Power,'" box, "Protest Movements, Black Panther Party Publications," San Francisco African American Historical and Cultural Society Archives.

108 Newton, *Revolutionary Suicide*, 71–72; Seale, *Seize the Time*, 24.

109 Seale, *Seize the Time*, 20–21; Newton, *Revolutionary Suicide*, 60–66.

110 Newton, *Revolutionary Suicide*, 81, 87–89. Also see folder, "People v. Newton Correspondence," box 17, HPN Papers.

111 Bobby Seale, interview by author. Jeffrey O. G. Ogbar argues that the Nation of Islam's emphasis on behavioral reform was another reason membership was unappealing (*Black Power*, 82–83).

112 Seale, *Seize the Time*, 27, 30–31; Fabio Rojas, *From Black Power to Black Studies: How a Radical Social Movement Became an Academic Discipline* (Baltimore: Johns Hopkins University Press, 2010), 38.

113 William Van Deburg, *New Day in Babylon: The Black Power Movement and American Culture, 1965–1975* (Chicago: University of Chicago Press, 1992), 152–55; Paul Alkebulan, *Survival Pending Revolution: The History of the Black Panther Party* (Tuscaloosa: University of Alabama Press, 2007), 8–13.

114 Clayborne Carson, SNCC *and the Black Awakening of the 1960s* (Cambridge, MA: Harvard University Press, 1981), 134–36, 101.

115 Tony Smith, *Thinking Like a Communist: State and Legitimacy in the Soviet Union, China and Cuba* (New York: Norton, 1987), 113, 155.

116 Frantz Fanon, *The Wretched of the Earth* (New York: Grove Press, 1963), 21, 93.

117 Newton, *Revolutionary Suicide*, 110.

118 Seale, *Seize the Time*, 59–63.

119 Seale, *Seize the Time*, 69.

120 Newton, *Revolutionary Suicide*, 73.

121 Seale, *Seize the Time*, 59.

122 See Murch, *Living for the City*, chapter 4; Martha Biondi, *The Black Revolution on Campus* (Berkeley: University of California Press, 2012).

123 "A Symposium on Black Power," box 3.55, SPC.

124 "The Challenge of Black Power," box 18.4b, SPC.

125 "What Black Power Means."

126 "Berkeley Conference on Black Power and Its Challenges," flyer, 28 October 1966, folder 18:46, SPC.

127 "Black Power Meet," *Flatlands*, 5–18 November 1966.

2. IN DEFENSE OF SELF-DEFENSE

1 Bobby Seale, *Seize the Time: The Story of the Black Panther Party and Huey Newton* (New York: Random House, 1968), 64–65.

2 Elendar Barnes, interview by author, 25 September 1997, tape recording, Brooklyn.

3 See Akinyele Omowale Umoja, *We Will Shoot Back: Armed Resistance in the Mississippi Freedom Movement* (New York: New York University Press, 2013).

4 Simon Wendt, *The Spirit and the Shotgun: Armed Resistance and the Struggle for Civil Rights* (Gainesville: University Press of Florida, 2007).

5 Robert Williams on "Radio Free Dixie," quoted in "'Negroes with Guns': A Radical Battle with Racism," interview of Sandra Dickson, NPR, 26 February 2006, http://www.npr.org/templates/story/story.php?storyId=5193906. Churchill Roberts, director, *Negroes with Guns: Rob Williams and Black Power*, DVD (Gainesville: Documentary Institute, College of Journalism and Communications, University of Florida, 2005).

6 John Henrik Clark, ed., *Malcolm X: The Man and His Times* (New York: Macmillan, 1969), 336–37.

7   Huey Newton, *Revolutionary Suicide* (New York: Harcourt Brace Jovanovich, 1973), 117.

8   "Police Vow Court Battle on Review," *Oakland Tribune*, 23 May 1966; "Police Affairs Committee," *Flatlands*, 30 July–13 August 1966.

9   "A Lot of You Young Cats," carton 18, folder 18:37, Social Protest Collection, BANC MSS 86/157 c, Bancroft Library, University of California, Berkeley; "Flatlands Profiles," *Flatlands*, 12 March 1966.

10 "Students at McClymonds in Walkout," *Oakland Tribune*, 19 December 1965.

11 Robert O. Self, *American Babylon: Race and the Struggle for Postwar Oakland* (Princeton, NJ: Princeton University Press, 2003), 210; "Police Brutality Review," *Flatlands*, 5–18 June 1966.

12 "The Official View," *Flatlands*, 5–18 June 1966.

13 *U.S. Riot Commission Report: Report of the National Advisory Commission on Civil Disorders* (New York: Bantam Books, 1968), 40. This commission was appointed by President Johnson on 27 July 1967 and was chaired by Otto Kerner, then governor of Illinois.

14 "Police Pressure Building Up in Oakland," *Movement*, September 1966; Mark Comfort, "Conditions in the Oakland Ghetto: Interview by Elsa Knight Thompson," 1967, cassette E2BB1309, Pacifica Radio Archives, Los Angeles.

15 "Police Vow Court Battle on Review," *Oakland Tribune*, 23 May 1966.

16 Scot Brown, *Fighting for Us: Maulana Karenga, the Us Organization, and Black Cultural Nationalism* (New York: New York University Press, 2003), 83; Keith A. Mayes, *Kwanzaa: Black Power and the Making of the African-American Black Holiday* (New York: Routledge, 2009), 221.

17 "Will Watts Secede?," *Movement*, July 1966; "There Is a Movement Starting in Watts," *Movement*, August 1966.

18 "A Night with the Watts Community Alert Patrol," *Movement*, August 1966.

19 "A Meeting with Brother Lennie," *Movement*, September 1966.

20 "Will Watts Secede?"

21 See Steve Estes, *I Am a Man! Race, Manhood, and the Civil Rights Movement* (Chapel Hill: University of North Carolina Press, 2005).

22 "Conversations with Chairman Bobby Seale," folder, "Bobby Seale–Herman Blake Manuscript," box 7, Huey P. Newton Foundation Papers, Special Collections, Green Library, Stanford University (hereafter HPN Papers).

23 Bobby Seale, interview by author, 13 October 1997, tape recording, Oakland, California.

24 Ruth Beckford, interview by author, 16 October 1997, tape recording, Oakland, California.

25 "The Black Scholar Interviews: Bobby Seale," *Black Scholar* 4, no. 1 (1972): 13.

26 Elendar Barnes, interview by author.

27 Judy (Hart) Jaunita, interview by author, 20 October 1997, tape recording, Oakland, California.

28 Emory Douglas, interview by author, 9 October 1997, tape recording, San Francisco, California.

29 Bill Jennings, interview by author, October 1997, tape recording, Sacramento, California.

30 Sherwin Forte, interview by author, 9 October 1997, tape recording, Oakland, California.

31 Sherwin Forte, interview by author.

32 Newton, *Revolutionary Suicide*, 121.

33 Emory Douglas, interview by author.

34 Sherwin Forte, interview by author.

35 David Hilliard and Lewis Cole, *This Side of Glory: The Autobiography of David Hilliard and the Story of the Black Panther Party* (Boston: Little, Brown, 1993), 109, 119.

36 Eldridge Cleaver, "The Courage to Kill: Meeting the Panthers," in *Post-Prison Writings and Speeches*, edited by Robert Scheer (New York: Vintage Books, 1969), 35–38.

37 Box, "Protest Movements, Black Panther Party Publications," folder, "Newsletter: 'Black Power,'" San Francisco African American Historical and Cultural Society Archives. Their armed stance quickly distinguished them from other local nationalist organizations, such as the Black Panther Party of Southern California. As the Oakland Panthers' local reputation grew, they came into growing conflict with the Black Panther Party of Northern California across the Bay. The BPPNC eventually changed its name after the Oakland Panthers insisted it either do so or merge with them.

38 Cleaver, "The Courage to Kill," 29–30.

39 Emory Douglas, interview by author.

40 See Newton, *Revolutionary Suicide*, 131–32; Seale, *Seize the Time*, 126–29.

41 Emory Douglas, interview by author.

42 Robert Scheer, ed., *Eldridge Cleaver: Post-Prison Writings and Speeches* (New York: Vintage Books, 1967), xv; Eldridge Cleaver, "Affidavit #1: I Am 33 Years Old," in *Post-Prison Writings and Speeches*, 3–4.

43 "Armed Black Brothers in Richmond Community," *Black Panther*, 25 April 1967.

44 Tarika Lewis, interview by author, 16 October 1997, transcript, Oakland, California.

45 Elendar Barnes, interview by author.

46 Judy (Hart) Juanita, interview by author.

47 Janice Garrett-Forte, interview by author, 9 October 1997, tape recording, Oakland, California.

48 Seale, *Seize the Time*, 83, 365.

49 Tarika Lewis, interview by author.

50 Angela LeBlanc-Ernest, "'The Most Qualified Person to Handle the Job': Black Panther Party Women, 1966–1982," in *The Black Panther Party (Reconsidered)*, edited by Charles Jones (Baltimore: Black Classic Press, 1998), 307–8.

51 *U.S. Riot Commission Report*, 143–44.

52 Huey Newton, *To Die for the People: The Writings of Huey P. Newton* (New York: Random House, 1972), 90, 85–86.

53 Newton, *To Die for the People*, 18–19, 14, 86, 18.

54 Seale, *Seize the Time*, 368–69.

55 Elendar Barnes, interview by author.

56 Emory Douglas, interview by author.

57 Bobby Seale, interview by author, 12 October 1997, tape recording, Oakland, California.

58 Seale, *Seize the Time*, 368–69.

59 Seale, *Seize the Time*, 366.

60 Philip S. Foner, ed., *The Black Panthers Speak* (New York: Da Capo Press, 1995), 5.

61 Jerry Belcher, "Oakland's Black Panthers Wear Guns, Talk Revolution," *San Francisco Examiner and Chronicle*, 30 April 1967.

62 Newton, *Revolutionary Suicide*, 142.

63 Emory Douglas, interview by author.

64 "Armed Black Brothers in Richmond Community," *Black Panther*, 25 April 1967.

65 Belcher, "Oakland's Black Panthers Wear Guns, Talk Revolution."

66 Bobby Seale, interview by author.

67 Newton, *To Die for the People*, 7–8.

68 Seale, *Seize the Time*, 153–60, 163.

69 Sherwin Forte, interview by author.

70 Emory Douglas, interview by author.

71 "The Truth about Sacramento," *Black Panther*, 15 May 1967.

72 Foner, *The Black Panthers Speak*, 14.

73 For examples of drawings of police as pigs, see *Black Panther*, 15 May 1967; "On Revolutionary Art," *Black Panther*, 20 June 1967.

74 Emory Douglas, interview by author.

75 Mary Williams, interview by author, 21 October 1997, tape recording, Oakland, California.

76 "Out of the Rank and File of the Black Panther Party: Interview with Terry Cotton," 3, unpublished article in author's possession.

77 Steve McCutchen, interview by author, 11 October 1997, tape recording, Oakland, California.

78 Newton, *Revolutionary Suicide*, 151, 154.

79 Newton, *To Die for the People*, 10–11.

80 Clayborne Carson, sncc and the Black Awakening of the 1960s (Cambridge, MA: Harvard University Press, 1981), 278–79.

81 Newton, *Revolutionary Suicide*, 184.

82 See Charles E. Jones, "The Political Repression of the Black Panther Party, 1966–1971: The Case of the Oakland Bay Area," *Journal of Black Studies* 18, no. 4 (1988): 415–34.

83 *Statutes of California*, 1967, vol. 2, p. 2463.

84 Jones, "The Political Repression of the Black Panther Party," 424.

85 "Panthers Expand 'Purge' in Move to Clear Up Image," *San Francisco Chronicle*, 14 January 1969, folder, "BPP Publicity and Misc, 1969," box 31, HPN Papers.

86 In his autobiography Newton recalls being shot by one officer and hearing other shots being fired as he passed out (*Revolutionary Suicide*, 171–76). For other accounts of this incident, see Michael Newton, *Bitter Grain: Huey Newton and the Black Panther Party* (Los Angeles: Holloway House, 1980), 43–52; Gene Marine, *The Black Panthers* (New York: Signet Books, 1969), 77–105.

87 Hilliard and Cole, *This Side of Glory*, 130–33.

88 Newton, *Revolutionary Suicide*, 187.

89 Foner, *The Black Panthers Speak*, 15–16.

90 Kathleen Cleaver, interview by author, 24 November 1997, tape recording, New York, New York.

91 Bobby Seale, interview by author.

92 Kathleen Cleaver, interview by author.

93 Bobby Seale, interview by author.

94 Janice Garrett-Forte, interview by author.

95 Kathleen Cleaver, interview by author.

3. MOVING ON MANY FRONTS

1 Henry Hampton and Steve Fayer, eds., *Voices of Freedom: An Oral History of the Civil Rights Movement from the 1950s through the 1980s* (New York: Bantam Books), 514.

2 "Affidavit #2 of Eldridge Cleaver," 12, folder, "Hilliard, David. People v.," box 25, Huey P. Newton Foundation Papers, Special Collections, Green Library, Stanford University (hereafter HPN Papers).

3 "Bobby Hutton Murdered," flyer, San Francisco African American Historical and Cultural Society Archives (hereafter SFAAHCS). See also Len Holt, *The Bobby Hutton Tribunal* (Berkeley: Tribunal Committee, 1968).

4 See various 1968 issues of the *Black Panther*, especially 5 October and 19 October.

5 Hampton and Fayer, *Voices of Freedom*, 513.

6 David Hilliard and Lewis Cole, *This Side of Glory: The Autobiography of David Hilliard and the Story of the Black Panther Party* (Boston: Little, Brown, 1993), 176–77, 151–52.

7 Sherwin Forte, interview by author, 9 October 1997, tape recording, Oakland, California.

8 Hilliard and Cole, *This Side of Glory*, 182–86.

9 "Out of the Rank and File of the Black Panther Party, interview with Terry Cotton," 3, unpublished article in author's possession.

10 Eldridge Cleaver, *Post-Prison Writings and Speeches*, edited by Robert Scheer (New York: Rampart Books, 1967), 74–75; "The Death of Protest; The Birth of Revolution," 2–4, box, "Protest Movements, Black Panther Party Publications," SFAAHCS.

11 Hampton and Fayer, *Voices of Freedom*, 514.

12 "Affidavit #2 of Eldridge Cleaver," 2–3.

13 Huey Newton, *To Die for the People: The Writings of Huey P. Newton* (New York: Random House, 1972), 11–12.

14 Folder, "Counterintelligence Program Case Histories FBI Files," box 68, HPN Papers.

15 Folder, "Counterintelligence Program Case Histories FBI Files," box 68, HPN Papers.

16 Ward Churchill and Jim Vander Wall, *The COINTELPRO Papers: Documents from the FBI's Secret Wars against Domestic Dissent* (Boston: South End Press, 1990), 107.

17 Elendar Barnes, interview by author, 25 September 1997, tape recording, Brooklyn.

18 Judy (Hart) Jaunita, interview by author, 20 October 1997, tape recording, Oakland, California.

19 Michele Russell, "Conversation with Ericka Huggins. Oakland, California, 4/20/77," p. 10, box 1, HPN Papers.

20 Bobby Seale, interview by author, 13 October 1997, tape recording, Oakland, California.

21 Kathleen Neal Cleaver, "Back to Africa: The Evolution of the International Section of the Black Panther Party (1969–1972)," in *The Black Panther Party (Reconsidered)*, edited by Charles Jones (Baltimore: Black Classic Press, 1998), 216–20.

22 Bobby Bowen, interview by author, 22 October 1997, tape recording, Oakland, California.

23 "Alameda, California Times-Star," folder, "Publicity File No. 6," box 53, HPN Papers.

24 Bobby Seale, interview by author.

25 "Community Mobilization for Huey Newton," folder, "Newton, Huey–MISC," box 52, HPN Papers.

26 "Intelligence Summary, May 21–May 28, 1968," folder, "Dellinger v. Mitchell 11596," box 5, Social Protest Collection, BANC MSS 86/157 c, Bancroft Library, University of California, Berkeley (hereafter SPC).

27 "FBI Intelligence Summary Nov 15–22, 1968," box 65, HPN Papers.

28 Terry Cotton, interview by author, 26 October 1997, Oakland, California.

29 Bobby Bowen, interview by author.

30 Janice Garrett-Forte, interview by author, 9 October 1997, tape recording, Oakland, California.

31 Bill Jennings, interview by author, 1 November 1997, tape recording, Sacramento. The 10-10-10 program was an organizing strategy by which one person organizes ten people, then those ten people each organize ten more, and so on.

32 Bill Jennings, interview by author.

33 Brenda Presley, interview by author, 22 October 1997, tape recording, Oakland, California.

34 Bobby Seale, interview by author.

35 Emory Douglas, interview by author, 9 October 1997, tape recording, San Francisco.

36 "National Organizational Structuer [sic] Black Panther Party," box 1, folder, "Organizational Chart, rules and armaments," Black Panther Party FBI Files, Manuscripts, Archives and Rare Books Division, New York Public Library, Schomburg Center for Research in Black Culture.

37   Kathleen Cleaver, interview by author, 24 November 1997, tape recording, New York.

38   Emory Douglas, "On Revolutionary Art," *Black Panther,* 20 October 1968.

39   Hilliard and Cole, *This Side of Glory,* 149.

40   "Counterintelligence Program Case Histories–FBI files," box 68, HPN Papers.

41   Bill Jennings, interview by author, 1 November 1997, tape recording, Sacramento.

42   Kathleen Cleaver, interview by author.

43   Aaron Dixon, interview by author, 19 October 1997, telephone.

44   "Letter from Seattle Panthers," *Black Panther,* 16 November 1968. See also Aaron Floyd Dixon, *My People Are Rising: Memoir of a Black Panther Party Captain* (Chicago: Haymarket Books, 2012).

45   Hampton and Fayer, *Voices of Freedom,* 520–21. See Jakobi Williams, *From the Bullet to the Ballot: The Illinois Chapter of the Black Panther Party and Racial Coalition Politics in Chicago* (Chapel Hill: University of North Carolina Press, 2013).

46   Mary Williams, interview by author, 21 October 1997, tape recording, Oakland, California.

47   Dick Cluster, ed., *They Should Have Served That Cup of Coffee: 7 Radicals Remember the 1960s* (Boston: South End Press, 1979), 50.

48   Bobby Seale, "Political Move: Huey Newton," *Black Panther,* 24 October 1968.

49   Bobby Seale, interview by author.

50   Manning Marable, *Race Reform and Rebellion: The Second Reconstruction in Black America, 1945–1990* (Jackson: University Press of Mississippi, 1991), 97–99.

51   Robert L. Allen, *Black Awakening in Capitalist America: An Analytic History* (Trenton, NJ: Africa World Press, 1990), 229.

52   Michele Russell, "Conversation with Ericka Huggins, Oakland, California, 4/20/77," p. 9, box 1, HPN Papers.

53   Churchill and Vander Wall, *The COINTELPRO Papers,* 124–25.

54   "Exhibit 6, 10/10/68," folder, "Freedom of Information Counterintelligence program against HPN," box 1, HPN Papers.

55   "Supplementary Detailed Staff Reports on Intelligence Activities and the Rights of Americans," 208, 206, folder, "FBI files," box 6, HPN Papers.

56   "Counterintelligence Program Case Histories–FBI files," box 68, HPN Papers.

57   Bobby Seale, *Seize the Time: The Story of the Black Panther Party and Huey Newton* (New York: Random House, 1968), 205–7.

58   Philip S. Foner, ed., *The Black Panthers Speak: The Manifesto of the Party. The First Complete Documentary Record of the Panthers' Program* (Philadelphia: J. B. Lippincott, 1970), 14–16.

59   "A Letter from Eldridge Cleaver," folder 25, carton 12, "Eldridge Cleaver Campaign Committee, 1968, SPC.

60   "BPP Ministry of Information Bulletins 1968–69," folder 8, carton 18, SPC. The police had arrested several leaders of "Stop the Draft Week." The "Oakland 7" were heralded as political prisoners by supporters. See W. J. Rorabaugh, *Berkeley at War: The 1960s* (New York: Oxford University Press, 1989), 115–21.

61   Seale, *Seize the Time,* 213.

62 Clayborne Carson, SNCC and the Black Awakening of the 1960s (Cambridge, MA: Harvard University Press, 1981), 266–72; Allen, Black Awakening in Capitalist America, 265–66.

63 Carson, SNCC and the Black Awakening of the 1960s, 280–82.

64 Bobby Seale, interview by author.

65 "Ministry of Information Black Paper," 3–4, folder, "BPP 1966–1972," carton 18, SPC.

66 Eldridge Cleaver, "Affidavit #1: I Am 33 Years Old," in Post-Prison Writings and Speeches, 1.

67 Bobby Seale, interview by author.

68 Carson, SNCC and the Black Awakening of the 1960s, 282; Allen, Black Awakening in Capitalist America, 250–51.

69 "Eldridge Cleaver campaign committee, 1969," folder 12, carton 25, SPC.

70 Churchill and Vander Wall, The COINTELPRO Papers, 127–28.

71 Carson, SNCC and the Black Awakening of the 1960s, 284–86; Allen, Black Awakening in Capitalist America, 267.

72 "Position Paper on Coalitions," folder, "Peace and Freedom Party–Area 1," carton 12, SPC.

73 "Control Your Local Police," folder, "BPP 1966–1972," carton 18, SPC.

74 "Huey Newton for U.S. Congress, Bobby Seale for State Assembly," no folder, SFAAHCS.

75 Janice Garrett-Forte, interview by author. See Williams, From the Bullet to the Ballot, chapter 4, for an extended discussion of the BPP's coalition politics in Chicago.

76 FBI memo, 14 October 1968, "Counterintelligence Program against Huey P. Newton," p. 2, exhibit 7, folder, "Counterintelligence Program against Huey P. Newton," box 1, HPN Papers.

77 "Exhibit 7, 10/14/68," folder, "Freedom of Information Counterintelligence program against HPN," box 1, HPN Papers.

78 "Report on Cleaver Rally," Black Panther, 16 November 1968.

79 "A Letter from Eldridge Cleaver," 2, folder 25, carton 12, SPC.

80 Cleaver, Post-Prison Writings and Speeches, 69.

81 Huey Newton, "Communique No. 1," Black Panther, 28 September 1968.

82 Seale, Seize the Time, 63.

83 Foner, The Black Panthers Speak, 3.

84 Bobby Seale, interview by author.

85 Bobby Seale, interview by author.

86 "FBI Intelligence Summary Nov 15–22, 1968," box 65, HPN Papers.

87 Ruth Beckford, interview by author, 16 October 1997, tape recording, Oakland, California.

88 Brenda Presley, interview by author.

89 Bobby Seale, interview by author.

90 "Grenades and Bombs: Anti-property and Anti-personnel," Black Panther, 16 November 1968.

91 Capt. Crutch, "Correcting Mistaken Ideas," Black Panther, 26 October 1968.

1 Kenneth O'Reilly, *Racial Matters: The FBI's Secret File on Black America, 1960–1972* (New York: Free Press, 1989), 298.

2 "Exhibit 15," file, "Freedom of Information Counterintelligence program against HPN," box 1, Huey P. Newton Foundation Papers, Special Collections, Green Library, Stanford University (hereafter HPN Papers).

3 "Supplementary Detailed Staff Reports on Intelligence Activities and the Rights of Americans," 189–95, folder, "FBI files," box 6, HPN Papers.

4 Thomas McCreary, interview by author, 25 September 1997, tape recording, Brooklyn.

5 "Interview with the Chief of Staff David Hilliard," *Black Panther*, 20 April 1969.

6 "Supplementary Detailed Staff Reports on Intelligence Activities and the Rights of Americans," 188.

7 "Justice for Huey Newsletter Summer 1976, No. 4," 4, box 42, HPN Papers.

8 According to Kathleen Cleaver, Seale surveyed the party in 1969 and found that women constituted two-thirds of membership. Kathleen Cleaver, "Women, Power and Revolution," in *Liberation, Imagination, and the Black Panther Party: A New Look at the Panthers and Their Legacy*, edited by Kathleen Cleaver and George Katsiaficas (New York: Routledge, 2001), 125. See also Bobby Seale, *Seize the Time: The Story of the Black Panther Party and Huey Newton* (New York: Random House, 1968), 403.

9 Brenda Presley, interview by author, 22 October 1997, tape recording, Oakland, California.

10 "Interview with the Chief of Staff David Hilliard."

11 Philip S. Foner, ed., *Black Panthers Speak: The Manifesto of the Party. The First Complete Documentary Record of the Panthers' Program* (Philadelphia: J. B. Lippincott, 1970), 5–6.

12 Kathleen Cleaver, interview by author, 24 November 1997, tape recording, New York.

13 Janice Garrett-Forte, interview by author, 9 October 1997, tape recording, San Francisco.

14 Seale, *Seize the Time*, 370.

15 "Black Panther Party Discipline, August 8, 1969," folder, "David Hilliard, FBI files," 1, box 32, HPN Papers.

16 "Reactionaries from the East Oakland Chapter," *Black Panther*, 23 March 1969.

17 Sherwin Forte, interview by author, 9 October 1997, tape recording, Oakland, California.

18 *The Church Committee Reports, Book III: Supplementary Detailed Staff Reports on Intelligence Activities and the Rights of Americans*, p. 222, accessed 15 June 2016, http://www.aarclibrary.org/publib/church/reports/book3/html/ChurchB3_0114b .htm.

19 "Re: Black Panther Party BPP Cleveland Division 1/23/70," folder, "David Hilliard, FBI files," box 32, HPN Papers.

20 See "Wiretap Transcript 1969," "May 31, 1969 Wiretap Transcript," "Wiretap Transcripts," "Wiretap Transcript March 19, 1969," all box 12, HPN Papers.

21 "Interview with the Chief of Staff David Hilliard."

22 Kathleen Cleaver, "Back to Africa: The Evolution of the International Section of the Black Panther Party (1969–1972)," 50, unpublished paper in author's possession.

23 "Message to Revolutionary Women," *Black Panther*, 9 August 1969; "Dear Comrade Brother 10/27/72," folder, "General Requests for material and/or specific info," box 24, HPN Papers.

24 Emory Douglas, interview by author, 9 October 1997, tape recording, San Francisco.

25 Bobby Bowen, interview by author, 22 October 1997, tape recording, Oakland, California.

26 Bobby Bowen, interview by author.

27 "Black Panther Party Discipline, August 8, 1969," folder, "David Hilliard's FBI files," 2–3, box 32, HPN Papers. Wiretap transcripts contain numerous references to Panthers being placed in "study hall" as a punishment for breaking rules; see "Wiretap Transcripts 1969," box 12, HPN Papers.

28 "Black Panther Party Discipline, August 8, 1969," folder, "David Hilliard's FBI files," 2–3, box 32, HPN Papers.

29 "Wiretap Transcripts 1969," box 12, HPN Papers.

30 Janice Garrett-Forte, interview by author.

31 "Supplementary Detailed Staff Reports on Intelligence Activities and the Rights of Americans," 218.

32 "Wiretap Transcripts 1969," box 12, HPN Papers.

33 "Wiretap Transcripts 3/14/69," box 12, HPN Papers.

34 "Intelligence Summary Nov 15–Nov 22, 1968," folder, "FBI Intelligence Summary, Nov 15–22, 1978," box 65, HPN Papers.

35 Ericka Huggins, interview by author, 21 October 1997, tape recording, Oakland, California.

36 "Wiretap Transcripts 1969," box 12, HPN Papers; "Hilliard Trouble," *San Francisco Sunday Examiner and Chronicle*, 11 December 1969.

37 Ericka Huggins, interview by author.

38 Emory Douglas, interview by author.

39 Brenda Presley, interview by author.

40 Mary Williams, interview by author, 21 October 1997, tape recording, Oakland, California.

41 Brenda Presley, interview by author.

42 Janice Garrett-Forte, interview by author.

43 Emory Douglas, interview by author.

44 Seale, *Seize the Time*, 403.

45 "Roberta Alexander at Conference," *Black Panther*, 2 August 1969.

46 Emory Douglas, interview by author.

47 "Black Panther Sisters Talk about Women's Liberation," *Movement*, September 1969.

48 "Roberta Alexander at Conference."

49 Mark Lane, "Huey Newton Speaks," interview, 4 June 1970, p. 2, box 1, HPN Papers.

50 "A Letter from Huey to the Revolutionary Brothers and Sisters about the Women's Liberation and Gay Liberation Movements," 3, folder, "MSS People's Revolutionary Intercommunalism," box 2, HPN Papers.

51 Interview with Huey Newton, 21 August 1970, folder, "The Whole World Revolution Will Be Kicked Off," box 15, HPN Papers.

52 "A Letter from Huey to the Revolutionary Brothers and Sisters about the Women's Liberation and Gay Liberation Movements," 4, 12, 3.

53 Ericka Huggins, interview by author.

54 "Our Enemies Friends Are Also Our Enemies," *Black Panther*, 9 August 1969.

55 "Letter to SAC, New York from Director," 2, 24 August 1970, folder, "Freedom of Information Counterintelligence Program against HPN," exhibit 41, box 1, HPN Papers.

56 "COINTELPRO, Reur airtel 8-11-70, from Director to SAC NY," 2, box 80, HPN Papers.

57 "Memo to FBI director from SAC SF," 31 August 1970, box 13, HPN Papers.

58 David K. Johnson, *The Lavender Scare: The Cold War Persecutions of Gays and Lesbians in the Federal Government* (Chicago: University of Chicago Press, 2004).

59 "9/9/70 Memo to SAC SF from Director FBI," 1, box 80, HPN Papers.

60 "Director FBI to SAC SF, 8/13/70," 1–2, box 13, HPN Papers.

61 "Airtel dated 8-10-70," 10, folder, "Counterintelligence Program against HPN," box 1, HPN Papers.

62 Amar Casey, interview by author, 28 October 1997, tape recording, Oakland, California. Joshua Bloom and Waldo Martin detail the debates about finances in the BPP and how they contributed to internal tensions; see *Black against Empire: The History and Politics of the Black Panther Party* (Berkeley: University of California Press, 2013), 352–58.

63 "Supplementary Detailed Staff Reports on Intelligence Activities and the Rights of Americans," 219–20; "FBI memo to SAC DF from Director of FBI. Dated 2-22-71," 2, box 80, HPN Papers.

64 "Supplementary Detailed Staff Reports on Intelligence Activities and the Rights of Americans," 220.

65 "FBI memo to SAC DF from Director of FBI. Dated 2-22-71," 2.

66 "FBI memo to SAC DF from Director of FBI. Dated 2-22-71," 3.

67 Pamela Hannah, interview by author, 20 November 1997, tape recording, Brooklyn.

68 David Hilliard and Lewis Cole, *This Side of Glory: The Autobiography of David Hilliard and the Story of the Black Panther Party* (Boston: Little, Brown, 1993), 310.

69 Bill Jennings, interview by author, 1 November 1997, tape recording, Sacramento.

70 Bobby Bowen, interview by author.

71 "To Comrade Servant from Comrade Candi," folder, "Letters not to be answered," box 23, HPN Papers.

72 For a full discussion of the Panthers' internationalism, see Yohuru Williams, "American Exported Black Nationalism: The Student Nonviolent Coordinating Committee, the Black Panther Party and the Worldwide Freedom Struggle, 1967–1972," *Negro History Bulletin* 60, no. 3 (1997): 13–20; Kathleen Neal Cleaver, "Back to Africa: The Evolution of the International Section of the Black Panther Party (1966–1972)," in *The Black Panther Party (Reconsidered)*, edited by Charles Jones (Baltimore: Black Classics Press, 1998), 211–54; Michael L. Clemons and Charles E. Jones, "Global Solidarity: The Black Panther Party in the International Arena," in Cleaver and Katsificas, *Liberation, Imagination, and the Black Panther Party*, 20–39; Kathleen Cleaver, "Mobilizing for Mumia Abu-Jamal in Paris," in Cleaver and Katsificas, *Liberation, Imagination, and the Black Panther Party*, 51–68.

73 Although the term *intercommunalism* quickly became institutionalized in the party's lexicon, comprehension and acceptance of this new ideological thrust among rank-and-file members was limited.

74 Huey Newton, *To Die for the People: The Writings of Huey P. Newton* (New York: Random House, 1972), 201–3.

75 "Repression Breeds Resistance: Huey Newton Talks to Sechaba," box 2, folder, "MSS People's Revolutionary Intercommunalism," HPN Papers.

76 Newton, *To Die for the People*, 178.

77 George Katsiaficas, ed., *Vietnamese Documents: American and Vietnamese Views of the War* (New York: Routledge, 1992), 135–36.

78 "9/9/70 Memo to SAC SF from Director FBI," 3.

79 "Sworn Statement by John Mitchell dated April 15, 1976," box 80, HPN Papers.

80 "Counterintelligence Program against Huey P. Newton," folder, "Counterintelligence Program against HPN," 11, box 1, HPN Papers.

81 "Memo to Mr. W. C. Sullivan from G. C. Moore April 9, 1970," 1, box 80, HPN Papers.

82 "Memo to Mr. C. D. Brennan from Mr. G. C. Moore, October 19, 1970," box 80, HPN Papers.

83 "Letter to Comrade Huey from Eldridge, December 20, 1970," box 36, HPN Papers.

84 "FBI Memo from SF to FBI Director March 3, 1970," 5, box 80, HPN Papers.

85 "Memo to SAC San Francisco from FBI Director, 1/20/71," box 80, HPN Papers; "Joint Communique," folder, "Communication Sheets," box 2, HPN Papers.

86 "FBI Memo from SF to FBI Director March 3, 1970," 9, 7–8.

87 "FBI Memo to FBI Director from SAC San Francisco, January 18, 1971," 1, 4, box 80, HPN Papers.

88 Hilliard and Cole, *This Side of Glory*, 299–300.

89 "Interview with L.A. P.O.W.'s," 12, folder, "Black Liberation Army," box 41, HPN Papers.

90 Pratt was charged with a Santa Monica murder that had taken place in December 1968. He claimed he was in Oakland at the time, but as an expelled member, an enemy of the people identified with the Cleaver faction, he received no support from Newton, which seriously compromised his alibi. His case became a cause célèbre that many supporters felt exemplified the role of the FBI in destroying

the Panthers. Pratt was released in 1997, after twenty-seven years of imprisonment, when a judge vacated his case. He subsequently won a settlement in a
wrongful imprisonment lawsuit. See "Elmer G. Pratt, Jailed Panther Leader, Dies
at 63," *New York Times*, 3 June 2011; Jack Olsen, *Last Man Standing: The Tragedy
and Triumph of Geronimo Pratt* (New York: Doubleday, 2000).

91   Kit Kim Holder, "The History of the Black Panther Party, 1966–1977: A Curriculum Tool for Afrikan American Studies," EdD diss., University of Massachusetts,
1990, 57.

92   Holder, "The History of the Black Panther Party, 1966–1977," 49–61.

93   *Black Panther*, 28 February, 7 March, and 18 April 1970.

94   "Organizing Self-Defense Groups," *Black Panther*, 6 April 1970; "Organizing Self-
Defense Groups, Part 3," *Black Panther*, 18 April 1970.

95   "Organizing Self-Defense Groups, Part 3."

96   "On the Purge of Geronimo from the Black Panther Party," *Black Panther*,
23 January 1971.

97   "On the Contradictions within the Black Panther Party," *Right On*, 3 April 1971.

98   "Memo from FBI Director to SAC Los Angeles, 2/9/71," 1–3, box 80, HPN Papers.

99   "Open Letter to Weathermen Underground from Panther 21," *East Village Other*,
19 January 1971. In another letter they argued that their first letter was a specific
response to the Weathermen, published in a medium frequented by the white
radical community. "We mention no party or group by name; nor did we intend
any specific or single group. So to all the noise and fuss about it, all that we can
say is, if the shoe fits, wear it!" "Message to the 3rd World from the New York
'21,'" *East Village Other*, 9 March 1971.

100 "On Eldridge and New York, Press Release," 9 February 1971, box 36, HPN Papers.

101 "UPI News Service, SF," box 13, HPN Papers.

102 "Memo to Director from New York, February 1971," 1–2, box 80, HPN Papers.

103 "Memo to SAC San Francisco from Director, FBI, 2/10/71," box 80, HPN Papers.

104 "Informative Note dated 3/4/71," box 80, HPN Papers.

105 "Memo from SAC SF to Director, 3/16/71," 1, box 80, HPN Papers; "Memo to
Legat, Ottawa from FBI Director, 3/4/70," 4, box 80, HPN Papers.

106 "Memo dated 3/16/71 from SAC SF to FBI director," 1–2, box 80, HPN Papers.

107 "Memo to SAC San Francisco from Director, FBI, 3/10/71," 1, box 80, HPN Papers;
"Memo from SAC SF to FBI Director, 3/16/71," 2.

108 *Sun Reporter*, 13 March 1971; *Berkeley Barb*, 12–18 March 1971; "Internal Dispute
Rends Panthers," *New York Times*, 7 March 1971, in folder, "Algiers Defection,"
box 2, HPN Papers.

109 "Statement by Central Committee Young Lords Party," 2, folder, "On Eldridge
and New York," box 36, HPN Papers.

110 "On the Contradictions within the Black Panther Party."

111 "On the Contradictions within the Black Panther Party."

112 Members of eight of these chapters joined with other dissident Panthers to
create the Black Liberation Army. Bobby Seale, interview by author, 13 October
1997, tape recording, Oakland, California.

113 "Memo to: All Progressive Journalists and Underground Newspapers from the Black Panther Party," 1, folder, "Info from Bobby and Ericka," box 14, HPN Papers.

114 "On the Contradictions within the Black Panther Party."

115 "Dep. Field Marshall Robert Webb Murdered by Huey's Assassins," folder, "On Eldridge and New York," box 36, HPN Papers.

116 "Memo, to Director from San Francisco," 1, box 80, HPN Papers; "Memorandum from FBI Headquarters to San Francisco and Chicago Field Offices, 3/25/71," box 80, HPN Papers.

117 "Memo, to Director from San Francisco," 4.

118 In a memo dated 10 May 1971, the FBI suggested that its investigation of Charles Garry, a BPP lawyer, staunch supporter, and frequent speaker on the party's behalf at fund-raisers, "be continued to identify his contacts and determine his daily activity. In view of his Communist Party (CP) background, it is necessary to ascertain if he is maintaining contact with the CP and if the CP is exerting any influence over the BPP through Garry" (folder, "Charles Garry FBI files," box 16, HPN Papers). Bert Schneider, a wealthy producer for Columbia Pictures who, according to the FBI, put up as much as $25,000 to be used as bail money for Panthers in Los Angeles jails on felony charges, was also targeted. Don Freed, an author and Panther supporter described by the FBI as a leading figure in the New Left responsible for organizing support for the Panthers in Los Angeles, also faced scrutiny. "Memorandum to Director, FBI from SAC, New Haven 7/20/71," box 34, "David Hilliard Case Information," HPN Papers.

119 Newton, *To Die for the People*, 51–53.

120 Bobby Bowen, interview by author.

121 "The Real Black Panther Party," folder, "The Real Black Panther Party," box 15, HPN Papers.

5. "REVOLUTION IS A PROCESS"

1 "Requests to Start Black Panther Party Centers," folder, "Requests to Start Black Panther Party Centers," box 14, Huey P. Newton Foundation Papers, Special Collections, Green Library, Stanford University (hereafter HPN Papers).

2 "George Jackson, Will, August 21, 1971," box 37, HPN Papers.

3 Dan Berger, *Captive Nation: Black Prison Organizing in the Civil Rights Era* (Chapel Hill: University of North Carolina Press, 2016), 141–61.

4 "Report by United States Department of Justice, FBI, November 5, 1971," 9, folder, "Huey P. Newton FBI File," box 21, HPN Papers.

5 Emory Douglas, interview by author, 9 October 1997, tape recording, San Francisco.

6 James Boggs, "The Revolutionary Struggle for Black Power," in *The Black Seventies*, edited by Floyd B. Barbour (Boston: Porter Sargent, 1970), 44, 45.

7 "The Real Black Panther Party," folder, "The Real Black Panther Party," box 15, HPN Papers.

8   Memo to Central Headquarters, Black Panther Party, from Massachusetts State Chapter, Black Panther Party, folder, "General Reports from Chapter & Branches," box 14, HPN Papers; "Notes from Central Body Meeting, October 2, 1972," folder, "Central Committee Info," box 10, HPN Papers.

9   Emory Douglas, interview by author.

10 "Panther answers to interrogatories," 19–24, box 80, HPN Papers.

11 Emory Douglas, interview by author.

12 Bobby McCall, interview by author, 14 October 1997, tape recording, San Francisco.

13 "Notes from Central Body Meeting, October 2, 1972."

14 "Huey Newton talks to French reporters/HPN on party ideology," 20 September 1974, tape recording, HPN Papers.

15 Survival nurse image, *Black Panther*, 21 March 1970.

16 "Free Food Program," *CoEvolution Quarterly*, no. 3 (Fall 1974): 29.

17 "Budget, 1971," folder, "Black Panther Party No-Profit Corporations Including Black United Front," box 34, HPN Papers.

18 "Free Ambulance Program," *CoEvolution Quarterly*, no. 3 (Fall 1974): 25.

19 "Sickle Cell Anemia Research Foundation," *CoEvolution Quarterly*, no. 3 (Fall 1974), 23. See Alondra Nelson, *Body and Soul: The Black Panther Party and the Fight against Medical Discrimination* (Minneapolis: University of Minnesota Press, 2011), chapters 3, 4.

20 Keith Power, "Help for the Elderly: Black Panther Escorts," *San Francisco Chronicle*, 5 December 1972, in folder, "US v. Hilliard re: Wiretap," box 26, HPN Papers.

21 "Funding Proposal: Seniors Against a Fearful Environment (SAFE)," 5, box 7, HPN Papers.

22 "Son of Man Temple," box 74, HPN Papers.

23 "Son of Man Temple," *CoEvolution Quarterly*, no. 3 (Fall 1974): 17.

24 "Son of Man Temple," tape recording, box 74, HPN Papers; "Son of Man Temple, David DuBois," tape recording, box 74, HPN Papers.

25 "Son of Man Temple, 8/26/73," tape recording, box 74, HPN Papers.

26 "Community Learning Center," *CoEvolution Quarterly*, no. 3 (Fall 1974), 13.

27 Michele Russell, "Conversation with Ericka Huggins, Oakland, California, 4/20/77," 17, box 1, HPN Papers.

28 "Letter, November 20, 1970," folder, "Letters requesting information," box 22, HPN Papers.

29 "Agreement, October 7, 1970," box 17, HPN Papers.

30 Letter to Newton and Seale from David Lubell, folder, "Huey's Personal File," box 18, HPN Papers.

31 Folder, "Property-General," box 3, HPN Papers.

32 "General Articles, Re: Youth Institute," box 48, HPN Papers.

33 "Articles of Incorporation for EOC filed on March 26, 1973," 1, folder, "EOC," box 4, HPN Papers.

34 Folder, "Huey's Personal File," box 18, HPN Papers.

35 "The Black Panther," *CoEvolution Quarterly*, no. 3 (Fall 1974): 36.

36 "Agreement between the BPP and David DuBois," employment contract, dated 1 January 1973, folder, "Information Regarding Our Paper," box 11, HPN Papers.

37 Memo dated 23 January 1973, folder, "Information Regarding Our Newspaper," box 11, HPN Papers; memo dated 2 February 1973, folder, "Information Regarding Our Newspaper," box 11, HPN Papers.

38 Folder, "Interviews," 27–28, box 5, HPN Papers.

39 Huey Newton, *To Die for the People: The Writings of Huey P. Newton* (New York: Random House, 1972), 53.

40 Billy X. Jennings, "Central Headquarters of the Black Panther Party 1971–1972," It's About Time: Black Panther Party Legacy and Alumni, accessed December 2015, http://www.itsabouttimebpp.com.

41 Newton, *To Die for the People*, 74.

42 Newton, *To Die for the People*, 68.

43 Newton, *To Die for the People*, 103.

44 Newton, *To Die for the People*, 107–8.

45 Bob Avakian, "Rise and Fall of the Panthers: End of the Black Power Era," *Workers Vanguard*, no. 4 (January 1972): 4–6; Charlene Mitchell, "Communist Party Defends Angela against Panther Party," *California Voice*, 28 September 1972.

46 Russell, "Conversation with Ericka Huggins," 12–13.

47 Folder, "Letters Requesting Information," box 22, HPN Papers.

48 Folder, "General requests for material and/or specific information," box 24, HPN Papers.

49 Letter to Huey Newton from Jane Huang, 21 May 1971, 1, folder, "Info on Churches," box 46, HPN Papers.

50 Letter from Sister Imagene Williams, 1–2, folder, "Info on Churches," box 46, HPN Papers.

51 "Panther Protection: Party Will Start Escort Service. Officials Ponder Motives," *Sacramento Bee*, 10 December 1972, in folder, "US v. Hilliard re: Wiretap," box 26, HPN Papers.

52 "Revolution Is the Solution," folder, "Standard Support letters sent out," box 22, HPN Papers, punctuation amended.

53 Manning Marable describes the sole-proprietorship, undercapitalized businesses run by black marginal worker-entrepreneurs in *How Capitalism Underdeveloped Black America* (Boston: South End Press, 1983), 156.

54 Unaddressed letter beginning "In May 1971, Cal Pak requested the assistance," folder, "CALPAC," box 45, HPN Papers.

55 "Black Capitalism Re-analyzed: Theoretical Analysis and Its Practical Application," 9 August 1971, folder, "MSS People's Revolutionary Intercommunalism," box 2, HPN Papers; Newton, *To Die for the People*, 110.

56 "Press Conference," 1–2, folder, "CALPAC," box 45, HPN Papers.

57 Newton, *To Die for the People*, 111.

58 "Attention Neighbor," folder, "CALPAC," box 45, HPN Papers.

59 "People's Boycott," folder, "CALPAC," box 45, HPN Papers.

60 "Ad Hoc Committee Meeting," 7, folder, "CALPAC," box 45, HPN Papers.

61 "Weekly Boycott Statistics," folder, "CALPAC," box 45, HPN Papers.

62 "For Immediate Release, January 15, 1972," folder, "CALPAC," box 45, HPN Papers.

63 "Memorandum of Agreement," 1, folder, "CALPAC," box 45, HPN Papers.

64 "Panthers to Help Store They Picketed," *San Francisco Chronicle*, 17 January 1972, in folder, "Articles Regarding Boycott," box 2, HPN Papers.

65 "Support the Businesses That Support Our Community," folder, "CALPAC," box 45, HPN Papers.

66 Letter to Huey P. Newton from California State Attorney General Evelle J. Younger, 13 March 1972, folder, "United Black Fund," box 34, HPN Papers.

67 "Letter to Department of Justice from Charles Garry," folder, "United Black Fund," box 34, HPN Papers.

68 "BPP Non-Profit Corporation Including Black United Front," box 34, HPN Papers.

69 "Articles of Incorporation," folder, "United Black Fund," box 7, HPN Papers.

70 "All Power to the People," 10 August 1972, folder, "United Black Fund," box 7, HPN Papers.

71 "The United Black Fund, Inc., Fundraising Activity," 2 October 1972, folder, "United Black Fund," box 7, HPN Papers.

72 "Ad Hoc Committee Meeting," folder, "CALPAC," box 45, HPN Papers.

73 "Letter to White Businesses," 2, folder, "CALPAC," box 45, HPN Papers.

74 Letter from Matsuko Ishida, 8 May 1973, folder, "Correspondence w/Committee to Support the Black Panther Party from Japan," box 85, HPN Papers.

75 Newton, *To Die for the People*, 56.

76 Amar Casey, interview by author, 28 October 1997, tape recording, Oakland, California.

77 Folder, "General Reports from Chapters and Branches," box 13, HPN Papers.

78 "Daily Report," folder, "General Info we have printed," box 14, HPN Papers.

79 See folder, "News of the Day," August 1972–February 1973, box 14, HPN Papers.

80 See box 14, HPN Papers.

81 "Memo to All Comrades of the Central Body, August 16, 1972," folder, "Central Committee Info," box 10, HPN Papers.

82 "Memo re: Agenda Items to be discussed," 22 May 1973, folder, "Central Committee Info," box 10, HPN Papers; "Notes from Central Body Meeting October 2, 1972."

83 "Agenda for Meeting with Responsible Comrades," 21 July 1972, folder, "Central Committee Info," box 10, HPN Papers.

84 "Notes from Central Body Meeting October 2, 1972."

85 Memo, 16 August 1972, folder, "Central Committee Info," box 10, HPN Papers.

86 "Innerparty Memorandum," 18 October 1972, box 14, HPN Papers. The following memos are also in box 14.

87 Bobby McCall, interview by author.

88 Ericka Huggins, "Servant: Insights and Poems," March 1972, box 14, HPN Papers.

89 Huggins, "Servant: Insights and Poems."

90 Letter to Comrade June from "your comrade, Paul," 14 March 1973, folder, "Legal Information: Party Cases," box 21, HPN Papers.

91 Memo from Joan Kelley to Comrade Servant, 31 October 1972, folder, "General Reports from Chapters and Branches," box 14, HPN Papers.

92 "Memo to all members of the Central Body August 28, 1973," folder, "Central Committee Info," box 10, HPN Papers.

93 "Memo to the Servant from the Editing Cadre," 3 January 1973, folder, "Information Regarding our Newspaper," box 11, HPN Papers.

94 See Innerparty Memoranda #1–#14, 29 July 1972–1 November 1972, box 14, HPN Papers.

95 "1973 Review Quiz No. 2," folder, "Central Committee Info," box 10, HPN Papers.

96 Skills survey, folder, "Central Committee Info," box 10, HPN Papers.

97 "Memo to Comrade June from Comrade Ericka," folder, "Central Committee Info," box 10, HPN Papers.

98 "Innerparty Memorandum #10," 4 October 1972, box 14, HPN Papers.

99 Reporters Transcript of Proceedings, 1 October 1976, in "The People of the State of California, Plaintiff vs. Stephen Mitchell Bingham, Hugo A. Pinell, John L. Spain, Luis N. Talamzntez, Fleeta Drumgo, David Johnson and Willie Tate, defendants," folder, "Johnny Spain," box 18, HPN Papers.

100 Memo from Joan Kelley to Central Committee, 22 May to 30 May [1972?], folder, "Legal Information—Party cases," box 21, HPN Papers.

101 "Inner Party Memorandum," 31 January 1974, box 14, HPN Papers.

102 Memo, 19 November 1973, folder, "Central Committee Info," box 10, HPN Papers.

103 "Sickle Cell Anemia Workers Harassed," *Black Panther*, 19 January 1974.

104 "Innerparty Memorandum #1, July 29, 1972," box 14, HPN Papers.

105 Steve Long, "The Rebirth of the Panthers," *Los Angeles Free Press*, 21 July 1972.

106 "The Black Panther Party Program, March 29, 1972 platform," folder, "Misc Articles," box 41, HPN Papers.

107 "The Black Panther Party Program, March 29, 1972 platform," 11.

108 Bobby Seale, *Seize the Time: The Story of the Black Panther Party and Huey Newton* (New York: Random House, 1968), 67.

109 "The Black Panther Party Program, March 29, 1972 platform," 11.

110 Seale, *Seize the Time*, 67–68.

111 "The Black Panther Party Program, March 29, 1972 platform," 11.

112 "The Black Panther Party Program, March 29, 1972 platform," 11.

113 "The Black Panther Party Program, March 29, 1972 platform," 11.

6. THE POLITICS OF SURVIVAL

1 Manning Marable, *Race, Reform and Rebellion: The Second Reconstruction in Black America, 1945–1990* (Jackson: University Press of Mississippi, 1991), 113; "The Black Scholar Book Reviews," *Black Scholar* 4, no. 1 (1972): 53.

2 Marable, *Race, Reform and Rebellion*, 121.

3   Letter to Robert N. C. Nix, U.S. congressman from Philadelphia, from Huey
    Newton, 12 April 1972, 1–2, folder, "Black Congressional Caucus," box 46,
    Huey P. Newton Foundation Papers, Special Collections, Green Library, Stanford
    University (hereafter HPN Papers).

4   "National Black Political Agenda," 1–2, folder, "National Black Political Conven-
    tion," box 7, HPN Papers.

5   "Black Politics in the 1970s," *Black Scholar* 4, no. 1 (1972): 22.

6   Folder, "National Black Political Convention," box 7, HPN Papers.

7   "West Magazine Interview with Huey P. Newton by Digby Diehl," *Los Angeles
    Times*, 6 August 1972, box 15, HPN Papers.

8   "Panthers Give Food to Poor," *San Francisco Examiner*, 30 March 1972.

9   "Central Committee Report," 6 March 1972, folder, "Black Community Survival
    Conference," box 14, HPN Papers.

10 "Memo re: Donations for Black Community Survival Conference,"
    17 March 1972, folder, "United Black Fund," box 34, HPN Papers.

11 "United Black Fund," box 34, HPN Papers; letter from Father Neil, 8 March 1972,
    folder, "Black Community Survival Conference," box 14, HPN Papers.

12 Steve Long, "The Rebirth of the Panthers," *Los Angeles Free Press*, 21 July 1972.
    The 8 April 1972 issue of the *Black Panther* estimated that nearly 16,000 people,
    mostly black, attended the conference; 11,120 registered to vote, and 13,282
    were tested for sickle cell anemia. However, an internal memo revealed a much
    lower figure: 2,071 were registered to vote and 3,687 were tested. This memo
    attributed low voter registration figures to the fact that on Wednesday a lot of
    young people attended who were too young to register and on the other nights
    a lot of people claimed to already be registered. See "Party Members Who Are
    Voter Registrars," folder, "Black Community Survival Conference," box 14, HPN
    Papers. In a memo Ericka Huggins stated that they registered a total of 2,725
    people to vote at the two conferences. See Memo from Ericka Huggins to the
    Servant, folder, "Voter Registration and Elections Committee," box 7, HPN
    Papers.

13 "Party Members Who Are Voter Registrars."

14 Speech for Voter Registration Conference, Oakland, 1, folder, "Black Community
    Survival Conference," box 14, HPN Papers.

15 Letter from Martin Kenner to Huey Newton, [1971?], folder, "Rev. Rep. in U.S.
    and Canada, Western Europe, e.g. China," box 41, HPN Papers.

16 "Black Panther Party Delegation's Book re: People's Republic of China upon
    Return," box 46, HPN Papers.

17 Press release, folder, "The Servants Visit to the People's Republic of China,"
    box 44, HPN Papers.

18 "Requests to Start Black Panther Party Centers," folder, "Requests to Start Black
    Panther Party Centers," box 14, HPN Papers.

19 "Innerparty Memorandum #13," 25 October 1972, 2, box 14, HPN Papers.

20 Bo Burlingham, "Huey Newton's Revival Meeting in Oakland," *Ramparts*,
    September 1972, box 44, HPN Papers.

21 Bob Manning, "The Black Panthers Anti-war Survival Conference," *Los Angeles Free Press*, 21 July 1972.

22 "Survival Petition," folder, "Anti-war African Liberation Voter Registration," box 44, HPN Papers.

23 "From the Anti-war, African Liberation Survival Conference," folder, "Mailing lists: before 1976," box 17, HPN Papers.

24 "Press Release," folder, "General Information Regarding Oakland, CA," box 41, HPN Papers.

25 Elaine Brown, *A Taste of Power: A Black Woman's Story* (New York: Pantheon Books, 1992), 324.

26 "Panthers Elected to Berkeley Anti-poverty Program," box 2, HPN Papers.

27 "Agenda for Meeting with Responsible Comrades 6/29/72," 1, folder, "Central Committee Info," box 10, HPN Papers.

28 "Bobby Seale Campaign Info," box 14A, HPN Papers.

29 "Innerparty Memorandum #3," box 14, HPN Papers; "Panther Protection: Party Will Start Escort Service. Officials Ponder Motives," *Sacramento Bee*, 10 December 1972, in folder, "US v. Hilliard re: Wiretap," box 26, HPN Papers; "Panthers Elected to Berkeley Anti-poverty Program."

30 "Panthers Win Berkeley OK," *Oakland Tribune*, 23 June 1972.

31 "Bobby Seale," folder, "General Information Regarding Oakland, California," box 41, HPN Papers; "The Black Panthers Anti-war Survival Conference," *Los Angeles Free Press*, 21 July 1972.

32 "Confidential Memo to Store Managers," folder, "General Information Regarding Oakland, California," box 41, HPN Papers.

33 "Memo dated September 25, 1972 from Concerned Citizens Committee, Inc.," folder, "Bobby Seale Campaign Info," box 14, HPN Papers.

34 "The Black Scholar Interviews: Bobby Seale," *Black Scholar* 4, no. 1 (1972): 7–16.

35 Press release, 30 January 1973, folder, "Bobby Seale Campaign Info," box 14A, HPN Papers.

36 "Black Panther Party, plaintiff, vs. Granny Goose Foods, Inc, et al., defendants," folder, "Black Panther Party v. Granny Goose," box 14, HPN Papers.

37 "Stipulation of Dismissal," folder, "Black Panther Party v. Granny Goose," box 14, HPN Papers.

38 "Cooperative Housing," *CoEvolution Quarterly*, no. 3 (Fall 1974): 40.

39 "Cooperative Housing," 40.

40 "Bobby Seale and Elaine Brown Unveil Fourteen Point Program for Economic Development of Oakland," 5 March 1973, folder, "Bobby Seale Campaign Info," box 14A, HPN Papers.

41 "Organizing a People's Campaign," *CoEvolution Quarterly*, no. 3 (Fall 1974): 53, 60–100.

42 "Notes from Central Body Meeting October 2, 1972," folder, "Central Committee Info," box 10, HPN Papers.

43 "Organizing a People's Campaign," 53, 60–100.

44 "Benefit Dance," folder, "Bobby Seale Campaign Info," box 14A, HPN Papers; "Community Committee to Elect Bobby Seale and Elaine Brown to City Offices of Oakland," folder, "Bobby Seale Campaign Info," box 14A, HPN Papers.

45 "Memo to Central Body re: Methods of Fundraising," folder, "Merritt College," box 7, HPN Papers.

46 "Organizing a People's Campaign," 54.

47 "Memo to Comrade Huey from Area 3/Russell Washington 24 July–31 July," folder, "Section Progress Reports," box 2, HPN Papers; "Daily Precinct Work Report," folder, "General Information we have printed," box 14, HPN Papers.

48 "Precinct Work Instruction Sheet," folder, "Voter Registration Elections Committee," box 7, HPN Papers.

49 "Report to Comrade Servant from Ericka Huggins 31 July 1972," folder, "Voter Registration Elections Committee," box 7, HPN Papers.

50 "Voter Registration Counts," folder, "Voter Registration Elections Committee," box 7, HPN Papers.

51 "Showdown in Oakland: Bobby Seale and Otho Green Battle to Become Mayor," *Jet*, 12 April 1973, in folder, "Bobby Seale for Mayor of Oakland," box 8, HPN Papers.

52 "Oakland: A Base of Operation. Part XXV: The Port of No Returns," *Black Panther*, 13 January 1973.

53 "Mass Voter Registration Meeting St. Augustine's Church 2/2/73," tape recording, box 74, HPN Papers.

54 "Vote for Survival," folder, "Bobby Seale Campaign Info," box 14A, HPN Papers.

55 "Re: White Community to Elect Bobby Seale and Elaine Brown," folder, "Bobby Seale Campaign Info," box 14A, HPN Papers.

56 "Bobby Seale Calls upon Oakland City Council to Become the First City in California to Provide Bilingual (English/Spanish) Ballots for Local Elections," folder, "Bobby Seale Campaign Info," box 14A, HPN Papers.

57 "Press Release, 29 March 1973," folder, "Bobby Seale Campaign Info," box 14A, HPN Papers.

58 "Memo from Elbert Howard, date 12/30/72 to Servant re: Section Report," folder, "Section Progress Reports," box 2, HPN Papers.

59 Flyer, folder, "Bobby Seale Campaign Info," box 14A, HPN Papers.

60 "The Black Scholar Interviews: Bobby Seale," 8–9.

61 "Memo from Elbert Howard re: North Peralta Community College 8/28/73," folder, "Merritt College," box 7, HPN Papers.

62 "Merritt Bobby Seale and Elaine Brown Landslide Election Committee," folder, "Bobby Seale Campaign Info," box 14A, HPN Papers.

63 "Reasons for Formation of Black Student Alliance (BSA)," folder, "Merritt College," box 7, HPN Papers.

64 Panthers James Mott and Michael Torrence, Laney College students, served as chair and cochair of the Alliance. See "Memo to Comrade from James Mott, October 4, 1972," folder, "Merritt College," box 7, HPN Papers; "Black Student Alliance," *CoEvolution Quarterly*, no. 3 (Fall 1974): 32.

65 Mailer, folder, "Bobby Seale Campaign Info," box 14, HPN Papers.

66 "Agenda for Meeting with Responsible Comrades 6/9/72," folder, "Central Committee Info," box 10, HPN Papers.

67 "The Black Scholar Interviews: Bobby Seale," 15.

68 "Seale's 'Revolt' Plans," *San Francisco Examiner*, 12 November 1972.

69 Brown, *A Taste of Power*, 327.

70 Letter from Japanese Committee to Support the Black Panther Party to Huey Newton, 8 May 1973, folder, "Correspondence with Committee to Support the Black Panther Party from Japan," box 85, HPN Papers.

71 Letter from Jørgen Dragsdahl to Huey Newton, [1973], folder, "Denmark Trip Info," box 40, HPN Papers.

72 "Election Victory Statement," folder, "Bobby Seale Campaign Info," box 14, HPN Papers.

73 "Run Off Election, May 17, 1973," *Oakland Tribune*, 18 April 1973.

74 Brown, *A Taste of Power*, 334.

75 "Section Progress Reports, July 23, 1973," 2, box 2, HPN Papers.

76 "Section Progress Reports," box 2, HPN Papers.

77 Memo to Comrade Huey from Area 3/Russell Washington 24 July–31 July," folder, "Section Progress Reports," box 2, HPN Papers.

78 "Section Progress Reports, September 6, 1973," box 2, HPN Papers.

79 Veronica "Roni" Hagopian, interview by author, 23 October 1997, tape recording, San Francisco.

80 Emory Douglas, interview by author, 9 October 1997, tape recording, San Francisco.

81 Letter from Johnny Stake, 3 May 1973, folder, "Central Committee Information," box 10, HPN Papers.

82 "Memo from Melainee King, March 10, 1973," folder, "General Reports from Chapters and Branches," box 14, HPN Papers.

83 "People's Free Medical Research Health Clinics," *CoEvolution Quarterly*, no. 3 (Fall 1974): 22.

84 "Health Cadre Reports," box 36, HPN Papers.

85 "People's Free Medical Research Health Clinics," 22.

86 "Health Cadre Reports," box 36, HPN Papers.

87 Memo, 27 March–5 April 1974, folder, "Health Cadre Reports," box 36, HPN Papers.

88 "Agenda Items to be discussed June 13, 1974," folder, "Central Committee Info," box 10, HPN Papers; "Innerparty Memorandum, March 21, 1974," box 14, HPN Papers.

89 "Innerparty Memorandum, April 11, 1974," box 14, HPN Papers.

90 "Huey P. Newton Testimony," 60, box 6, HPN Papers.

91 Bobby Bowen, interview by author, 22 October 1997, tape recording, Oakland, California.

92 See memos and letter, folder, "Denmark Trip Info," box 40, HPN Papers.

93 See full text of Newton's papers in folder, "General Papers, 1973–4," box 49, HPN Papers.

94 Steve McCutchen, interview by author, 11 October 1997, tape recording, Oakland, California.

95 "Newton Is Arrested for Assault," *Daily Independent Journal*, 28 April 1972; "2 More Charges against Newton," *San Francisco Chronicle*, 5 May 1972; "Marlon Scott vs. The Servant," box 80, HPN Papers.

96 Bobby Seale, interview by author, 13 October 1997, tape recording, Oakland, California.

97 "Memo to: All Centers/Facilities/Survival Programs in the Bay Area from Roosevelt Hilliard re: Drinking and Smoking (marijuana), February 28, 1973," folder, "Directives," box 14, HPN Papers.

98 "BPP Possession of Firearms," box 68, HPN Papers.

99 "Memo to Central Body from Brenda Bay," folder, "Central Committee Info," box 10, HPN Papers.

100 Darron Perkins, interview by author, 23 October 1997, telephone.

101 Brown, *A Taste of Power*, 321.

102 Thomas McCreary, interview by author, 25 September 1997, tape recording, Brooklyn.

103 Bobby McCall, interview by author, 14 October 1997, tape recording, San Francisco.

104 Amar Casey, interview by author, 28 October 1997, tape recording, Oakland, California.

105 Bobby Bowen, interview by author.

106 "Memo to All Coordinators/General Cadre from Central Committee of the Black Panther Party, March 31, 1973," folder, "Central Committee Information," box 10, HPN Papers.

107 Brown, *A Taste of Power*, 320.

108 Veronica "Roni" Hagopian, interview by author.

109 Terry Cotton, interview by author, 26 October 1997, tape recording, Oakland, California.

110 Bobby Bowen, interview by author.

111 David Horowitz, "Some Thoughts on Party Structure," 1, box 47, HPN Papers. Horowitz repudiated the Panthers in the mid-1970s and in 2016 leads a conservative think tank. See David Horowitz, *Radical Son: A Generational Odyssey* (New York: Free Press, 1997).

112 Horowitz, "Some Thoughts on Party Structure," 1.

113 Terry Cotton, interview by author.

114 Emory Douglas, interview by author.

115 See "Innerparty Memorandum," 5 April 1973–24 January 1974, box 14, HPN Papers.

116 Emory Douglas, interview by author.

117 "Innerparty Memorandum, January 10, 1973," box 14, HPN Papers.

118 Brown, *A Taste of Power*, 320.

119 Brown, *A Taste of Power*, 320–21, 353.

120 "Notes, Central Body meeting, March 6, 1974," folder, "Central Committee Info," box 10, HPN Papers.

121 Letter to Huey Newton from David Hilliard, folder, "Misc: David at Vacaville," box 62, HPN Papers. Newton's behavior had become increasingly erratic;

see "Letter from June Hilliard to David Hilliard Thursday March 1," folder, "Correspondence to David Hilliard re: expulsion," box 68, HPN Papers.

122 See David Hilliard and Lewis Cole, *This Side of Glory: The Autobiography of David Hilliard and the Story of the Black Panther Party* (Boston: Little, Brown, 1993), 332, 372–73.

123 Letter to Huey Newton from David Hilliard, folder, "Misc: David at Vacaville," box 62, HPN Papers.

124 Bill Jennings, interview by author, 1 November 1997, tape recording, Sacramento.

125 Bill Jennings, interview by author.

126 "Inspection Check List," folder, "Central Committee Info," box 10, HPN Papers.

127 Bobby Seale, interview by author.

128 Terry Cotton, interview by author.

129 Amar Casey, interview by author.

130 Bobby Bowen, interview by author.

131 "Federal Bureau of Investigation, Date of Transcription November 20, 1973," folder, "Black Panther Party Possession of Firearms," box 68, HPN Papers.

132 Memo, 26 November 1973, 13, folder, "Black Panther Party Possession of Firearms," box 68, HPN Papers.

133 Brown, *A Taste of Power*, 332–33, 329.

134 Ollie A. Johnson III, "Explaining the Demise of the Black Panther Party: The Role of Internal Factors," in *The Black Panther Party (Reconsidered)*, edited by Charles Jones (Baltimore: Black Classic Press, 1998), 407.

135 Bobby Bowen, interview by author.

136 "Position Paper," box 46, HPN Papers.

137 Memorandum to SAC, San Francisco, from Supervisor Gary L. Penrith, folder, "Black Panther Party Possession of Firearms," box 68, HPN Papers.

138 "Pat Hilliard Tells Huey Newton That (David) Lubell," box 13, HPN Papers.

139 "Telephone Communications in the Black Panther Party," folder, "Central Committee Information," box 10, HPN Papers.

140 "Huey P. Newton Testimony," 16, box 6, HPN Papers.

141 "Declaration of Joan Kelley," box 6, HPN Papers.

142 "Declaration of Joan Kelley," box 6, HPN Papers.

143 Steve McCutchen, interview by author.

144 *Justice for Huey Newsletter* 1, no. 1 (1974), folder, "Newton, Huey. Tax Liability Matter," box 30, HPN Papers.

145 "Complaint for Declaratory and Injunctive Relief," 2, folder, "Hilliard, David. Prison Letters 4/1/72," box 25, HPN Papers.

146 "Complaint for Declaratory and Injunctive Relief."

147 "Panthers Lose Bid against IRS," *San Francisco Chronicle*, 16 April 1975, in folder, "Freedom of Information Act," box 4, HPN Papers.

148 "At San Francisco, California," box 80, HPN Papers.

149 "Report by George R. Zeigler, San Francisco Office 1/7/75," folder, "Huey P. Newton Legal Brief," box 18, HPN Papers.

150 "FBI memo to Director from SAC San Francisco, 10/2/74," folder, "Huey P. Newton Legal Brief," box 18, HPN Papers.

151 Ericka Huggins, interview by author, 21 October 1997, tape recording, Oakland, California.

152 Brown, *A Taste of Power*, 192.

153 "FBI memo to Director from SAC San Francisco, 10/2/74."

154 Brown, *A Taste of Power*, 355.

155 "We're Going to Eat at the Machinery Piece by Piece," *Common Sense*, 16 November 1976, 5.

156 Brown, *A Taste of Power*, 363–67.

157 Folder, "Panthers and Sickle Cell Anemia," 106, box 80, HPN Papers.

158 Brown refused to change her vote to Jimmy Carter after Jerry Brown released his delegates to Carter at convention. She criticized Carter's supporters and argued that the Democratic Party had abandoned black people and that black people should build an independent party of their own. Quote from John Jacobs, "Local Demo Delegates Reminisce," *Daily Californian*, 23 July 1976, 3, in folder, "General Articles on the Black Panther Party," box 4, HPN Papers.

159 "Council Praises New Business Panel," *Oakland Tribune*, 1 September 1976, in folder, "Freedom of Information Act," box 4, HPN Papers.

160 Michael K. Martin, "Panther Chairperson Brown Accepts OCED Appointment," *California Voice*, 11 December 1976, in folder, "Grove-Shafter City Center Project," box 4, HPN Papers.

161 Martin, "Panther Chairperson Brown Accepts OCED Appointment."

162 "Grove-Shafter Settlement," *Oakland Tribune*, 18 October 1975; Harre W. Demoro, "Relocation Funds Ordered: Grove Shafter gets a Break," *Oakland Tribune*, 7 February 1976.

163 "Grove-Shafter Clears Big Hurdle," *Oakland Tribune*, 6 September 1978.

164 "Consolidated Application Info./State Department of Education Comprehensive Program Planning," folder, "Wilson's Donation List," box 17, HPN Papers; Robert O. Self, *American Babylon: Race and the Struggle for Postwar Oakland* (Princeton, NJ: Princeton University Press, 2003), 309–16.

165 "We're Going to Eat at the Machinery Piece by Piece," 5.

166 Amar Casey, interview by author.

7. "I AM WE"

1 "Justice for Huey P. Newton and the Black Panther Party," box 41, Huey P. Newton Foundation Papers, Special Collections, Green Library, Stanford University (hereafter HPN Papers).

2 Committee for Justice for Huey P. Newton and the Black Panther Party, letterhead, folder, "Committee for Justice for Huey P. Newton, Folder 1," box 42, HPN Papers; memo from Gwen Fountaine, 23 August 1977, folder, "Justice for Huey Thank You Letters," box 28, HPN Papers.

3   *I Am We*, no. 4 (Summer 1976), folder, "Committee for Justice for Huey P. Newton, Folder 1," box 42, HPN Papers.

4   *I Am We*, 2.

5   "Justice for Huey P. Newton and the Black Panther Party," box 41, HPN Papers.

6   Elaine Brown, "Committee for Justice for HPN," *Counterspy*, Spring 1976, in box 42, HPN Papers.

7   "Civil Action No. 76-2205, Jury Trial Demanded," box 80, HPN Papers.

8   Jay Peterzell, "COINTELPRO in Court," *Center for National Security Studies* 4, no. 3 (1978), in box 65, HPN Papers.

9   Minutes from Central Body Meeting, 10 July 1977, folder, "Central Body Meetings," box 5, HPN Papers.

10 Memo from Lulla Hudson to Gwen Newton, 17 September 1977, folder, "Justice for Huey Thank You Letters," box 28, HPN Papers.

11 Memo to Elaine from Molly, 17 March 1977, folder, "Justice for Huey Thank You Letters," box 28, HPN Papers.

12 "Committee for Justice—Some Ideas," folder, "Justice for Huey Thank You Letters," box 28, HPN Papers.

13 Memo to Huey and Gwen from Molly, folder, "Committee for Justice for Huey P. Newton, Folder 1," box 42, HPN Papers.

14 Ericka Huggins, interview by author, 21 October 1997, tape recording, Oakland, California.

15 Directive, 11 August 1977, folder, "Directives," box 4, HPN Papers.

16 "Elaine Resigns from the Black Panther Party," box 35, HPN Papers.

17 Elaine Brown, *A Taste of Power: A Black Woman's Story* (New York: Pantheon Books, 1992), 448–50.

18 See newspaper articles in folder, "Articles regarding 1977 trials," box 4, HPN Papers.

19 "Elaine Resigns from the Black Panther Party."

20 Letter to EOC from Phyllis Jackson, folder, "EOC," box 14, HPN Papers.

21 Steve McCutchen, interview by author, 11 October 1997, tape recording, Oakland, California.

22 "Panther Chief Quits for Personal Reasons," *San Francisco Examiner*, 22 November 1977, in box 4, HPN Papers.

23 "Black Panther Party Falters: Leadership Crisis," *Oakland Tribune*, 27 November 1977, in folder, "Articles regarding 1977 Trials," box 4, HPN Papers.

24 "Elaine Resigns from the Black Panther Party."

25 "Panther Furor Spurs Audit by City," *Oakland Tribune*, 4 November 1977, in folder, "Articles regarding 1977 Trials," box 4, HPN Papers.

26 Letter from Lionel Wilson to Elaine Brown, 1 November 1977, folder, "OCS Weekly Reports," box 4, HPN Papers.

27 "Justice for Huey," 1 January 1968, folder, "Committee for Justice for Huey P. Newton, Folder 1," box 42, HPN Papers.

28 Newton's Testimony, box 6, HPN Papers.

29 "Declaration of Huey P. Newton," folder, "Court Transcript," box 21, HPN Papers.

30 "Declaration of Joan Kelley August 1977," 149, box 6, HPN Papers.

31 "Declaration of Elaine Brown August 1977," box 6, HPN Papers.

32 "Declaration of Fred Hiestand," box 6, HPN Papers.

33 Notes, folder, "Montclarion Article," box 5, HPN Papers.

34 "East Oakland Ghetto Blooms with Growth of Black Panther School," *Jet*, 5 February 1976, in folder, "OCS Brochure," box 4, HPN Papers.

35 "29 July 1977 Corporate Overview EOC," folder, "EOC," box 4, HPN Papers.

36 Notes, folder, "OCS Montclarion Article," box 5, HPN Papers.

37 "Oakland Community School, Instructor Handbook," box 66, HPN Papers.

38 "29 July 1977 Corporate Overview EOC."

39 "Oakland Community Learning Center News, November 1979," folder, "Oakland Community School Weekly Reports," box 4, HPN Papers.

40 Flier dated 23 November 1976, file "Misc Articles," box 41, HPN Papers.

41 "Panther Furor Spurs Audit by City"; "Audit Report as of Oct 31, 1977," folder, "EOC," box 4, HPN Papers.

42 "Audit Report as of Oct 31, 1977."

43 "Audit Report as of Oct 31, 1977."

44 "29 July 1977 Corporate Overview EOC."

45 "29 July 1977 Corporate Overview EOC."

46 Ericka Huggins, untitled poem, folder, "Ericka's Poems," box 5, HPN Papers. Huggins said she did not give Newton this poem until several months later because she was afraid he would not understand it at the time.

47 "Huey P. Newton speaks to BPP Members on Return to Cuba 8/13/77," cassette tape, HPN Papers; responses to Newton's inquiry are in the folder "Reports on Comrades," box 14, HPN Papers.

48 Steve McCutchen, interview by author.

49 "Memo to: Huey from: Dale re: Women in the Perty [*sic*]," 4 October 1977, folder, "Reports on Comrades," box 14, HPN Papers.

50 "Memo to: Huey from: Dale re: Women in the Perty."

51 "Memo to: the Servant from: Comrade JoNina Abron," 10 August 1977, folder, "Reports on Comrades," box 14, HPN Papers.

52 "Memo to: the Servant from: Comrade JoNina Abron."

53 Memo from Roni Hagopian, 21 August 1977, folder, "Reports on Comrades," box 14, HPN Papers.

54 Memo from Amar Casey and Melvin Dickson, 12 August 1977, folder, "Reports on Comrades," box 14, HPN Papers.

55 "Memo to: the Servant from: Arlene Clark," 9 August 1977, folder, "Reports on Comrades," box 14, HPN Papers.

56 See Letter about Comradely Criticism, 1 May 1979, folder, "Reports on Comrades," box 14, HPN Papers.

57 "Central Body Info," box 5, HPN Papers.

58 "Inner Party Memorandum," 31 March 1978, box 4, HPN Papers.

59 "Editing and Distribution Report, August 4, 1978," folder, "The Black Panther Party Newspaper," box 35, HPN Papers.

60 "Memo to All Coordinators from JoNina" 11 April 1978, folder, "Innerparty Memorandum," box 4, HPN Papers.

61 Memo to Huey from JoNina, 2 October 1978, folder, "Innerparty Memorandum," box 4, HPN Papers.

62 "Editing and Distribution Report, August 4, 1978."

63 "Memo to Huey from Amar Casey," 31 July 1978, folder, "Innerparty Memorandum," box 4, HPN Papers,

64 James Abron, interview by author, 6 October 1997, tape recording, Oakland, California.

65 "Memo to Huey from Ericka re: Collective Parents meeting," box 4, HPN Papers.

66 Amar Casey, interview by author, 28 October 1997, tape recording, Oakland, California.

67 "Memo to Huey from Austin A and Steve E," folder, "Innerparty Memorandum," box 4, HPN Papers.

68 "Memo from JoNina to Huey," 8 May 1978, folder, "The Black Panther Party Newspaper," box 35, HPN Papers.

69 "Memo to Huey from Austin," 30 March 1978, folder, "Innerparty Memorandum," box 4, HPN Papers.

70 "Memo from JoNina to Huey/Larry," 9 January 1979, folder, "The Black Panther Party Newspaper," box 35, HPN Papers.

71 "Memo to Newton," 30 January 1979, folder, "The Black Panther Party Newspaper," box 35, HPN Papers.

72 Report, 11 July 1979, folder, "OCS Weekly Reports," box 4, HPN Papers.

73 "Memo from JoNina to Huey," 7 June 1979, folder, "The Black Panther Party Newspaper," box 35, HPN Papers.

74 Memo to Sheldon Otis from Elaine Brown, 25 July 1977, folder, "Bay Area Properties," box 30, HPN Papers.

75 "OCLC Meeting, 1 September 1979," folder, "OCS Weekly Reports," box 4, HPN Papers.

76 Bobby McCall, interview by author, 14 October 1997, tape recording, San Francisco.

77 "Party Members (as of Feb 15, 1979)," folder, "Central Body Meetings," box 5, HPN Papers.

78 "Oakland Community Learning Center Meeting," 24 January 1979, folder, "EOC," box 4, HPN Papers.

79 Folder, "EOC," box 4, HPN Papers.

80 "OCLC Mtg notes, 2/3/79," folder, "EOC," box 4, HPN Papers.

81 "OCLC Mtg notes, 2/3/79."

82 Memo from OCS to Huey, 23 March 1979, folder, "OCS Weekly Reports," box 4, HPN Papers.

83 "Oakland Community Learning Center News," November 1979, folder, "ocs Weekly Reports," box 4, HPN Papers.

84 "oclc Meeting Notes," 1 March 1979, folder, "eoc," box 4, HPN Papers.

85 Report, 10 March 1979, folder, "ocs Weekly Reports," box 4, HPN Papers.

86 Report, 11 July 1979, folder, "ocs Weekly Reports," box 4, HPN Papers.

87 Memo from Central Body Meeting, 15 September 1979, folder, "Central Body Meetings," box 5, HPN Papers.

88 Amar Casey, interview by author.

89 "Letter to Huey from Beatrice Kelly re: Request to complete Masters Degree," 18 January 1978, folder, "Reports on Comrades," box 14, HPN Papers.

90 "Letter to Huey from Lonnie Dee," folder, "Reports on Comrades," box 14, HPN Papers.

91 Letter by Lulla Hudson (Smokie), 20 February 1979, folder, "Reports on Comrades," box 14, HPN Papers.

92 "Letter to Huey from Tommye Williams," folder, "Reports on Comrades," box 14, HPN Papers.

93 Steve McCutchen, interview by author.

94 Steve McCutchen, interview by author.

95 "Letter to Central Body from Austin Allen," folder, "Reports on Comrades," box 14, HPN Papers.

96 "Letter to Huey from Amar Casey," folder, "Reports on Comrades," box 14, HPN Papers.

97 "Letter to Huey from Amar Casey."

98 Report, 1 May 1979, folder, "Reports on Comrades," box 14, HPN Papers.

99 Report, 1 May 1979, folder, "Reports on Comrades."

100 Report, 1 May 1979, folder, "Reports on Comrades."

101 Ericka Huggins, interview by author.

102 "Memo from JoNina to Huey," 1 October 1980, box 69, HPN Papers.

103 Memo from Oakland Community School, 20 February 1979, folder, "Party Property," box 4, HPN Papers; "oclc Meeting Notes," folder, "eoc," box 4, HPN Papers.

104 "Oakland Community School Graduation 1980," box 68, HPN Papers.

105 "Funding Terms and Conditions per Child Development Programs 1982–83," box 66, HPN Papers.

106 Committee for Justice for Huey P. Newton and the Black Panther Party Solicitation letter, Dear Friend from JoNina Abron, 14 April 1980, folder, "1974 cases, Huey," box 28, HPN Papers.

107 "oclc Meeting Notes," 28 March 1979, folder, "eoc," box 4, HPN Papers.

108 Innerparty Memorandum, 6 April 1979, box 4, HPN Papers.

109 "Memo to Huey from JoNina 7 August 1980," folder, "1974 cases, Huey," box 28, HPN Papers.

110 "Ex-Panther Newton in Court on Charges of Stealing Funds," *Oakland Tribune*, 16 October 1986.

111 "Amended Complaint against Newton, Alexander, Long, Moore," box 69, HPN Papers.

112 Steve McCutchen, interview by author.

113 The building that housed the OCS would be sold one year later. "IRS Reports to EOC," folder, "IRS Reports to EOC," box 18, HPN Papers.

CONCLUSION

1 Folder, "West Magazine Interview with Huey P. by Digby Diehl—LA Times," box 15, HPN Papers.

Bibliography

MANUSCRIPT COLLECTIONS

Howard University Library Archives, Moorland Spingarn Research Center, The Civil Rights Documentation Project.

Huey P. Newton Foundation Papers, Special Collections, Green Library, Stanford University.

New York Public Library, Schomburg Center for Research in Black Culture.

Black Panther Party, Harlem Branch Collection.

Black Panther Party FBI Files, Manuscripts, Archives and Rare Books Division.

San Francisco African American Historical and Cultural Society Archives.

Social Protest Collection, Bancroft Library, University of California, Berkeley.

University of California, Berkeley, Survey Research Center. "Poverty and Poverty Programs in Oakland: Selected Results from the 701 Household Survey of Oakland." Vol. 24 of SRC M. 1967. Reprinted August 1968. Oakland Public Library.

INTERVIEWS

Abron, James. Interview by author, 6 October 1997, tape recording, Oakland, California.

Barnes, Elendar. Interview by author, 25 September 1997, tape recording, Brooklyn.

Beckford, Ruth. Interview by author, 16 October 1997, tape recording, Oakland, California.

Bowen, Bobby. Interview by author, 22 October 1997, tape recording, Oakland, California.

Casey, Amar. Interview by author, 28 October 1997, tape recording, Oakland, California.

Cleaver, Kathleen. Interview by author, 24 November 1997, tape recording, New York.

Coates, Paul. Interview by author, 13 November 1997, telephone.

Cotton, Terry. Interview by author, 26 October 1997, Oakland, California.

Dixon, Aaron. Interview by author, 19 October 1997, telephone.

Douglas, Emory. Interview by author, 9 October 1997, tape recording, San Francisco.

Forte, Sherwin. Interview by author, 9 October 1997, tape recording, Oakland, California.

Garret-Forte, Janice. Interview by author, 9 October 1997, tape recording, Oakland, California.

Hagopian, Veronica "Roni." Interview by author, 23 October 1997, tape recording, San Francisco.

Hannah, Pamela. Interview by author, 20 November 1997, tape recording, Brooklyn.

Huggins, Ericka. Interview by author, 21 October 1997, tape recording, Oakland, California.

Jennings, Bill. Interview by author, 1 November 1997, tape recording, Sacramento.

Lewis, Tarika. Interview by author, 16 October 1997, transcript, Oakland, California.

Juanita, Judy (Hart). Interview by author, 20 October 1997, tape recording, Oakland, California.

McCall, Bobby. Interview by author, 14 October 1997, tape recording, San Francisco.

McCreary, Thomas. Interview by author, 25 September 1997, tape recording, Brooklyn.

McCutchen, Steve. Interview by author, 11 October 1997, tape recording, Oakland, California.

Perkins, Darron. Interview by author, 23 October 1997, telephone.

Presley, Brenda. Interview by author, 22 October 1997, tape recording, Oakland, California.

Seale, Bobby. Interview by author, 13 October 1997, tape recording, Oakland, California.

Williams, Mary. Interview by author, 21 October 1997, tape recording, Oakland, California.

SECONDARY SOURCES

Abu-Jamal, Mumia. *We Want Freedom: A Life in the Black Panther Party*. Cambridge, MA: South End Press, 2004.

Abu-Jamal, Mumia, and Kathleen Cleaver. *We Want Freedom: A Life in the Black Panther Party*. Cambridge, MA: South End Press, 2008.

Ahmad, Muhammad. *We Will Return in the Whirlwind: Black Radical Organizations 1960–1975*. Chicago: Charles H. Kerr, 2007.

Albert, Judith Clavir, and Stewart Edward Albert. *The Sixties Papers: Documents of a Rebellious Decade*. New York: Praeger, 1984.

Alkebulan, Paul. *Survival Pending Revolution: The History of the Black Panther Party*. Tuscaloosa: University of Alabama Press, 2007.

Allen, Robert L. *Black Awakening in Capitalist America: An Analytic History*. Trenton, NJ: Africa World Press, 1990.

Andrews, Lori B. *Black Power, White Blood: The Life and Times of Johnny Spain*. New York: Pantheon Books, 1996.

Anthony, Earl. *Picking Up the Gun: A Report on the Black Panthers*. New York: Dial Press, 1970.

Arend, Orissa. *Showdown in Desire: The Black Panthers Take a Stand in New Orleans*. Fayetteville: University of Arkansas Press, 2009.

Aretha, David. *Black Power*. Greensboro, NC: Morgan Reynolds, 2012.

Austin, Curtis J. *Up against the Wall: Violence in the Making and Unmaking of the Black Panther Party*. Fayetteville: University of Arkansas Press, 2006.

Baron, Harold M. "Racism Transformed: The Implications of the 1960s." *Review of Radical Political Economics* 17 (1985): 10–33.

Baruch, Ruth-Marion, and Pirkle Jones. *Black Panthers, 1968.* Los Angeles: Greybull Press, 2002.

Baruch, Ruth-Marion, and Pirkle Jones. *The Vanguard: A Photographic Essay on the Black Panthers.* Boston: Beacon Press, 1970.

Basgen, Brian. "History of the Black Panther Party." Marxists Internet Archive. Accessed 30 July 2009. https://www.marxists.org/history/usa/workers/black-panthers/.

Bass, Paul, and Douglas W. Rae. *Murder in the Model City: The Black Panthers, Yale, and the Redemption of a Killer.* New York: Basic Books, 2006.

Beale, Francis. "Double Jeopardy: To Be Black and Female." In *The Sixties Papers: Documents of a Rebellious Decade*, edited by Judith Clavir Albert and Stewart Edward Albert, 500–508. New York: Praeger, 1984.

Berger, Dan. *Captive Nation: Black Prison Organizing in the Civil Rights Era.* Chapel Hill: University of North Carolina Press, 2016.

Bingham, Howard L. *Howard L. Bingham's Black Panthers 1968.* Los Angeles: Ammo, 2009.

Biondi, Martha. *The Black Revolution on Campus.* Berkeley: University of California Press, 2012.

Blackburn, Sara, ed. *White Justice: Black Experience Today in American Courtrooms.* New York: Harper Colophon Books, 1971.

Black Panther Party. *Sista's Speak Up: Selected Interviews, Reflections and Writings from the Women of the Black Panther Party on Their Experiences with Patriarchy, Sexism, Imprisonment and Revolutionary Struggle.* Cincinnati: Books 4 Prisoners Crew, 2005.

Black Panther Party Alumni. "It's about Time: Black Panther Legacy and Alumni." Accessed 31 July 2011. http://www.itsabouttimebpp.com/home/home.html.

"Black Panther Sisters Talk about Women's Liberation." *The Movement*, September 1969.

"The Black Scholar Interviews: Bobby Seale." *Black Scholar* 4, no. 1 (1972): 7–16.

Blake, John. *Children of the Movement: The Sons and Daughters of Martin Luther King, Jr., Malcolm X, Elijah Muhammad, George Wallace, Andrew Young, Julian Bond, Stokely Carmichael, Bob Moses, James Chaney, Elaine Brown, and Others Reveal How the Civil Rights Movement Tested and Transformed Their Families.* Chicago: Lawrence Hill Books, 2004.

Blauner, Robert. "Internal Colonialism and Ghetto Revolt." *Social Problems* 16 (Spring 1969): 393–408.

Bloom, Jack M. *Class, Race, and the Civil Rights Movement.* Indianapolis: Indiana University Press, 1987.

Bloom, Joshua, and Waldo E. Martin. *Black against Empire: The History and Politics of the Black Panther Party.* Berkeley: University of California Press, 2013.

Boggs, James. "The Revolutionary Struggle for Black Power." In *The Black Seventies*, edited by Floyd B. Barbour, 33–48. Boston: Porter Sargent, 1970.

Bradford, Amory. *Oakland's Not for Burning.* New York: David McKay, 1968.

Breitman, George, ed. *Malcolm X Speaks.* New York: Grove Press, 1965.

Brent, William Lee. *Long Time Gone: A Black Panther's True-Life Story of His Skyjacking and Twenty-Five Years in Cuba.* New York: Times Books, 1996.

Broussard, Albert S. *Black San Francisco: The Struggle for Racial Equality in the West 1900–1954*. Lawrence: University Press of Kansas, 1993.

Brown, Elaine. *A Taste of Power: A Black Woman's Story*. New York: Pantheon Books, 1992.

Brown, Scot. *Fighting for Us: Maulana Karenga, the Us Organization, and Black Cultural Nationalism*. New York: New York University Press, 2003.

Bukhari, Safiya, and Laura Whitehorn. *The War Before: The True Life Story of Becoming a Black Panther, Keeping the Faith in Prison and Fighting for Those Left Behind*. New York: Feminist Press at the City University of New York, 2010.

Bush, Rod, ed. *The New Black Vote: Politics and Power in Four American Cities*. San Francisco: Synthesis, 1984.

———. *We Are Not What We Seem: Black Nationalism and Class Struggle in the American Century*. New York: New York University Press, 1999.

Carmichael, Stokely, and Charles Hamilton. *Black Power: The Politics of Liberation in America*. New York: Vintage Books, 1967.

Carson, Clayborne. *SNCC and the Black Awakening of the 1960s*. Cambridge, MA: Harvard University Press, 1981.

Chevigny, Paul. *Cops and Rebels: A Study of Provocation*. New York: Pantheon Books, 1972.

Churchill, Ward. *To Disrupt, Discredit and Destroy: The FBI's Secret War against the Black Panther Party*. New York: Routledge, 2009.

Churchill, Ward, and Jim Vander Wall. *Agents of Repression: The FBI's Secret Wars against the Black Panther Party and the American Indian Movement*. Cambridge, MA: South End Press, 2002.

Clark, John Henrik, ed. *Malcolm X: The Man and His Times*. New York: Macmillan, 1969.

Cleaver, Eldridge. "The Fire Now: Field Nigger Takes Over the Black Power Movement." *Commonweal*, 14 June 1968, 375–77.

———. "Letter from Jail." *Ramparts*, 15 June 1968, 17–21.

———. *Post-Prison Writings and Speeches*. Edited by Robert Scheer. New York: Rampart Books, 1967.

———. "Requiem for Nonviolence." *Ramparts*, May 1968, 48–49.

———. *Soul on Ice*. New York: Delta Trade Paperbacks, 1999.

Cleaver, Eldridge, and Kathleen Cleaver. *Target Zero: A Life in Writing*. New York: Palgrave Macmillan, 2006.

Cleaver, Kathleen, and George Katsiaficas. *Liberation, Imagination, and the Black Panther Party: A New Look at the Panthers and Their Legacy*. New York: Routledge, 2001.

Cluster, Dick, ed. *They Should Have Served That Cup of Coffee: 7 Radicals Remember the 1960s*. Boston: South End Press, 1979.

Coleman, Jeffrey Lamar. *Words of Protest, Words of Freedom: Poetry of the American Civil Rights Movement and Era*. Durham, NC: Duke University Press, 2012.

Collier-Thomas, Bettye, and V. P. Franklin. *Sisters in the Struggle: African American Women in the Civil Rights–Black Power Movement*. New York: New York University Press, 2001.

Conway, Marshall, and Dominque Stevenson. *Marshall Law: The Life and Times of a Baltimore Black Panther*. Oakland, CA: AK Press, 2011.

Crosby, Emilye. *A Little Taste of Freedom: The Black Freedom Struggle in Claiborne County, Mississippi.* Chapel Hill: University of North Carolina Press, 2005.

Crowe, Daniel Edward. *Prophets of Rage: The Black Freedom Struggle in San Francisco, 1945–1969.* New York: Garland, 2000.

Cruse, Harold. *The Crisis of the Negro Intellectual: A Historical Analysis of the Failure of Black Leadership.* New York: William Morrow, 1984.

Cunningham, David. "The Pattering of Repression: FBI Counterintelligence and the New Left." *Social Forces* 82 (2003): 209–40.

Daniels, Douglas Henry. *Pioneer Urbanites: A Social and Cultural History of Black San Francisco.* Philadelphia: Temple University Press, 1980.

Davenport, Christian. *Media Bias, Perspective, and State Repression: The Black Panther Party.* Cambridge: Cambridge University Press, 2010.

Davis, Alprentice David Emory. *Urchin Society: The Memoirs of a Black Panther Cub.* Bloomington, IN: Xlibris, 2010.

Davis, Angela. *Angela Davis: An Autobiography.* New York: International, 1974.

Dimitroff, Georgi. *United Front against Fascism.* Marxist Pamphlet No. 3. New York: New Century, 1935.

Dixon, Aaron Floyd. *My People Are Rising: Memoir of a Black Panther Party Captain.* Chicago: Haymarket Books, 2012.

Douglas, Emory, Bobby Seale, Sam Durant, and Sonia Sanchez. *Black Panther: The Revolutionary Art of Emory Douglas.* New York: Rizzoli, 2007.

Estes, Steve. *I Am a Man! Race, Manhood, and the Civil Rights Movement.* Chapel Hill: University of North Carolina Press, 2005.

Fanon, Frantz. *Toward the African Revolution.* New York: Grove Press, 1967.

———. *The Wretched of the Earth.* New York: Grove Press, 1963.

Fergus, Devin. "I Am Not Gonna Shuffle and Dance, I Don't Have to Grin When Ain't Nothing Funny, and I Am Not Going to Scratch When I'm Not Itching: The Origins and Early Development of the Black Panther Party in North Carolina." MA thesis, North Carolina State University, 1994.

———. *Liberalism, Black Power, and the Making of American Politics, 1965–1980.* Athens: University of Georgia Press, 2009.

Fletcher, Jim, Tanaquil Jones, and Sylvere Lortinger, eds. *Still Black, Still Strong: Survivors of the War against Black Revolutionaries.* New York: Semiotext(e), 1993.

Flood, Dawn Rae. "A Black Panther in the Great White North: Fred Hampton Visits Saskatchewan, 1969." *Journal for the Study of Radicalism* 8, no. 2 (2014): 21–49.

Foner, Philip S., ed. *The Black Panthers Speak: The Manifesto of the Party. The First Complete Documentary Record of the Panthers' Program.* New York: Da Capo Press, 1995.

Forbes, Flores A. *Will You Die with Me? My Life and the Black Panther Party.* New York: Atria Books, 2006.

Freed, Donald. *Agony in New Haven: The Trial of Bobby Seale, Ericka Huggins and the Black Panther Party.* New York: Simon and Schuster, 1973.

Freeman, Jo. "From Freedom Now! to Free Speech: The FSM's Roots in the Bay Area Civil Rights Movement." In *The Free Speech Movement: Reflections on Berkeley in the*

1960s, edited by Robert Cohen and Reginald E. Zelnik, 73–82. Berkeley: University of California Press, 2002.

Fujino, Diane. *Samurai among Panthers: Richard Aoki on Race, Resistance, and a Paradoxical Life.* Minneapolis: University of Minnesota Press, 2012.

Gidding, Paula. *When and Where I Enter: The Impact of Black Women on Race and Sex in America.* New York: Bantam Books, 1984.

Gilmore, Stephanie. *Feminist Coalitions: Historical Perspectives on Second-Wave Feminism in the United States.* Urbana: University of Illinois Press, 2008.

Glover, Danny, and Emory Douglas. *The Black Panther Party for Self Defense: The Protest Art of Emory Douglas.* New York: Rizzoli, 2007.

Gore, Dayo F., Jeanne Theoharis, and Komozi Woodard. *Want to Start a Revolution? Radical Women in the Black Freedom Struggle.* New York: New York University Press, 2009.

Haas, Jeffrey. *The Assassination of Fred Hampton: How the FBI and the Chicago Police Murdered a Black Panther.* Chicago: Lawrence Hill Books, Chicago Review Press, 2010.

Haines, Herbert H. *Black Radicals and the Civil Rights Mainstream, 1954–1970.* Knoxville: University of Tennessee Press, 1988.

Haley, Alex. *The Autobiography of Malcolm X.* New York: Ballantine Books, 1964.

Hall, Jacquelyn Dowd. "The Long Civil Rights Movement and the Political Uses of the Past." *Journal of American History* 91 (2005): 1233–63.

Hall, Simon. "On the Trail of the Panther: Black Power and the 1967 Convention of the National Conference for New Politics." *Journal of American Studies* 37 (2003): 59–78.

Hampton, Henry, and Steve Fayer, eds. *Voices of Freedom: An Oral History of the Civil Rights Movement from the 1950s through the 1980s.* New York: Bantam Books, 1990.

Harris, Jessica C. "Revolutionary Black Nationalism: The Black Panther Party." *Journal of Negro History* 86 (2001): 409–21.

Haskins, James. *Power to the People: The Rise and Fall of the Black Panther Party.* New York: Simon and Schuster Books for Young Readers, 1997.

Hausler, Donald. "Blacks in Oakland: 1852–1987." Public History Room, Oakland Public Library, Lakeshore Branch.

Hayes, Edward. *Power Structure and Urban Policy: Who Rules in Oakland?* New York: McGraw-Hill, 1972.

Heath, G. Louis, ed. *The Black Panther Leaders Speak: Huey P. Newton, Bobby Seale, Eldridge Cleaver and Company Speak Out through the Black Panther Party's Official Newspaper.* Metuchen, NJ: Scarecrow Press, 1976.

Hilliard, David, ed. *The Black Panther: Intercommunal News Service, 1967–1980.* New York: Atria, 2007.

———. *The Black Panther Party: Service to the People Programs.* Albuquerque: University of New Mexico Press, 2008.

Hilliard, David, and Lewis Cole. *This Side of Glory: The Autobiography of David Hilliard and the Story of the Black Panther Party.* Boston: Little, Brown, 1993.

Hilliard, David, Cornel West, and the Dr. Huey P. Newton Foundation. *The Black Panther Party: Service to the People Programs.* Albuquerque: University of New Mexico Press, 2008.

Hilliard, David, Keith Zimmerman, and Kent Zimmerman. *Huey: Spirit of the Panther.* New York: Thunder's Mouth Press, 2006.

Hinton, Elizabeth Kai, and Manning Marable. *The New Black History: Revisiting the Second Reconstruction.* New York: Palgrave Macmillan, 2011.

Hogan, Wesley C. *Many Minds, One Heart: SNCC's Dream for a New America.* Chapel Hill: University of North Carolina Press, 2007.

Holder, Kit Kim. "The History of the Black Panther Party, 1966–1977: A Curriculum Tool for Afrikan American Studies." EdD diss., University of Massachusetts, 1990.

hooks, bell. *Ain't I a Woman: Black Women and Feminism.* Boston: South End Press, 1981.

Hopkins, Evans D. *Life after Life: A Story of Rage and Redemption.* New York: Free Press, 2005.

Horne, Gerald. *Fire This Time: The Watts Uprising and the 1960s.* Charlottesville: University Press of Virginia, 1995.

Howard, Elbert. *Panther on the Prowl.* Self-published, 2002.

Hulett, John, and Stokely Carmichael. *The Black Panther Party: Speech by John Hulett, Interview with Stokely Carmichael, Report from Lowndes County.* New York: Merit, 1966.

Jackson, George. *Blood in My Eye.* Baltimore: Black Classics Press, 1990.

———. *Soledad Brothers: The Prison Letters of George Jackson.* New York: Lawrence Hill Books, 1994.

Jeffries, Hasan Kwame. *Bloody Lowndes: Civil Rights and Black Power in Alabama's Black Belt.* New York: New York University Press, 2009.

Jeffries, J. L. *Black Power in the Belly of the Beast.* Urbana: University of Illinois Press, 2006.

———. *Comrades: A Local History of the Black Panther Party.* Bloomington: Indiana University Press, 2007.

———. *Huey P. Newton: The Radical Theorist.* Jackson: University Press of Mississippi, 2002.

———. *On the Ground: The Black Panther Party in Communities across America.* Jackson: University Press of Mississippi, 2010.

Johnson, Marilynn S. *The Second Gold Rush: Oakland and the East Bay in World War II.* Berkeley: University of California Press, 1993.

Jones, Charles E., ed. *The Black Panther Party (Reconsidered).* Baltimore: Black Classic Press, 1998.

———. "The Political Repression of the Black Panther Party, 1966–1971: The Case of the Oakland Bay Area." *Journal of Black Studies* 18, no. 4 (1988): 415–34.

Jones, J. "Creating Revolution as We Advance: The Revolutionary Years of the Black Panther Party for Self-Defense and Those Who Destroyed It." PhD diss., Ohio State University, 2006.

Jordan, June. "Black History as Myth." In *Civil Wars.* Boston: Beacon Press, 1981.

Joseph, Jamal. *Panther Baby: A Life of Rebellion and Reinvention.* Chapel Hill, NC: Algonquin Books, 2012.

Joseph, Peniel E. *The Black Power Movement: Rethinking the Civil Rights–Black Power Era.* New York: Routledge, 2006.

———. "Dashikis and Democracy: Black Studies, Student Activism, and the Black Power Movement." *Journal of African American History* 88 (2003): 182–203.

———. *Neighborhood Rebels: Black Power at the Local Level*. New York: Palgrave Macmillan, 2010.

———. *Waiting 'til the Midnight Hour: A Narrative History of Black Power in America*. New York: Henry Holt, 2006.

Keating, Edward M. *Free Huey!* Palo Alto, CA: Ramparts Press, 1970.

Killian, Lewis M. *The Impossible Revolution? Black Power and the American Dream*. New York: Random House, 1968.

King, Mary. *Freedom Song: A Personal Story of the 1960s Civil Rights Movement*. New York: William Morrow, 1963.

King, Robert Hillary. *From the Bottom of the Heap: The Autobiography of Black Panther Robert Hillary King*. Oakland, CA: PM Press, 2009.

Lannon, Albert Vetere. *Fight or Be Slaves: The History of the Oakland–East Bay Labor Movement*. New York: University Press of America, 2000.

Lazerow, Jama, and Yohuru Williams. *In Search of the Black Panther Party: New Perspectives on a Revolutionary Movement*. Durham, NC: Duke University Press, 2006.

Lemke-Santangelo, Gretchen. *Abiding Courage: African American Migrant Women and the East Bay Community*. Chapel Hill: University of North Carolina Press, 1996.

———. "Deindustrialization, Urban Poverty and African American Community Mobilization in Oakland 1945 through the 1990s." In *Seeking Eldorado: African Americans in California*, edited by Lawrence De Graaf, Kevin Mulroy, and Quintard Taylor, 343–76. Seattle: University of Washington Press, 2001.

Lincoln, C. Eric. *The Black Muslims in America*. 3rd edition. Grand Rapids, MI: Wm. B. Eerdmans, 1994.

Lockwood, Lee. *Conversations with Eldridge Cleaver: Algiers*. New York: McGraw-Hill, 1970.

Lumsden, Linda. "Good Mothers with Guns: Framing Black Womanhood in the Black Panther, 1968–1980." *Journalism and Mass Communication Quarterly* 86, no. 4 (2009): 900–922.

Major, Reginald. *A Panther Is a Black Cat*. Baltimore: Black Classic Press, 2006.

Mantler, Gordon Keith. *Power to the Poor: Black-Brown Coalition and the Fight for Economic Justice, 1960–1974*. Chapel Hill: University of North Carolina Press, 2013.

Marable, Manning. *How Capitalism Underdeveloped Black America*. Boston: South End Press, 1983.

———. *Race, Reform, and Rebellion: The Second Reconstruction in Black America, 1945–1990*. Jackson: University Press of Mississippi, 1991.

Marable, Manning, and Leith Mullings. *Let Nobody Turn Us Around: Voices of Resistance, Reform, and Renewal. An African American Anthology*. Lanham, MD: Rowman and Littlefield, 2000.

Marine, Gene. *The Black Panthers*. New York: Signet Books, 1969.

Martin, Waldo. "Holding One Another: Mario Savio and the Freedom Struggle in Mississippi and Berkeley." In *The Free Speech Movement*, edited by Robert Cohen and Reginald E. Zelnik, 83–102. Berkeley: University of California Press, 2002.

Massey, Douglas, and Nancy Denton. *American Apartheid: Segregation and the Making of the Underclass*. Cambridge, MA: Harvard University Press, 1993.

Matlin, Daniel. "'Lift Up Yr Self!': Reinterpreting Amiri Baraka (LeRoi Jones), Black Power, and the Uplift Tradition." *Journal of American History* 93 (2006): 91–116.

Mayes, Keith A. *Kwanzaa: Black Power and the Making of the African-American Black Holiday*. New York: Routledge, 2009.

McCartney, John T. *Black Power Ideologies: An Essay in African-American Political Thought*. Philadelphia: Temple University Press, 1992.

McCutchen, Steve. *We Were Free for a While: Back to Back in the Black Panther Party*. Baltimore: PublishAmerica, 2008.

Meier, August, Elliot Rudwick, and John Bracey Jr., eds. *Black Protest in the Sixties*. Princeton, NJ: Marcus Wiener, 1991.

Miller, Paul T. *The Postwar Struggle for Civil Rights: African Americans in San Francisco 1945–1975*. New York: Routledge, 2009.

Moore, Gilbert. *A Special Rage*. New York: Harper and Row, 1967.

Morris, Aldon D. *The Origins of the Civil Rights Movement*. New York: Free Press, 1984.

Murch, Donna Jean. *Living for the City: Migration, Education, and the Rise of the Black Panther Party in Oakland, California*. Chapel Hill: University of North Carolina Press, 2010.

Nadasen, Premilla. *Welfare Warriors: The Welfare Rights Movement in the United States*. New York: Routledge, 2005.

Nadasen, Premilla, Jennifer Mittelstadt, and Marisa Chappell. *Welfare in the United States: A History with Documents, 1935–1996*. New York: Routledge, 2009.

Nelson, Alondra. *Body and Soul: The Black Panther Party and the Fight against Medical Discrimination*. Minneapolis: University of Minnesota Press, 2011.

Nelson, Jill. *Police Brutality: An Anthology*. New York: Norton, 2000.

Newton, Huey. *Revolutionary Suicide*. New York: Writers and Readers, 1973.

——. *To Die for the People: The Writings of Huey P. Newton*. New York: Random House, 1972.

——. *War against the Panthers: A Study of Repression in America*. New York: Harlem River Press, 1996.

Newton, Huey P., David Hilliard, Donald Weise, and Frederika Newton. *The Huey P. Newton Reader*. New York: Seven Stories Press, 2003.

Newton, Michael. *Bitter Grain: Huey Newton and the Black Panther Party*. Los Angeles: Holloway House, 1980.

Ogbar, Jeffrey Ogbonna Green. *Black Power: Radical Politics and African American Identity*. Baltimore: Johns Hopkins University Press, 2004.

Olsen, Jack. *Last Man Standing: The Tragedy and Triumph of Geronimo Pratt*. New York: Doubleday, 2000.

Ongiri, Amy Abugo. *Spectacular Blackness: The Cultural Politics of the Black Power Movement and the Search for a Black Aesthetic*. Charlottesville: University of Virginia Press, 2010.

O'Reilly, Kenneth. *Racial Matters: The FBI's Secret File on Black America, 1960–1972*. New York: Free Press, 1989.

Pearson, Hugh. *The Shadow of the Panther: Huey Newton and the Price of Black Power in America*. Boston: Addison-Wesley, 1994.

Peterson, Franklyn. "The Deacons: They Fight for Survival." *Sepia*, May 1967, 10–14.

Peterzell, Jay. "COINTELPRO in Court." *Center for National Security Studies* 4, no. 3 (1978): 1–5.

Pressman, Jeffrey L., and Aaron B. Wildavsky. *Implementation: How Great Expectations in Washington Are Dashed in Oakland: Or, Why It's Amazing That Federal Programs Work at All, This Being a Saga of the Economic Development Administration As Told by Two Sympathetic Observers Who Seek to Build Morals on a Foundation of Ruined Hopes.* Berkeley: University of California Press, 1973.

Rafalko, Frank J. *MH/CHAOS: The CIA's Campaign against the Radical New Left and the Black Panthers.* Annapolis, MD: Naval Institute Press, 2011.

Raines, Howell. *My Soul Is Rested: The Story of the Civil Rights Movement in the Deep South.* New York: Penguin Books, 1983.

Rhodes, Jane. *Framing the Black Panthers: The Spectacular Rise of a Black Power Icon.* New York: New Press, 2007.

Rhomberg, Chris. *No There There: Race, Class, and Political Community in Oakland.* Berkeley: University of California Press, 2004.

Robinson, Cedric J. *Black Marxism: The Making of the Black Radical Tradition.* London: Zed Books, 1983.

Rojas, Fabio. *From Black Power to Black Studies: How a Radical Social Movement Became an Academic Discipline.* Baltimore: Johns Hopkins University Press, 2010.

Rorabaugh, W. J. *Berkeley at War: The 1960s.* New York: Oxford University Press, 1989.

Ross, James Robert, ed. *The War Within: Violence or Nonviolence in the Black Revolution.* New York: Sheed and Ward, 1971.

Sales, William W. *From Civil Rights to Black Liberation: Malcolm X and the Organization of Afro-American Unity.* Boston: South End Press, 1994.

Schanche, Don. *The Panther Paradox: A Liberal's Dilemma.* New York: David McKay, 1970.

Scheer, Robert, ed. *Eldridge Cleaver: Post-Prison Writings and Speeches.* New York: Vintage Books, 1967.

Seale, Bobby. *A Lonely Rage: The Autobiography of Bobby Seale.* New York: Times Books, 1978.

———. *Seize the Time: The Story of the Black Panther Party and Huey Newton.* Baltimore: Black Classic Press, 1991.

Self, Robert O. *American Babylon: Race and the Struggle for Postwar Oakland.* Princeton, NJ: Princeton University Press, 2003.

Shakur, Assata. *Assata: An Autobiography.* Chicago: Lawrence Hill Books, 1987.

Shames, Stephen, and Charles E. Jones. *The Black Panthers.* New York: Aperture Foundation, 2006.

Sheehy, Gail. *Panthermania: The Clash of Black against Black in One American City.* New York: Harper and Row, 1971.

Sinclair, John, Allen Ginsberg, Gary Grimshaw, Bobby Seale, and Jim Semark. *Guitar Army: Rock and Revolution with MC5 and the White Panther Party.* Los Angeles: Process, 2007.

Slate, Nico. *Black Power beyond Borders: The Global Dimensions of the Black Power Movement.* New York: Palgrave Macmillan, 2012.

Smith, Jennifer B. *An International History of the Black Panther Party*. New York: Garland, 1999.

Smith, Tony. *Thinking Like a Communist: State and Legitimacy in the Soviet Union, China and Cuba*. New York: Norton, 1987.

Spencer, John P. *In the Crossfire: Marcus Foster and the Troubled History of American School Reform*. Philadelphia: University of Pennsylvania Press, 2012.

Tabor, Michael Cetewayo. "Capitalism Plus Dope Equals Genocide." Accessed 18 June 2016. https://www.marxists.org/history/usa/workers/black-panthers/1970/dope.htm.

Tate, Gayle T., and Lewis A. Randolph. *The Black Urban Community: From Dusk till Dawn*. New York: Palgrave Macmillan, 2006.

Taylor, Quintard. "African American Men in the American West, 1528–1990." *Annals of the American Academy of Political and Social Science* 569 (2000): 102–19.

Theoharis, Jeanne, and Komozi Woodard. *Groundwork: Local Black Freedom Movements in America*. New York: New York University Press, 2005.

Thevenin, R. "The Single Greatest Threat: A Study of the Black Panther Party, 1966–71." PhD diss., Michigan State University, 2006.

Tyson, Timothy B. "Robert F. Williams, 'Black Power,' and the Roots of the African American Freedom Struggle." *Journal of American History* 85, no. 2 (1998): 540–70.

UC Berkeley Library et al. "UC Berkeley Library Social Activism Sound Recording Project: The Black Panther Party." Accessed 30 July 2009. http://www.lib.berkeley.edu/MRC/pacificapanthers.html.

Umoja, Akinyele Omowale. *We Will Shoot Back: Armed Resistance in the Mississippi Freedom Movement*. New York: New York University Press, 2013.

U.S. Riot Commission Report: Report of the National Advisory Commission on Civil Disorders. New York: Bantam Books, 1968.

Van Deburg, William L. *Modern Black Nationalism: From Marcus Garvey to Louis Farrakhan*. New York: New York University Press, 1997.

———. *New Day in Babylon: The Black Power Movement and American Culture, 1965–1975*. Chicago: University of Chicago Press, 1992.

Van Peebles, Mario, Ula Y. Taylor, and J. Tarika Lewis. *Panther: A Pictorial History of the Black Panthers and the Story behind the Film*. New York: Newmarket Press, 1995.

Wallace, Michele. *Black Macho and the Myth of the Superwoman*. 1979. New York: Verso, 1990.

Ward, Churchill, and Jim Vander Wall. *The COINTELPRO Papers: Documents from the FBI's Secret Wars against Domestic Dissent*. Boston: South End Press, 1990.

Washburn, Amy. "The Pen of the Panther: Barriers and Freedom in the Prison Poetry of Ericka Huggins." *Journal for the Study of Radicalism* 8, no. 2 (2014): 51–78.

West, Guida. *The National Welfare Rights Movement: The Social Protest of Poor Women*. New York: Praeger, 1981.

West, Michael O., William G. Martin, and Fanon Che Wilkins. *From Toussaint to Tupac: The Black International since the Age of Revolution*. Chapel Hill: University of North Carolina Press, 2009.

Wheeler, B. Gordon. *Black California*. New York: Hippocrene Books, 1993.

Williams, Jakobi. *From the Bullet to the Ballot: The Illinois Chapter of the Black Panther Party and Racial Coalition Politics in Chicago.* Chapel Hill: University of North Carolina Press, 2013.

———. "Racial Coalition Politics in Chicago: A Case Study of Fred Hampton, the Illinois Black Panther Party, and the Origin of the Rainbow Coalition." PhD diss., University of California, Los Angeles, 2009.

Williams, Rhonda Y. *The Politics of Public Housing: Black Women's Struggles against Urban Inequality.* New York: Oxford University Press, 2004.

Williams, Yohuru. *Black Politics/White Power: Civil Rights, Black Power, and the Black Panthers in New Haven.* St. James, NY: Brandywine Press, 2000.

Williams, Yohuru R., and Jama Lazerow. *Liberated Territory: Untold Local Perspectives on the Black Panther Party.* Durham, NC: Duke University Press, 2008.

Wilson, J. "Free Huey: The Black Panther Party, the Peace and Freedom Party, and the Politics of Race in 1968." PhD diss., University of California, Santa Cruz, 2003.

Winston, Henry. *Strategy for a Black Agenda: A Critique of New Theories of Liberation in the United States and Africa.* New York: International, 1973.

Witt, Andrew. *The Black Panthers in the Midwest: The Community Programs and Services of the Black Panther Party in Milwaukee, 1966–1977.* New York: Routledge, 2007.

Wolfe, Tom. *Radical Chic and Mau-Mauing the Flak Catchers.* New York: Bantam Books, 1999.

World History Archives. "The History of the Black Panther Party." Accessed 31 July 2009. http://www.hartford-hwp.com/archives/45a/index-be.html.

Youth of the Rural Organizing and Cultural Center. *Minds Stayed on Freedom.* Boulder, CO: Westview Press, 1991.

Index

Note: Page numbers in *italics* indicate illustrations.